PRAISE FOR *TAKINGPOINT*

"The experience that members of the military, like Brent, are bringing to industry are critical. For those that want to deepen their understanding of the lessons today's veterans have learned, and how those lessons can make us all better leaders, Brent is a person you'll want to listen to!"

General Stanley McChrystal, U.S. Army (Retired)

Managing Partner, McChrystal Group

"Victorious warriors win *first* and then go to war. So should business leaders. Gleeson is amazing. Full stop. Take one look at his bio and it's obvious that excellence is woven into his DNA. What becomes obvious in reading *TakingPoint*, though, is that it can become woven into ours as well. No matter what industry you're in, it will face change. By outfitting you with a set of brilliant, battlefield-proven principles, *TakingPoint* will help you meet that change head-on and guide your team to success. *TakingPoint* is hands-down one of the best leadership books I have ever read."

Brad Thor

#1 *New York Times* bestselling author of *Use of Force*

"With every page I turned of *Taking Point*, I was struck by how much Brent Gleeson's ten principles apply to the entrepreneurs and business leaders we serve at *Inc*. As a Navy SEAL, Brent has seen these principles work in the most trying circumstances imaginable—in BUD/S training, in the crucible of combat and in his own successful businesses. That makes this one of the most credible business books I've seen in a long while. If you're a leader in today's incredibly fluid business world, you are called on to take point every day. And when you do, you can't do any better than to be guided by the blueprint Brent lays out in this remarkable book."

Eric Schurenberg

President and Editor-in-Chief, *Inc.* Media

"Brent Gleeson gets it. He's done many amazing things in his still young career and, in *TakingPoint*, demonstrates deep insight into how things *really* work best in life and in business . . . especially in highly fluid and chaotic environments. His philosophy about the importance of culture and engagement—light-years beyond the traditional lazy platitudes about empowerment—are ideas that desperately need to be put to work in this new century."

Jeff Campbell

Former Chairman/CEO of Burger King Corporation

Chairman Emeritus at San Diego's Chairmen's Roundtable

"The ability to successfully lead organizational change is a skill all leaders need now more than ever. In *TakingPoint*—inspired by Navy SEAL principles of discipline, accountability, resiliency and agility—Brent Gleeson shares his unique combination of tactics and strategies all leaders and managers need in today's more volatile and unsettled business environment."

Congressman Scott Taylor
Former Navy SEAL

"This book is a must-read for any business leader or manager! In a rapidly evolving business environment driven by new innovations and increasing consumer expectations, the Navy SEAL philosophy of 'becoming comfortable being uncomfortable' is a key message that resonated with me. Controlling what is seemingly uncontrollable in a company becomes a key to its existence. Brent clearly organizes and prioritizes cultural fundamentals and initiatives that will benefit companies at any stage of its life cycle and seamlessly connects the SEAL's ethos to real-life examples, highlighting the necessity of an empowered organization that must be held accountable for this empowerment."

Todd Hymel
CEO, Volcom

"This is the first business book that I couldn't put down! Brent's vivid storytelling perfectly captures the Navy SEAL experience and makes it relatable to any business leader by defining leadership, culture, discipline, accountability and most importantly—adaptability. This book provides powerful principles for leading organizational transformation—but most impressively, it's honest. Every member of my global organization will receive this book."

Quinn Lyzuun
Deputy CEO, Optos

"With humor and deep insight about how to effect crucial changes necessary to lead teams in an accelerating world, Brent takes point once again to show business leaders the way."

Mark Divine
Navy SEAL, Commander (Retired)
NYT bestselling author: *The Way of the SEAL* and *Unbeatable Mind*
Founder, Unbeatable Mind and SEALFIT

"This is the best book on culture and leading change in an organization I have ever read. Gleeson has spoken to our senior leaders many times in Hong Kong, Sydney, Singapore and Charlotte. He has shared with us how the principles that forge Navy SEAL culture can be applied in any organization—especially as it relates to business transformation. *TakingPoint* captures it all!"

Matthew Koder
President, Asia Pacific, Major Global Bank

"This is one of the most credible and entertaining business and leadership books I have ever read. As we all know, change is inevitable. The key to a successful business is how we, as leaders, manage the constant change. The ten principles in *TakingPoint* provide an extremely valuable road map for any leader to successfully navigate their teams through the rapid waters of change. *TakingPoint* truly delivers the best practices any leader or manager needs to help a team accept change, grow stronger, communicate better, and become more efficient and effective. *TakingPoint* is most definitely a must-read for anyone regardless of where they are at in their careers."

Alisha L. Nowlin

Senior Executive, Global Aerospace and Defense Company

"Brent does a masterful job of using his broad leadership background as a Navy Seal, entrepreneur, and business consultant to create a powerful approach to leading change in today's fast-paced business environment. He intimately grasps the importance of culture and the driving impact it has on strategy, engagement and execution. The transitions from Navy SEAL experiences to those in business also make this a very entertaining read! Amazing book!"

Gordon Lansford, III

President & CEO, JE Dunn Construction

"I watched many men attempt Navy SEAL Hell Week but few stood out like Brent Gleeson. True leaders rise to the occasion during the brutal crucible of Navy SEAL training. This book brilliantly captures the principles that forge SEAL culture and translates them into actionable methodologies for leading business transformation. *TakingPoint* provides powerful tools any business leader or manager needs to lead through uncertainty—from the battlefield to the boardroom."

David Goggins

Navy SEAL (Retired)

Endurance Athlete

"*TakingPoint* perfectly captures the principles our special operations warriors use every day and applies them to building resilient and agile organizations in today's business environment. Brent helped transform our group of high-performing senior leaders into one aligned team through the TakingPoint program outline in this amazing book."

Ryan Cork

Senior Director, Heart & Vascular Institute, Cleveland Clinic

"*TakingPoint* is a powerful model all leaders and managers should embrace in order to inspire themselves and their teams to lead and win. Brent Gleeson translates the SEAL's core principles into an actionable business guide for leading successful and lasting transformation in any organization."

Jim Guscette

Senior Vice President, CommUSA, Inc.

"*TakingPoint* is fantastic! Brent identifies well the necessary elements needed to engage in and manage change in today's uncertain environment. Applicable for business, non-profit and military organizations, Brent combines his upbringing, education, military and business experiences to capture what's required to 'lead through change.' Additionally, I'm humbled by Brent's unwavering support of the SEAL Family Foundation; he is an engaged Board Member who provides his time, talent and treasure to support our mission of building resilient families in Naval Special Warfare. Thank you, Brent; the Navy SEAL community is better for your continued service."

William R. Fenick

Captain, U.S. Navy (Ret.)

Executive Director, SEAL Family Foundation

"For those charged with the responsibility of leading their teams or organizations through transformative change, *TakingPoint* is a must read. Smart, focused and immediately applicable, it is one of the most comprehensive books on the topic of leadership. As my company forges its way through major transformation, the ten principles outlined in the book are spot-on. *TakingPoint* has provided an excellent shoreline for successfully leading my organization through its major transformation."

Tom Whaley

Regional Director, NetApp, Inc.

"Wow! What an incredible book. Brent Gleeson has put together a masterful story of leadership, service and sacrifice. Every leader, manager and executive in this country needs to stop what they are doing and grab a copy of *TakingPoint*. It's a perfect blueprint for how to build highly successful, elite organizations."

Sean Parnell

New York Times bestselling author of *Outlaw Platoon*

TAKING POINT

A NAVY SEAL'S 10 FAIL-SAFE PRINCIPLES FOR LEADING THROUGH CHANGE

BRENT GLEESON

TOUCHSTONE

New York   London   Toronto   Sydney   New Delhi

Touchstone
An Imprint of Simon & Schuster, Inc.
1230 Avenue of the Americas
New York, NY 10020

First Touchstone hardcover edition February 2018

TOUCHSTONE and colophon are registered trademarks of Simon & Schuster, Inc.

For information about special discounts for bulk purchases, please contact Simon & Schuster Special Sales at 1-866-506-1949 or business@simonandschuster.com.

The Simon & Schuster Speakers Bureau can bring authors to your live event. For more information, or to book an event, contact the Simon & Schuster Speakers Bureau at 1-212-698-8888 or visit our website at www.simonspeakers.com.

Interior design by Bryden Spevak

Manufactured in the United States of America

10 9 8 7 6 5 4 3 2 1

Library of Congress Cataloging-in-Publication Data is available.

ISBN 978-1-5011-7678-4
ISBN 978-1-5011-7680-7 (ebook)

To our brave servicemen and servicewomen
who willingly go into harm's way;
to the bold business leaders facing transformation;
and to my incredible wife, Nicole,
and our three amazing children:
Tyler, Ryder, and Parker Rose

CONTENTS

PART 3: WINNING THE CHANGE FIGHT

FOREWORD

I first met Brent in early 2002 when he checked in to SEAL Team 5 and was assigned to our platoon along with another guy from his BUD/S class. He was now one of our "new guys." I got to know him well during our workup (platoon-level training) and his background intrigued me.

Like me, he had attended college prior to enlisting in the Navy. He had also spent time in "corporate America" before making the transition into the Navy. I was curious as to why he left a lucrative job as a financial analyst to join the Teams? It seemed he felt called to a higher purpose like the rest of us.

Brent played the new guy role well. He was smart, mature, listened, and was eager to accept advice and constructive criticism when mistakes were made. Having already been at the Team for a couple years, I took Brent under my wing and showed him the ropes.

The aftermath of the 9/11 attacks sent a shock wave through the NSW (Naval Special Warfare) community. Everyone wanted to take the fight to the enemy and seek retribution for those cowardly acts of terrorism. As the Navy SEAL Ethos states, "We train for war and fight to win." It was time to put that training to the test.

These were tumultuous times of great uncertainty. The war in Afghanistan had kicked off and it was already becoming clear that our initial expectations of a swift victory were fading away. It seemed the war would be long and brutal with potentially no clear end in sight. Stories and intelligence reports were filtering in from the front lines each day. Lessons learned the hard way were already being applied to our training. Our transformation had begun.

Later that year, word began circulating that a conflict in Iraq was imminent. We took our training very seriously and hoped that we could join the fight soon. Many of our SEAL brothers had headed downrange to Afghanistan, and now those who had not yet deployed to a combat zone were anxious to see how things would unfold.

Our minds were racing. How would we sustain two complex wars in two very different environments and against very different enemies? Were we prepared? What would need to change to ensure victory? The answers to these questions would be revealed sooner than we thought.

At this point, we didn't yet know if we would be deploying to PACOM (U.S. Pacific Command) or CENTCOM (U.S. Central Command). Needless to say, we prayed that our task unit would be sent to CENTCOM—where all the action was. We were elated when we got the news that we were going to Iraq.

The 2003 invasion of Iraq lasted from March 20 to May 1, 2003, and signaled the start of the Iraq War, which was labeled Operation Iraqi Freedom by the United States. Prior to March 19, the mission in Iraq was called Operation Enduring Freedom, a carryover from the War in Afghanistan. The invasion consisted of twenty-one days of major combat operations, in which a combined force of troops from the United States, the United Kingdom, Australia and Poland invaded Iraq and deposed the Ba'athist government of Saddam Hussein. The invasion phase consisted primarily of a conventionally fought war which included the capture of the Iraqi capital, Baghdad, by American forces with the implicit assistance of the United Kingdom, alongside Australia and Poland.

The invasion was preceded by an airstrike on the presidential palace in Baghdad on March 20, 2003. The following day, coalition forces launched an incursion into Basra Province. While the special operations forces (including SEAL Team 3) launched an amphibious assault from the Persian Gulf to secure Basra and the surrounding petroleum fields, the main invasion army moved into southern Iraq, occupying the region and engaging in the Battle of Nasiriyah on March 23.

SEAL Team 3 pushed north to Baghdad with conventional forces, then headed back to Ali al Salem airbase in Kuwait. Our task unit from Team 5 took over in early April 2003.

This was our first combat tour.

I didn't know it yet, but my career would lead me on twelve more combat tours. Brent and I put our training to the test as we worked closely together night after night on what became a very busy deployment— performing what were dubbed "capture or kill" missions. When we returned, I screened for the selection and training program for our Tier 1 unit and was accepted. Due to the operational tempo of that command, we didn't see each other for years. We kept in touch as much as possible, but the timing of our different schedules precluded much contact.

As is the unfortunate nature of our business, we later reconnected in Dallas, at the memorial service for Chris Kyle (Navy SEAL and author of *American Sniper*). Brent had been out of the Teams for a while, attended graduate school, and become a successful entrepreneur. I had recently left the Teams and published my #1 *New York Times* bestseller, *No Easy Day*. From that day forward, we have stayed in contact and traveled together with our families.

Since leaving the Navy, like Brent, I have applied that vast knowledge and principles for building high-performance organizations to the business world through speaking, consulting, and launching my own companies. Brent and I often discuss our theories on how the post-9/11 special operations transformation can be applied to organizations in today's more complex and uncertain business environment.

I experienced these transformations as a Navy SEAL team leader and in working very closely with coalition forces, other branches of the military and our agency partners. It quickly became very apparent that to move at the speed these wars require, there needed to be a significant transformation in mindset, organizational approach and even the culture of the military in its entirety. As the transformation unfolded, the culture of the special operations community started to align better with the mission and strategy. And as that mission narrative continually became more singular and aligned, we realized that it was indeed possible to transform into a modern twenty-first-century organization that could defeat a dangerous and much more decentralized enemy.

We, too, had to become more adaptive and decentralized. Over the years we were able to create a new operational framework that allowed for decentralized decision-making, a seamless flow of transparent communication, and breaking down vertical and horizontal silos that impeded true collaboration.

I spent more years in the Teams than Brent, but his application of these principles in his own businesses and in working with other global organizations is what validates their rationality. The ten *TakingPoint* principles are not theories from business school or a management textbook. Through trial and error, successes and failures, years of research and testing ideas in his weekly columns in *Forbes* and *Inc.*, Brent has become a well-respected thought leader in this space.

The question he answers in this book is essentially: *How can leaders and managers transform their mindsets, align culture with specific business strategies, and successfully lead lasting organizational transformations?*

Our many conversations on these topics as they relate to both special operations and business organizations across the world—and I've worked closely with many—led us to the conclusion that these methodologies need to be captured in a book. There are many books on "change management" but most are not necessarily as applicable to today's volatile and ever-changing business landscape. And most simply teach how to *manage* change, not how to transform a culture and lead lasting change.

In my second book, *No Hero*, I offer similar battle-tested leadership concepts that can be applied in any organization. But what I like about *TakingPoint* and the principles you will learn in the following pages is that they are focused on a single mission: to transform an organization into something better. To achieve true alignment behind one vision, communicate that vision concisely and build empowered networks of teams with leaders at all levels. To create disciplined groups made up of fully engaged star players all pulling in the same direction. Resilient teams that accept and embrace change.

The refreshing reality about this book is that it is not another combat book disguised as a business leadership book. Brent has a deep understanding of today's business challenges and has tested these theories in his own companies—organizations repeatedly earning a spot on the *Inc.* 500 list of fastest-growing companies for many consecutive years. That's a track record you can't fake. Unlike many books, the principles in *TakingPoint* actually teach you *how* to implement these practices in any organization.

This book helps leaders and managers better understand the unique differences between those two disciplines (leadership and management) and how they relate to leading change. The *TakingPoint* model offers any organization the opportunity to not become one of the statistics of failed organizational transformation. The principles and supporting case studies contained in the following chapters address some of the most critical questions of modern business:

> *How must we transform our organizations so that we can grow, compete, and thrive in the new environment?*

> *What new mindsets, cultures, systems, and processes are needed to succeed and win?*

> *What tools and approaches do leaders need to navigate the murky waters of change?*

And what are the potential financial returns that come with
properly fulfilling a vision for change?

In my opinion, organizations with a burning desire to thrive in today's increasingly complex world will need to adopt new ways of thinking, new structures, new systems, and the behaviors to make those systems work.

If you are a leader—or have a desire to be one—and want to avoid the pitfalls of failed transformation efforts and need a road map for success, this is it.

—MARK OWEN, former Navy SEAL Team leader,
#1 *New York Times* bestselling author of *No Easy Day* and *No Hero*,
founder of Front Sight Focus

PREFACE

The four CH-47 Chinook helicopters flew low and fast over the barren desert, filled with two SEAL platoons and Polish special operators on our way to the target—a massive hydroelectric power plant and dam that had been seized by retreating Iraqi forces.

Our mission was to assault, capture, and hold the plant until conventional Army forces arrived. The intelligence regarding the size and makeup of the enemy force protecting the plant wasn't very detailed. Their intent, however, was to destroy the dam, resulting in mass power and electrical outages and to flood the land below. Our mission was to ensure this didn't happen.

And even though this was our first combat mission in Iraq, we hadn't even deployed "in-country" yet. We were actually staged at Ali Al Salem Air Base in Kuwait doing our turnover with SEAL Team 3 when we were handed this mission.

As the HRST (helicopter rope suspension techniques) master in my platoon, my initial job was to prepare the helicopters and supervise the fast rope insert onto the target. I was sitting on a tight coil of thick green nylon rope next to the open door of the helicopter, monitoring our progress toward the insert point. Sweat was pouring down my face. Although it was midnight, the air temperature was approximately 90 degrees.

The night sky was clear and illuminated by a full moon—something that made it easier for us to see the landscape below but also made our helos nicely silhouetted targets for the enemy. Hills, dunes, and palm groves scattered the land beneath us. We had been in flight for about three hours—legs numb and bodies stiff. But all—who were awake—maintained total focus.

"Ten minutes out," came the call over our radios.

Now all were awake. Each man passed the signal down the line—ten fingers—and checked weapons, radios and NVGs (night-vision goggles). Each man double-checking the gear of the man next to him. We all put on our thick welding gloves that protected our hands from the intense friction that came from sliding down the nylon rope.

"Five minutes."

Now, we were all on our feet, getting ready for the exit. Hearts beating a little faster. The intense focus permeating our minds, each man envisioning his mission responsibilities. We had been rehearsing for a week—day and night—for this mission. The helo crew chief and platoon commander leaned out to confirm our target location.

"One minute."

Each man passed the signal—one index finger extended. Heart hammering, I grabbed the coiled fast rope, lifted it up and got ready to throw it out. The plant was enormous, stretching out across the horizon in front of us. Even the intense buzzing from our helicopter's spinning rotors didn't drown out the noise of the rushing river below us.

We had thirty SEALs and a troop of Polish GROM—Poland's elite special forces warriors. There was no way to know what was facing us, but anybody who was in that building and the surrounding structures had no idea what they were in for, either. We'd all trained for years for this moment. It was time for the training wheels to come off.

Twenty feet above our landing zone, the helo came to a steady hover, and I threw the rope out.

Every man down the line gave a thumbs-up. With one final fist bump, we were ready to go. In rapid succession, each SEAL—carrying sixty pounds of gear—launched himself with well-trained precision out into the black abyss, grabbing the thick rope and sliding quickly down into the tornado of swirling sand below.

Ready to take the fight to the enemy.

What This Book Is, and What It Isn't

Fast-forward fifteen years.

I completed my somewhat brief but busy SEAL career and attended graduate school at the University of San Diego. Using the guiding principles I learned in the Teams, I have created multimillion-dollar companies that have made the Inc. 500 list of America's fastest growing private companies for many consecutive years.

My SEAL training, combat experience and business acumen make me uniquely qualified to share the kinds of strategies we're all going to need in an intensely volatile and unsettled business environment.

In these pages, I'll share some of the stories from my active-duty SEAL experience (although intentionally brief in nature and light on details), but this is not a war memoir, or a combat book disguised as a business leadership book. I'm humbled and honored to have served with some of the world's greatest warriors. But my contribution to the ongoing war on terror pales in comparison to that of many of my brothers—who have fought longer, are still fighting, or have made the ultimate sacrifice. This is also why a portion of the proceeds from this book will being going to the SEAL Family Foundation. I continue to serve in a different capacity by sitting on the board of the foundation and mentoring young men into the SEAL program.

There are plenty of fantastic books detailing the heroic stories of our SEAL brotherhood, like *No Easy Day, American Sniper, Fearless, Lone Survivor,* and many more—all stories that needed to be told by men better deserving than I. I've been in combat and experienced the horrors of war-torn countries around the world. I've lost friends, attended countless funerals and I've taken life.

This book is not about that.

This book is designed to give you a prescriptive model for navigating the complexities of change in any organization. Whether you're a leader, manager or a team member, the principles outlined in this book are a set of tools that I have developed through lessons learned on both literal and figurative battlefields.

I definitely had some unique experiences in the SEAL Teams and I've had success in the business world. But my intent is not to make this sound like a lecture from somebody who knows it all. I consider myself a lifelong learner who still has a long way to go. My "wisdom" comes from making plenty of costly mistakes. SEAL training, wartime experience, and graduate school provided a solid foundation, but nothing compares to cutting your teeth in the real world of entrepreneurship and business leadership—as it applies to learning how to build a winning organization designed to achieve great financial returns. And leadership—especially amidst uncertainty—is arguably one of the hardest disciplines to define and master.

It is a humbling journey, and I want to give you the best advice I can to help you avoid some of the landmines and prepare your organization for inevitable changes—to build resilient teams well prepared for anything.

TakingPoint is organized into a series of proven, step-by-step tools and models that can be applied in any business environment. They aren't complicated, but they require a shift in mindset, culture and organizational approach. Successful application and execution can't happen without accountability, team engagement, discipline, and resiliency.

Why This Book? Why Now?

The post-9/11 reality has permeated the entire world.

Whether we're talking about the Naval Special Warfare community, the United States military in its entirety, or the global business environment, the operative word is "change."

To put a finer point on it—constant and dynamic change.

Plenty of books, research reports and articles try to capture the rapidly shifting trends in the global marketplace, today's workforce, and the ever-evolving rules organizations need to live by to survive.

But unless you learn how to be comfortable with the discomfort of the unsettled nature of change itself, no amount of strategy or tactics will lead you to the win.

The workforce is changing. It's becoming more digital, more diverse and more reliant on advanced technology. At the same time, business expectations, needs, and demands are evolving faster than most organizations can keep up with. Most companies have yet to truly understand how to harness these emerging technologies so they translate to greater efficiencies. They are forced to grow faster, leaving less time to focus on the details of their financial strategy—reducing resources and causing leaders and managers to do more with less.

Is that a challenge?

Sure.

But it's also an opportunity.

If you thrive in those situations, you will dominate the vast majority of leaders, managers, and teams who are trying to figure out how to *avoid* change. Leaders today have the opportunity to reimagine their approach to talent acquisition, organizational structure, and even the discipline of leadership itself to take advantage of change, not shrink from it.

Need proof?

Data from the U.S. Bureau of Labor Statistics and other sources show that productivity growth remains low despite the introduction of new technology into the business environment. In fact, since the 2008 recession, growth in business productivity—gross domestic product per hour worked—stands at its lowest rate.

We have more tools than ever before, but we're in the middle of a time of great disruption. Companies that aren't resilient and agile are breaking down, and new ones are arriving to replace them.

The *TakingPoint* principles in this book will give you an operating manual for navigating what we called a VUCA environment in the Teams—volatile, uncertain, complex, and ambiguous. The principles, anecdotes and case studies contained in this book reflect the shifts in mindsets and behaviors necessary to lead, manage, inspire, and engage the twenty-first-century workforce.

Leading change is not a new function of leadership and management, but the approach to successful transformations has shifted. You won't see the term "change management" used in this book. Why? Because true, lasting change must be inspired and evangelized from the top. It must permeate every aspect of a business, and the people in it.

It can't simply be managed, it must be led.

The Navy SEAL community holds close the values of teamwork, trust, accountability, shared vision, communication, discipline, and resiliency. My hope is that by the time you finish this book, you'll have the tools to instill those values and influence lasting change in your organization or wherever you are.

—BRENT GLEESON
Rancho Santa Fe, CA
August 12, 2017

TAKINGPOINT

INTRODUCTION

My journey to the SEAL Teams may not have been as conventional as some.

Some join the Navy immediately following high school or college and attempt to go through Basic Underwater Demolition/SEAL training (BUD/S—the first six months of the training pipeline). Many before they are even old enough to buy a beer. For me, I had never given serious thought to joining the Navy until after college.

Until then, I had what you would call a "normal" life. I attended high school at Jesuit College Preparatory School of Dallas, followed by college at Southern Methodist University, where I studied finance and economics. During that time I also had the privilege of studying at Oxford University in England, which influenced me to become a writer. When I graduated in 1999, I had already accepted a job as a financial analyst with a global real estate investment company. I accepted the offer just before Christmas break during my senior year, so let's just say my class attendance during that last semester was subpar.

One of my fraternity brothers who was a year behind me in school was determined to join the Navy and try out for the SEAL program after he graduated. And so during his senior year, I trained with him. I had played rugby for four years in college, so it was a great way to maintain my fitness and help a friend prepare for a rough journey.

As time went on, I became more and more fascinated with the culture and values of the Naval Special Warfare community. I was reading everything I could find, from the earliest history of the Underwater Demolition Teams (UDT) in World War II to operations in Korea, Vietnam, and the Middle East. I was attracted to the idea of challenging myself to become a part of one of the most elite, highest-performance teams in the world.

My mindset was transforming.

I would sit at my desk on the forty-second floor of a high-rise office building in downtown Dallas, staring out the window, counting the minutes until I could leave and go train with my friend. It's embarrassing to admit, but toward the end of the day I would walk quickly through the office with an empty manila folder, looking busy and focused—so I hopefully wouldn't get tasked with a new project at 5:45 p.m. It rarely worked. I was the new guy.

Maybe not what an employer is looking for in a star player, but I was becoming fixated on something greater than myself. Each night, I would put on my running shoes, throw on a backpack containing swim fins and goggles and run four miles from my uptown apartment to the SMU pool. We would swim for an hour and do calisthenics such as push-ups, pull-ups, burpees and sit-ups. Then I would run four miles home. On the weekends, we had a strength training regimen followed by running ten to twenty miles around White Rock Lake. We ran marathons and earned our skydiving licenses. Each day our dedication to this singular mission increased.

Eventually, I decided to live a life without regret. I quit my job, and my friend and I spent several more months training in the mountains, in Colorado. There would be no hiking or horseback riding on this trip. My parents had a house in the Gold Link neighborhood in Crested Butte, Colorado, which became our training facility. We carved out a training ground in the woods behind the house and suspended thick climbing ropes thirty feet high in the tall cypress trees. We used a chain saw to cut eight-foot logs from fallen trees and would run each day for miles through the mountain passes, carrying them on our shoulders. We'd swim in ice-covered lakes and spend hours a day training at 10,000 feet so we'd be ready.

In 2000, I enlisted in the Navy. Like many SEALs with college degrees, I chose to not attend OCS (Officer Candidate School) because enlisting was a faster path to BUD/S. During basic training in Great Lakes, Illinois, you take the physical test to qualify for BUD/S. It involves a 500-meter swim, 1.5-mile timed run in boots, push-ups, pull-ups, and sit-ups. Candidates are not expected to simply meet the minimum standards—which most don't—they are expected to blow them out of the water. I can't remember how many guys tried out that day, but there were many. The swim test began like a flurry of salmon battling to make it upstream. Some couldn't even complete the swim. Limp, exhausted bodies literally being pulled from the pool. It was astonishing. All I remember is that only three of us were sitting in the office that afternoon getting orders to BUD/S. Me, my friend from college and one other guy. The rest of boot camp flew by.

We had earned our ticket to the show.

After a month of "A" school (the school teaching you a trade in the Navy, because most won't become SEALs) in San Diego, we were given a couple weeks of leave. I went back to Dallas to mentally prepare for the journey ahead.

Two weeks later, I distinctly remember the feeling of anticipation I had as my plane flew over the downtown skyline on its approach into San Diego International Airport. The sun was glistening off the bay and my mind was racing. I remember thinking what a beautiful place this was to endure such misery.

I checked in to a hotel on Harbor Drive just a few minutes from the airport that Thursday evening. That would prove to be a sleepless night. The next morning, my buddy and I hopped in a cab and headed to the Naval Special Warfare Center in Coronado to check in. Driving over the Coronado Bridge felt like the point of no return. I had heard rumors that instructors would make you "hit the surf" and get wet, sandy, and miserable as soon as you arrived. So it seemed it would prove to be an interesting morning.

The journey had begun—or so we thought.

We walked into the lobby and approached the front desk. Behind it sat two clean-cut young gentlemen. Clearly, early-stage BUD/S students standing "watch" on the quarterdeck. Apparently, it was a holiday weekend, so they told us to come back on Tuesday! It was both a relief and a bit anticlimactic. We held up in a dingy but rather expensive motel down the street for the next few days—dreaming of the impending doom ahead.

So, as destiny dictated, a couple of fraternity brothers from SMU joined BUD/S class 235 in the fall of 2000. Of all the adventures and challenges I would end up experiencing as a SEAL, I remember those days at the beginning of BUD/S vividly.

I can still picture the other guys filtering in, and the experience of everybody sizing each other up. We all knew that only a small percentage of people would end up getting through. We were strangers, but at the end of it, a small group of us would be blood brothers, forever.

Hollywood generally portrays SEALS in one way—big, ripped guys who look like they just walked off the football field or climbed out of an Olympic swimming pool. But the reality is that nobody looking at a BUD/S class on the first day can really tell who will still be standing at the end. Some of the biggest and fittest guys—ones who looked like they came off a recruiting poster—were the ones who placed their green helmets on the ground and rang the bell to give up on the first day—the formal and humbling ceremony for those that quit. Recruits who were unbelievable swimmers and runners quit the first week, or the first day of Hell Week—the relentless torture chamber that organically separates the candidates who can push through physical and psychological pain from those who can't.

Everything about SEAL training is designed to test your mental and physical fortitude, and see how you can adapt to constantly changing conditions. Each class is divided into "boat crews" consisting of six enlisted students and one officer. As candidates would quit, boat crews would get rearranged. You were constantly building and rebuilding your team and adapting to new teammates—and they to you.

The culture taught us that change was a given, and that the strongest embraced change and used it to their advantage.

I made it through BUD/S without incident or any severe injuries and was preparing to begin SQT (SEAL Qualification Training—the advanced portion of the training pipeline). The attacks on the World Trade Center and Pentagon on September 11, 2001, occurred just days before we checked in to SQT. In the space of a few hours, we went from being a peacetime force to an organization constantly preparing for and executing missions all over the world. To being in a constant state of change.

I've seen and done things I will never forget, though my contribution pales in comparison to so many. When I finished my time as a SEAL, I decided I wanted to merge my special operations experience with "real world" education to start the next phase of my life—as an entrepreneur. While attending graduate school at the University of San Diego, I launched my first company.

As I was building that business, I read every book and watched every presentation I could find on leadership, organizational development, culture and business transformation—all tools I knew I would need. And I dove deep into the literature and reports produced by the top consulting firms that companies hire to help them solve their complicated strategic problems. There was clearly no shortage of awareness and willingness on the part of organizational leaders, and there were plenty of resources. But clearly, navigating growth and change wasn't easy.

So why do so many organizations fall significantly short of realizing their potential?

The numbers are grim.

Research shows that more than two-thirds of all significant organizational transformation efforts fail or fall short of meeting the intended objectives. Companies try every day to fix cultural problems, change their target markets, revise their product mixes, adapt to new competitive challenges, and undertake dozens of other transformative steps. You've heard about the success stories, like Apple and Amazon. But the failures outnumber them exponentially.

I built my own organizations on the premise that change was a natural part of the business cycle—and that hiring, training, communicating, engaging, measuring, and rewarding in a way that reinforced that principle was the best way to produce the desired culture and results. The success of that approach is reflected by the results—building some of the fastest-growing companies in the country. But it hasn't been easy or void of major challenges.

One of the first valuable principles you learn after joining a SEAL Team is how the team learns from its successes and failures. After every mission, the team conducts an AAR (after-action review)—a post mortem debrief where we analyze performance and results. Lessons learned are applied to the operating strategy. When the data supports the potential need for a shift in tactics, that information is disseminated quickly across the organization.

Between my time in the Teams, in academia, and in the business world, I've spent almost twenty years figuring out what works and what doesn't—and how transformations can succeed and last. And why they fail.

The result is a ten-principle model, *TakingPoint*, that is the only guide of its kind. It is a step-by-step playbook for surviving and thriving in the uncertain business landscape of the twenty-first century. The strategies we're going to talk about are the same ones I share with my consulting clients like PayPal, Bank of America Merrill Lynch, Boeing, Nestlé, Care Fusion, The North Face, and Raytheon. They're the principles that have transformed the special operations community in this post-9/11 reality. And they have helped Fortune 500 companies overcome what seem to be almost insurmountable challenges.

When a SEAL platoon is on a mission, the man in front is the point man—he's "taking point"—leading the team into what are almost always volatile, complex, and unpredictable situations. My goal with this book is to give anybody the tools to take point in their own organization and the ability to vigorously lead change, not just manage it.

This matters wherever you fall on your org chart.

Why?

In large part, most organizational change efforts fail because they happen in overmanaged, under-led command-and-control environments. The existing structures and culture impede forward progress. In overmanaged companies, when leadership sees a crisis looming, knee-jerk reactions can often become the norm—making uninformed decisions and giving different orders to different groups of people. And while many might be under the misconception that all military units operate in command-and-control environments, that's not the case. In special operations, we have made a diligent effort to decentralize controls and decision-making mechanisms. Varying leadership responsibilities are disseminated down the chain of command.

Lasting and productive change is certainly led from the top, but it works because the entire ecosystem is operating with the appropriate and aligned mindset. All hands are on the rope pulling in the same direction. It is a collective process that takes buy-in, engagement and contribution from everybody. You have to learn to master your role—whether you're the Team's commanding officer, platoon leader, or the frontline soldier.

We will build that mindset together. It will take discipline and accountability, and some parts of the process will cause discomfort. As we say in the SEAL Teams, we will all have to "get comfortable being uncomfortable." I know this from my own career as a leader of organizations that had the inevitable growing pains that all companies experience. It isn't as easy as flipping a few pages and giving yourself a pep talk.

But at the end of this journey, your business "kit bag" will have the tools and weapons you will need to step confidently onto the business battlefield of change. You'll be more ready for the job we're all going to have for better or worse in the modern economy.

Change agent.

PART 1

BUILDING A CHANGE CULTURE

Not all organizations are naturally ready for making significant changes. Regardless of the size of the company or its existing systems, structures, and culture, leading organizational change usually comes with at least a little bit of culture shift.

And although Part 1 is about building a culture that is more nimble and adaptive by improving trust and accountability, it doesn't just end there. Building or improving the culture is a constant evolution, with the majority of the lasting culture changes happening toward the end of a transformation process. This is because it takes time for mindsets and behaviors to evolve significantly enough for the "new ways of doing things" to actually be ingrained in the culture.

The culture of the Naval Special Warfare community is a very distinct and well-defined organism. But it didn't happen overnight. It evolved through years of conflict, sacrifice, discipline, and training. We have applied lessons learned to changing or improving how we do things—all which impact culture.

Part 1 reveals the critical importance of weaving trust and accountability into the fabric of an organization's culture in order to prepare the business for lasting—and even ongoing—change. The principles and tools explained will better equip any organization to build a strong culture—one that aligns with a specific strategic vision—and navigate the volatile and uncertain waters of change.

1

CULTURE:
THE CHIEF ENABLER OF CHANGE

Brave men have fought and died building the proud tradition and
feared reputation that I am bound to uphold.
—NAVY SEAL ETHOS

Culture—and its application to strategy and results—is now a core focus of great organizations that "get it." Volumes of research from global consulting firms coupled with my own experiences as a business owner and consultant point to the fundamental belief that there is a distinct correlation between culture and financial performance.

But many companies fall significantly short in doing four things: (1) clearly defining their culture, (2) managing that culture, (3) aligning culture with strategy and desired results, and (4) leveraging culture during times of change.

In the *2017 Global Deloitte Human Capital Trends* report, senior executives and human resources professionals from across the globe rated the areas of culture, engagement, and retention as "urgent." Due to globalization, emerging technology, a wider array of employment opportunities, and organizational transparency driven by sites like LinkedIn,

Glassdoor, and Indeed, the power is in the hands of the job-seeker, not the employer. And today's workforce—and top talent—cares deeply about the culture, values, purpose, and work environment of the organizations they seek to join. This reality provides a significant opportunity for those who can define and manage culture successfully.

And culture has a significant impact on engagement, which is critical for driving change—which we will dive deeply into in Chapter 7. According to Gallup's State of the Global Workplace report, only 15 percent of employees worldwide are engaged in their jobs—meaning that they are emotionally invested in committing their time, talent and energy in adding value to their team and advancing the organization's initiatives.

More Gallup research shows that employee disengagement costs the United States upwards of $550 billion a year in lost productivity. So one could see why this is both a serious problem that most leaders and managers face with today's workforce—but also an amazing opportunity for companies that learn to master the art of engagement, especially as it relates to culture and leading change. And the companies that rank the highest on sites like Glasdoor do so in large part because they are cited as doing a great job of defining and managing culture.

This is why managing culture—and aligning culture with strategy—is now more important than ever.

An organization that has a clearly articulated culture which aligns with their core strategic objectives?

Naval Special Warfare—home to the Navy SEAL and SWCC (Special Warfare Combatant-Craft Crewmen) teams.

The Navy SEAL training and selection process is now widely depicted in many books, movies, and online resources. But you really can't understand the almost surreal essence of this environment unless you experience it for yourself. BUD/S is the first six months of the long training pipeline and is designed to begin the development process of the most elite and sophisticated special operators—warriors who are aligned behind a clear and concise mission narrative.

To defeat our nation's enemies.

The irony is that the training after BUD/S only becomes more challenging—and peak performance is everything. The small handful of students who graduate from BUD/S go on to SQT, which consists of many more months of arduous training. The students are constantly under the microscope, being tested on their physical and tactical performance in all things Naval Special Warfare.

As the saying goes, *you either manage your culture or it will manage you.* The NSW community does a very deliberate and thorough job of building, managing, and protecting our *culture*—the shared beliefs, mindsets, values and rituals that have been forged over decades of relentless training and brutal combat. Like any organization, it isn't perfect and we have our flaws. But our culture is not haphazard, it's by design—it's what fuels our ability to be nimble, adapt to change, and defend this great nation from those who wish to destroy us.

If you make it through training—and that's a big *if*, since only a few out of every beginning class of two hundred or so candidates survives to the end—your fellow SEALs know you're coming in with an extreme level of training, toughness, and willingness to be a part of the most feared and elite special operations fighting force in existence.

They know you're a "culture fit."

The training evolutions and experiences are designed to equip SEAL Teams with the ability to perform at an elite level in situations where lives are at stake and conditions are constantly changing. The ability to communicate well, move swiftly to the sound of gunfire and make decisions amidst uncertainty.

My first overseas tour with SEAL Team 5 was in 2003. We were mostly operating in and around Baghdad, Ar Ramadi and Al Fallujah. We worked out of a compound inside one of Saddam Hussein's former palaces near the Baghdad airport. The compound was surrounded by fifteen-foot walls—the tops covered in razor wire. The compound was about three quarters of a mile long and a quarter mile deep. It had several buildings on its East and West ends that were formerly the living quarters for staff working at the palace.

When we arrived, there was no infrastructure yet in place, so we lived in the abandoned buildings, sleeping on top of our North Face sleeping bags—atop dirty mattresses. It was miserably hot during the day and almost as bad at night. The mosquitos were relentless. Army soldiers guarded the exterior while we rotated on watch internally. There was only one way in and out. It was a fairly secure base. Although one morning we woke to the sound of mortar rounds impacting the wall on the east end. It's a pretty funny sight to see a bunch of well-built warriors in underwear, flip flops and body armor racing eagerly into battle. But it was over as quickly as it began. Our Army brothers manning the guard tower on the northeast corner dispatched the attacker with a few bursts from their SAWs (squad automatic weapon).

One of our first missions in Baghdad was to capture a high-ranking Iraqi general who was allegedly—according to our agency intelligence partners—hiding out in a nearby neighborhood. In a lawless, bombed-out city, much of the information we used to plan a mission came from what we call "ground intelligence"—working closely with our agency partners who developed local assets to obtain information on enemy positions and movements. It's almost impossible to properly vet every tip and piece of "valuable" information you receive, even with our extremely important agency partners working round the clock. So every time we left the relative safety of our compound, we had to be prepared for anything.

On this particular mission, we left our compound in our specially modified Humvees and a black suburban at 1 a.m. and rendezvoused with conventional forces—that "owned" the AO (area of operation)—at the Arch of Triumph in central Baghdad just outside of the neighborhood where the target house was located. After going over the plan one last time, the convoy drove to the predetermined *set point* where those of us on the assault team reconfigured ourselves in the Humvees for a speedy exit.

We had learned that most houses in this area had walls five or six feet high surrounding them. The only option for getting in was to find a way over the wall, or to go through a very noisy metal gate. So we started using some very unglamorous but extremely useful handmade ladders constructed out of 2x4s. We had also discovered the difficulties of getting in and out of our vehicles with our full battle gear on. So we had made some "modifications"—removing the doors and rear roofs. We welded steel running boards along the sides to stand on—like you see SWAT teams do as they approach a target. Two SEALS would stand on each side running board, holding the ladders, while two more sat on the tailgate.

As soon as we neared the target house, the primary assault team quickly dismounted from the vehicles. Once we were over the wall and lined up along the side of the house—rifles pointing in all directions searching for threats—our lead breacher pulled a bundle of explosives from a pouch along his right calf and set the charge to blow open the door.

"Three, two, one. Execute. Execute. Execute."

The charge blew, sending glass from the windows flying over our heads—finding every piece of skin not covered by clothing or gear. The concussive blast violently shook every man's body. We dynamically flooded the house, but at every floor, not only did we not find our HVT (high-value target), we didn't find anybody.

So far, the house was empty.

I was on the third floor with my chief and one of our point men calling for more guys to assist with the final clearance. That's when the call came over the radio to "collapse security"—get out of the house and back to the vehicles. As we headed for the door, more information came in. The informant had pegged the wrong house. The target was actually a few houses east on the same street, but our window of time to get our HVT was closing.

We came out of the house a somewhat disorganized group, lugging ladders and equipment down an unfamiliar road in the dark, leaving a smoking mess at the front of the first house from the two-pound block of C4 explosive we used to breach the door. The sense of urgency now at an all-time high. The SEAL combat credo is *speed, surprise, and violence of action*—and we had just given away the element of surprise. Thanks to all the noise we had made, shadowy figures were starting to appear on the rooftops. The whole neighborhood was awake and alert. The problem with this complex environment is that you have no idea who is good or bad. There are 360 degrees of potential threats.

We hustled as fast as we could to the next house. The breaching team (breacher and two point men) set another charge while half the platoon was still coming over the wall. Time was of the essence. Now with the threat level higher, everyone was going in. The charge blew and we surged forward. But this one didn't blow the door all the way. There was a secondary security door behind the main door.

The breacher, frustrated but calm, announced, "Failed breach—we need to manually breach."

The newest guys on the Team are allowed the pleasure of carrying the heaviest, most awkward equipment, which meant at this time I quickly moved to the door and removed the 30-pound, gas-powered metal-cutting saw that was strapped to my back. I set it down, got it started and began cutting through the thick mess of twisted metal. Sparks flying everywhere—again, finding every piece of exposed skin. Small burning holes started emerging on my black balaclava mask.

Time was of the essence. The problem with a failed breach is that it gives enemy fighters inside time to prepare for the fight.

Once we made it in, we began flooding the rooms on the first floor. The primary HVT was actually hiding in the first room off to the right of the main entrance and had thrown his AK-47 on the ground. A couple of our guys made quick work of detaining him with black plastic flex cuffs, and one stayed behind to hold security on him.

While this was happening, another group of us began stacking on the main stairs leading up to the second floor. This was a winding marble staircase—which left anyone coming up completely exposed to threats from an elevated position on the landing above. We moved up slowly, suppressed rifles scanning our fields of fire. All of a sudden, we began taking heavy fire from an enemy shooter who was in a barricaded position around the corner on the second floor, only ten feet away. Dozens of 7.62 mm rounds were whizzing past our heads and pounding the walls around us—marble and plaster flying everywhere. We immediately returned fire.

Bang-bang-bang-click!

My rifle jammed, and I quickly transitioned to my SIG Sauer 9 mm pistol—quickly but smoothly moving my rifle with my left hand to my left hip while removing my pistol from its holster on my right hip. The point man made the call to move back down and reset. As we did, our corpsman (highly trained Navy SEAL combat medic) took a round right through the base of his night-vision goggles, only a half inch above the lip of his helmet. He stumbled a bit but was able to keep moving down. It wasn't until the next day when he saw his helmet that he realized what had happened—and how close he had come to the end of the game.

We threw several flash-bang grenades up and over onto the landing—*BOOM! BOOM! BOOM!*—and then proceeded back up, scanning the smoky area through the green hue of our NVGs. Due to smoke and dust, visibility had diminished substantially. My NVGs were doing me no favors at this point, so I flipped them up on my helmet. We continued clearing the building and looking for the shooter. My platoonmate and I peeled left down the hallway and entered a back bedroom on the right. A smoking AK-47 lay on the floor. A quick clearance revealed the shooter's hiding place behind a dresser on the left side of the room. We pulled him out, slammed him on the floor, and placed the thick plastic cuffs on his wrists.

Target secure.

So how do we continue to dominate the battlefield and defeat a dangerous, decentralized enemy? In large part because of our well-defined culture. A culture that matches our strategic vision. To win.

I'm not trying to make that mission sound especially dangerous, heroic, or disorganized. It's like so many others I went on during my time in the Teams, and SEALs are running much more complex missions as you read this chapter.

It's what happened immediately after that mission and every other one that reinforces my point about culture. A core tenet of our culture is that it is one of constant learning based on the foundation of transparency and ongoing feedback—something lacking in most civilian organizations. That element of our culture is what drives performance, accountability, and mission success.

Our culture aligns with our strategy.

When we got back to the compound after the operation, soaked in sweat, we immediately stowed our gear and went into a room for our traditional after action review.

Plenty of organizations review their work and perform postmortems, but the way we do it in the SEAL Teams is unique. We do it constantly. When we go into that room, every sailor leaves his rank at the door. You go in as equals, and everybody is free to speak his mind. Transparency is key. The newest member of the team can ask a team leader or platoon commander why he made a certain call, or an experienced operator can make a point about how a certain tactic can be improved for the next mission.

The brutal honesty and transparency serve two very important purposes. If something goes wrong—whether it is the way the mission was planned, decisions that were made or the on-target execution—it is addressed immediately. Lives are on the line, which makes the concept of "best practices" something more than a corporate catchphrase. It also reinforces the culture of trust, communication, and accountability. You will be heard, and if you bring forth a good point, it will be respected. But this level of transparency only works because it's ingrained in our culture. It's a ritual that supports our learning process.

Developing and protecting the culture is one of the most sacred parts of any high-performance team, but if you listen to a lot of conversation in the business world, "culture" isn't much more than a soft buzzword that gets put up on a PowerPoint slide once or twice a year—even though most smart business leaders understand its critical importance.

Winning organizations know that treating culture like an afterthought isn't just foolish.

It's detrimental.

Because leaders who don't actively create the best culture for their organization and its mission will end up with a culture anyway. It will be the haphazard total of its employees' thoughts and experiences—based on everything from how they're treated and rewarded to behavior that is tolerated and where they sit.

But high-performance organizations don't leave those kinds of details to chance. They make the conscious decision to *build* and *define* a culture that attracts and retains the right team members, promotes the organization's values and reinforces those values throughout the company with consistent action. And their culture is aligned with specific strategic objectives—culture matches strategy.

This consistency of action relates to all decisions, large and small. My friend and client Gordon Lansford runs JE Dunn Construction, one of the largest commercial builders in the country. When he took over as CEO, one of his core missions was to establish a culture of transparency, honesty, and accountability. And he was determined to show that the people are JE Dunn's greatest asset.

We have a saying in the SEAL Teams—"Take care of your gear and your gear will take care of you." Similarly, when you take care of your people, they will in turn take care of you (the business). Gordon, like other great business leaders, understands that if you take care of your people, they will take care of the customers—which leads to positive financial returns.

And great financial returns equals happy shareholders.

One of the ways he did this was by changing the way employees are evaluated—separating it from the usual career development process. For example, candidates seeking upward mobility in management must have a record of behavior showing that the company's people have been their primary consideration. Over the past three years, by focusing on promoting a culture of open communication, trust and accountability—and rewarding these behaviors consistently and publically—the company has seen measurable growth and the financial returns to prove it. And more important, you can feel it when you walk into the office.

It's much more than a catchphrase.

One of the unfortunate side effects of the economic downturn that began between 2006 and 2008 is that it has caused many organizations to manage out of fear. Because of the uncertainties in the marketplace—and the very real threats to many companies' survival—many, many leaders see the concept of "culture" and the tasks of defining and managing it as luxuries that only get attention once more concrete and easier-to-measure objectives are handled. This has resulted in many organizations making misaligned tactical decisions and being heavy on *management* and light on *leadership*—which is the antithesis of companies that navigate change successfully.

That's a shortsighted view, because the organizations that dominate their segment do it specifically by defining and managing culture! Culture is a significant part of the strategy. It is the single greatest differentiating factor between mediocre performers and the organizations that operate at the top.

As Gordon Lansford says, if you focus on your "people practices" and put the team first, the other issues tend to work themselves out.

When you define the culture you want for your organization, align it with the vision and strategy, and establish it authentically, you will have built the single most powerful tool for navigating *change*. You will be building a team that can adapt and thrive in adversity—which is something every organization has to do just to survive. And while organizational change doesn't need to happen in such rapid succession as in urban combat, adaptability is key for success.

THE TAKINGPOINT PRINCIPLE

In his new book, *One Mission*, Chris Fussell (former Navy SEAL officer and partner at the McChrystal Group) provides an in-depth description about the special operations community's need for culture transformation. Special Operations and the military as a whole entered these post-9/11 conflicts essentially as a slower moving, very siloed twentieth-century organization. Many things would have to change in order to sustain and win the fight against much more decentralized enemies to become a modern, adaptive twenty-first-century organism. Silos had to be broken down and communication needed to flow more seamlessly. All of this would eventually result in a shift in mindset and culture transformation. The "new" culture needed to align with the new vision and support a singular mission narrative.

So why is this so important to talk about how culture impacts change?

Because so many organizations fall short of their transformation objectives. There is a common thread among the highest-performing organizations that prioritizing culture beats business strategy every time. I'd like to take that theory a step further. For companies that will thrive in the twenty-first century—*culture will BE the strategy*. Obviously, culture is not the only element of a successful business strategy, but it will start playing a much more significant role, garnering more attention, time, and investment.

According to a 2013 survey of more than 22,000 business executives by the Katzenbach Center at Strategy&, 84 percent of leaders understand the key point I just mentioned—that culture plays a critical role in leading and managing change, and overall business performance.

But the survey also revealed that more than two-thirds of organizational change efforts fail because they don't recognize and use the strengths of the internal culture while shoring up the weaknesses. Leaders are recognizing that their organizations need to do something to adapt to a new market reality, but they're failing to execute those changes more than half the time because they mishandle the cultural components of the team. As Chris intelligently points out in his book, if the new mindsets and behaviors hadn't eventually become ingrained in the culture, the transformation wouldn't have been fulfilled—or lasted.

We will dive more deeply into culture's role in organizational transformation in the following pages, but let's first take a look at why culture is so critically important—and not just as it applies to change, but as it applies to building winning companies.

As I pointed to earlier, defining and managing culture is more important than ever—especially since 2017 Gallup research has employee disengagement at a whopping 67 percent, with only 15 percent of the workforce as defined as engaged, and 18 percent who are actively disengaged—working against the organization. You can see why this is a serious problem. But also an opportunity for those who learn to master the art of culture management.

Culture is reflective of leadership and culture is what drives engagement.

- Weak culture not aligned with strategy = low engagement.

- Strong culture aligned with strategy = high engagement.

According to *Fortune*'s Best Companies list and Glassdoor's Best Places to Work list (data compiled through employee surveys), organizations like HubSpot, Netflix, Apple, Google and many more rate the highest, primarily due to how actively they focus on maintaining a great culture. For example, Netflix's *Culture Manifesto* is one of the most widely viewed documents on the Internet. And most of the companies that are winning when it comes to culture and being the "best places to work" are doing so by actually being the best PLACES to work. They invest heavily in cultural experiences and the workplace environment.

It didn't take long when I came back to the civilian world after my time in the SEAL Teams to see this corporate reality.

The economy was in shambles. Companies were going out of business, and those that were still clinging on were definitely not focusing on what could be misconstrued as these "softer-side" management strategies. And I certainly didn't begin my career as an entrepreneur prioritizing these things either.

The first company I started was a search engine for finding new home developments across the globe—basically an early version of Trulia or Zillow. We grew it into a substantial business but it wasn't the best timing as the housing market was on the brink of disaster. We eventually raised more money and launched what became a large marketing agency that would make the prestigious *Inc.* 500 list for many consecutive years—and still is.

Leading a rapidly growing company is a great problem to have but comes with all of the growing pains one could imagine. Fast growth in an even faster-changing industry requires an extremely nimble organization with leaders that embrace and evangelize change. We were running into some of the inevitable growth barriers I had read about in my favorite business books and learned about in graduate school. It was time to make a change.

I resolved that I would use some of the tools I learned in the Teams to avoid making those same mistakes that failed organizations regret. By combining those tools with some valuable lessons learned on the business battlefield, I built the Culture-Driven Transformation (CDT) model, which is the first step on the *TakingPoint* performance blueprint you're learning about in this book. I will take you through this model and how to apply it in the following pages of this chapter.

The goal is simple, but it takes hard work to achieve it. Instead of dealing with change as a massive disrupting force within the organization—a crisis that needs to be survived—I teach organizations how to develop a culture that sees and understands change as *part* of the culture. A culture that meshes perfectly with the business strategy and desired results.

The steps we will talk about will ensure that your team develops a different way of seeing challenges and opportunities. You can use your existing culture to drive change and get better results—by turning up the volume on the positive aspects of the culture and improving or eliminating the negative aspects—instead of trying to eradicate your current culture and replace it completely.

It's a mindset shift, not an organ transplant.

It is important to say right up front that you will not hear some Pollyanna speech from me about how some Navy SEAL "magic" will make all the risks and uncertainties that come with changes in the marketplace go away. Even the best-run, highest-performing organizations struggle with change and culture's role in transformation.

But organizations (and leaders) that have seen the most growth, survived the stiffest competition and stood the test of time have become comfortable with the discomfort of change—and they lead that change *intentionally* with the strength of their culture.

APPLICATIONS FROM THE BATTLEFIELD
TO THE BOARDROOM

I completed my BUD/S training just a couple weeks before 9/11. My class was literally days away from beginning SQT. I saw firsthand the deliberate, aggressive, and massive transformation the special operations community went through after the attacks. The new reality required a significant shift in organizational structure and approach. We went from an essentially peacetime fighting force to one that has been involved in nonstop conflicts for more than sixteen years—and not to mention constant change.

The Navy has spent millions on market research and studies in an attempt to identify key drivers and the physical and mental traits required to successfully complete our training pipeline. We have constantly applied lessons learned on the battlefield to making adjustments to various strategies and tactics. Like any organization, all of this has some level of impact on the culture.

But even with that dedicated effort of time, money, and attention, the system still hits snags. Culture doesn't change instantly, just because somebody orders it. In that way, the Naval Special Warfare community is similar to many organizations in the business world. The best intentions and a seemingly open-ended budget aren't enough if you want to successfully embrace change, upgrade your culture, and thrive in an uncertain environment.

In fact, it wasn't until 2005 that the Navy SEAL Ethos was created at a two-day leadership offsite event on San Clemente Island. Our ethos is essentially the culture statement that guides who we are and why we exist. We had been constantly operating in VUCA environments for four years. VUCA (volatile, uncertain, complex, ambiguous), as I mentioned previously, is an acronym originally coined by the U.S. military and is now widely used in the global business community. But these new environments require new mindsets and a renewed focus on change.

The same is true for today's business landscape. Some of the biggest roadblocks to successful change strategies? Lack of leadership alignment on the vision, change battle fatigue, skill deficits, external market factors, and undisciplined leaders (and therefore undisciplined teams).

All of these issues are things we're going to talk much more in depth about later, but it's important to introduce them now because of how critical they are to understanding the value of a culture-based approach.

You don't have to look very hard to see plenty of real-life examples of change exhaustion. Almost every organization is faced with human capital challenges inside and outside the company—from creating a team to managing customers and clients. Information moves faster now than ever before, which makes it easier to make well-informed decisions—assuming that data is being properly managed and disseminated—but also to create disruption. Disrupting a market can make a company billions of dollars, but disrupting your team can cause an extreme amount of stress—and fatigue.

According to the *2017 Deloitte Global Human Capital Trends* report I referenced earlier, 60 percent of employees feel "overwhelmed" by the mass amounts of messaging and communication they receive. Simplicity must become the new normal and a core function of communicating a vision for change.

All this information and change happens very quickly, and very few organizations have the training and skill set to survive it—let alone exploit it. So many organizations find themselves learning how to manage change *as it happens*, which is sort of like learning how to fly by getting behind the controls of a jetliner when it's already up in the air. You need to train new skills and strategies *before* you need them, not in the middle of a crisis. And change can't just be managed, it must be inspired and led.

Change starts with many important leadership decisions. One of the most surprising things civilians learn about the SEAL community is the lack of "authoritarian" leadership at the platoon or troop level. There is no question who is in charge and we have hierarchies, but leaders are interested in receiving the best information possible, no matter where it comes from. The unfortunate reality of the civilian world is that management teams often make decisions from the bunker—without gathering valuable intelligence from frontline team members to inform those decisions. Nor do they gather feedback after the fact to make any necessary adjustments. Mistrust and confusion ensues. Almost nothing corrodes a culture faster.

Maybe you have been in a situation like this. You're part of a management team that has been tasked by senior leaders with rolling out an important new initiative—say developing a new product line. During the initial briefing, brows start to furrow, and inquisitive glances begin darting around the room. It seems that the new plan doesn't really fit the company's culture and value system, and it doesn't match a real area of expertise. It seems to stray from the core functions that make the company great. And there is no mentioning of any sort of culture shift to align with the new strategy. No real vision—just a misaligned tactical move in an attempt to capture some market share in a space that may not even be appropriate.

What happens next? What does it mean?

Down through the organization, people are wondering. Are there things happening that we don't know about? Why are we doing this? Is this a knee-jerk reaction to something else that's not working? Maybe leadership's new "pet project" to make more money?

There could be fantastic reasons—ones that mean the difference between survival and bankruptcy. But transformations require a significant reflection and explanation about the "why," and a strategy that matches the company's cultural strengths. Otherwise, resistance will immediately set in, and the change plan might ultimately fail.

In their book, *Diagnosing and Changing Organizational Culture: Based on the Competing Values Framework*, Kim Cameron and Robert Quinn provide tools and instruments for diagnosing culture and strategies for changing organizational culture and behaviors. Years of their research point to the fact that most organizational cultures fall into one of four categories:

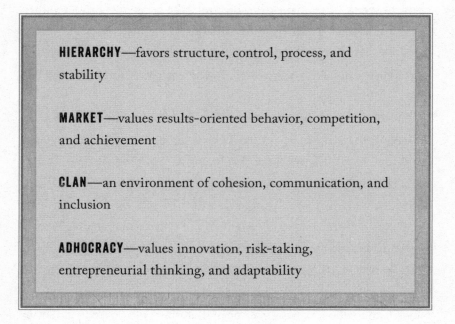

HIERARCHY—favors structure, control, process, and stability

MARKET—values results-oriented behavior, competition, and achievement

CLAN—an environment of cohesion, communication, and inclusion

ADHOCRACY—values innovation, risk-taking, entrepreneurial thinking, and adaptability

I would add that these cultures are most likely at least moderately "managed." Many organizations seem to be made up of a bit of each of these themes.

Based on the *TakingPoint* principles outlined in this book, an adhocracy will lead change better than organizations that fall into the other categories based primarily on those elements of innovation, risk-taking, and adaptability.

This is where the CDT model comes in. By following its six steps, organizations can first identify the positive and negative aspects of their culture, then take well-defined, concrete action.

The first step in the model is to *Define the High-Level Vision for Transformation*.

We will dive deeper into the intelligence gathering and mission planning phases in later chapters, but before you can understand how culture can truly become the chief enabler of change, you need to define the vision for transformation. If you can at least clearly articulate the results the organization is currently getting versus the results it needs to be getting, you're off to a good start.

For example, if a company has had a long history of being a sales-focused organization but light on quality and delivery, the leadership team will need to redefine how they approach the business if they ever want to go to the next level or have a healthy exit strategy. A new high-level vision for transformation might be a renewed focus on the customer, quality, and efficiency. Once that is defined, the company knows the direction it needs to head—and the cultural behaviors that will take them there.

The next step is to perform a *Culture Diagnostic Analysis*.

Before every mission you perform in the SEAL Teams, gathering as much valuable intelligence is critical for understanding what you will be dealing with and how you plan the mission. What details can we learn about the AO (area of operation)? Who lives there? How many enemy fighters can we expect on target? How many noncombatants? What weapons do they have? Will they have a QRF (quick reaction force) nearby? What resources and assets will we have at our disposal? The more information the better, especially when you know some of the intelligence may be flawed.

When you have a thorough understanding of the landscape, resources, and tools at your disposal, you're in the best position to make better decisions.

The purpose of performing this diagnostic is to identify the culture strengths and weakness—the strengths that can be leveraged and the weaknesses that will impede progress. There are several ways to go about this. For example, you can use a combination of anonymous surveys, interviews, and open forums both at specific levels within the company and company-wide to get some of the answers you're looking for. And while a more formal culture diagnosis used to be owned by a relatively small grouping of psychology and consulting firms, more and more tools are becoming available from online platforms to mobile applications— all designed to allow the employer (leaders and managers) to maintain an almost constant pulse on culture and sentiment. Some of these tools include Culture Amp, TinyHR, BlackbookHR, Achievers, Globoforce, BetterCompany, Glint, Officevibe, Waggl, Canary and RelatedMatters. These types of tools matter now more than ever with today's workforce and younger generations, because they are real-time and can be accessed from any device.

For the purpose of this model, if you're deploying a survey, the questions should be culture- and behavior-focused, such as details about the positive aspects of the environment and what can be improved. How would you define our culture? Where does communication fall short? What do you perceive the levels of trust are within the organization? Do we really embody our core values or do we just pretend to? What do our customers, competitors, and others outside the organization say about our culture? Does what they say align with what we perceive reality to be? Does the culture align well with our strategic vision? Do the cultural experiences we create have real value and align with the vision of the company—or do they have little or no impact—a negative impact? Do the existing HR mechanisms and career-pathing programs support the behaviors we are trying to enforce?

These surveys can be customized to gather information in key areas, but you should always leave room for general comments and feedback. I have found this to be where the best and most specific information comes from. And the applications I mentioned previously can help streamline the process and allow for ongoing feedback.

Whatever the results, the data should be used to make the best possible decisions about how culture will fuel change efforts and what parts of the culture should simultaneously be improved.

Next, you must perform a *Team Engagement Audit*.

It is a common understanding of a vast majority of leaders that the employees are a company's most important asset. But in reality, that is true only when the majority of the workforce is fully engaged in their work. If not, they are either adding minimal value or actively working against the organization. You must have a keen understanding of the human capital you have to work with before stepping onto the change battlefield.

There are three types of employees in any organization:

ENGAGED (15 PERCENT OF THE WORKFORCE). These employees are loyal and emotionally committed to the organization. They are in roles where they excel and where their talents are truly leveraged. They enthusiastically invest in their work and take on responsibilities outside of their job description. They are generally more likely to become emerging leaders and will stay with an organization much longer than disengaged employees. These are the team members that will drive change.

NOT ENGAGED (67 PERCENT OF THE WORKFORCE). These employees can be difficult to identify, because they are often relatively happy and satisfied in their role. However, they do the bare minimum and are not invested in the company's mission, vision, values or goals. They are less likely to be customer-focused and are not concerned about productivity or company profitability. These team members are both a threat and great opportunity—because with the proper approach, they can be transformed into engaged employees that thrive in the organization—and help fuel change.

ACTIVELY DISENGAGED (18 PERCENT OF THE WORKFORCE). We have all worked alongside these people. They are consistently negative, create a toxic environment, dominate their manager's time and are usually vocal about their unhappiness. What's worse, is they are often subject-matter experts well respected in their unique skill set. And because of that, they often have significant influence over others. These employees can easily spread toxicity throughout an organization and can rarely be transformed into true "A" players. These employees will work against change and need to be removed.

Most studies point to the fact that employee engagement has a direct impact on productivity and profitability. That seems self-evident, yet many managers still struggle to define, measure and improve engagement in their teams.

HOW DO MANAGERS KNOW WHO IS ENGAGED? Their team members need to be able to confidently state the following:

- I know what is expected of me and my work quality.

- I have the resources and training to thrive in my role.

- I have the opportunity to do what I do best—every day.

- I frequently receive recognition, praise and constructive criticism.

- I trust my manager and believe they have my best interests in mind.

- My voice is heard and valued.

- I clearly understand the mission and purpose and how I contribute to each.

- I have opportunities to learn and grow both personally and professionally.

I will provide you with the tools and process for improving engagement in Chapter 7.

The next step in the CDT model is to *Define the Mindsets and Behaviors That Will Drive the Desired Results*.

In any transformation, mindsets and behaviors must first change in order for the culture to begin shifting in the needed direction—the direction that will fulfill the high-level vision for transformation. In the SEAL Teams or any business organization, culture is all about the beliefs, behaviors, and actions of those on the team. If you want to use the strongest aspects of the current culture as a jumping-off point, you have to be able to identify which ones are *prime movers*—the ones that will help lead change.

In the SEAL Teams, one of the most powerful aspects of our culture is that of accountability. We train for war and fight to win. Failure to perform your job functions in training or on the battlefield isn't tolerated. That mindset helps drive the actions that need to be taken to be in a constant state of evolution—and to get the results we desire. We hold ourselves and others accountable to do what needs to be done to accomplish the mission. Leaders hold their teams accountable and the team holds them accountable. This is how we build teams that are stronger than the sum of their parts.

Other positive aspects of our culture are transparency and adaptability. We communicate well and learn fast. There is no time for passive-aggressive behavior or unwillingness to make changes at the individual or team level. When we realized that the culture of the special operation community had to shift in order to sustain and defeat decentralized enemies in the post-9/11 world, we relied heavily on these culture strengths to lead change.

When a company is going through a transformation, there will obviously be behaviors that need to continue, change, or stop. If you're facing a crisis—or even if you're just enthusiastic about fixing some core functions of the business—sometimes the natural response is to tackle the entire to-do list all at once, thereby piling on a laundry list of new priorities on top of the existing priorities.

That's a mistake. In BUD/S you quickly learn to "eat the elephant one bite at a time." If you focus on all of the difficult evolutions you have to pass before graduation, you'll lose your mind. Picking just a few key mindset and behavioral changes to make at a time helps fend off *change battle fatigue* (which we'll talk about more in Chapter 8) and lets the team focus on a few main initiatives. When you give a blizzard of directives and initiatives, it dilutes the message, stresses the team out, and makes it way more likely that *nothing* gets changed. That's why I prefer the concept of prioritization over multitasking. Multitasking really just means you are most likely doing many things poorly all at once.

The fourth critical step in the CDT model is about *Inspiring a Connection to the Mission.*

In Chapter 6 you'll learn about the process for defining and communicating a compelling vision for change. This is how leaders inspire a connection to the mission. From the minute you start BUD/S training, the core SEAL mission is laid out. And from day one, you're fully committed and bought in or you're drummed out as fast as you can ring a bell. By the time you make it through training and go "downrange," every single person is intimately connected to the cause.

One team with one fight.

You're probably not putting your people through that kind of intense physical and mental training, and your corporate missions probably aren't life-or-death. But the philosophy still holds. When you're changing things about your organization, the goal is to create a positive outcome, right? Improving speed, efficiency, quality, culture, internal and external communication and so on. So communicating what the change is about, why it's necessary, what the positive outcomes will be and what everyone's role is in effecting the change isn't optional. It's a crucial part of the process, and something that needs to be done repeatedly from start to finish. You won't connect your team to the cause if they don't know the five W's (who-what-when-where-*WHY*).

Through this process of explanation and connection, you prime the team to want to follow you into battle—to the win. Which means you need to *define* the win. Repeatedly.

I've consulted with many organizations that have missed this key component. In a sales job, for example, setting "wins" is easy. You can tell a person he or she needs to generate this many leads, sell X number of products, or generate Y amount of revenue. But on non-sales teams, the wins might not be as clear-cut. Still, it's the leader's job to set the goalposts, so the team can begin to develop a plan for how they will accomplish the mission. It fosters collaboration, motivation, and *connection.*

The fifth step is to assign *Change Evangelists* and develop *Team Networks*.

Real change is led from the top, but it will work only if the vision and primary strategic initiatives touch every part of the business—and involve everybody from the boardroom to the front line. Not everybody will see the vision or agree with the strategy—especially if they feel like their input either wasn't solicited or was ignored. And I'll provide you the tools for proper execution in later pages when we discuss the importance of alignment and participation.

Even those who buy in and understand the goals often need guidance to make sure their energetic efforts aren't aimed in the wrong place! Authoritarian, micromanaging leaders like to think they can lay down the law and everybody will fall in line—and that they can keep eyes on the entire team. That's a recipe for disaster. You can't make too many generalizations about the workforce as a whole, but one you *can* make is that employees and job-seekers who were born in the 1980s and 1990s can't be managed like their older counterparts. They must to be led in a different way, and you have to groom that buy-in. If you don't, you'll get distrustful team members who tune out the message.

Any successful transformation effort needs trusted and respected team members "evangelizing" the vision and strategy throughout the ranks. This starts with what I call a *transformation task force* and grows outward. The transformation task force should be made up of a healthy cross section of senior leaders and well-respected subject matter experts from across the organization. This will most likely start with your pool of "engaged" team members.

Their mission? To lead the change process. A cross-functional team whose core function is to help lead the transformation by leveraging the positive aspects of the company culture, activating key managerial tasks and communicating the vision consistently.

The best change evangelists don't just help make the mission work on their own. They recruit other evangelists to join the cause, which results in networks of people across the organization getting behind the cause and organically sharing the story of the new vision—an ecosystem of people communicating an aligned narrative to the edges of the organization. These evangelists can be a driving force for turning the "disengaged" into leaders of change.

It would be nice to think that all this communication and solidarity spreads organically, without any specific effort. But it *does* take effort—diligent effort. In the companies that I've started, I created transformation task forces whose specific responsibility was to promote the horizontal sharing of information—peer to peer, not down from the mountaintop, so to speak. They become the primary change evangelists and chief recruiters of more evangelists.

A transformation task force should be given a specific mission and the resources to complete that mission. One of their most powerful weapons is a creative communication strategy. During change, there is no such thing as overcommunicating. During a major restructuring in one of my companies, a subcommittee within the transformation task force was called *Culture Club*. It was a group of volunteer team members who best embodied the culture and values of the organization—the fully engaged. How do I know this? Because they volunteered! Their mission: to continue to build a great culture and use creative internal and external communication strategies for communicating the vision for change. And they had a blast doing it. They were change evangelists who creatively designed networks where an aligned narrative could thrive and spread.

Culture Club was given the autonomy to create multichannel communication tools that kept the whole company energized and focused on the long-term win. They used social media for communicating quick wins. They launched a video contest where team members reflected on their favorite parts of the company culture. They hosted live events and team-building experiences designed to bring everyone together. But most important, we always aligned these activities with what we were trying to accomplish. These cultural experiences were designed to support the beliefs and actions that would get desired results.

The sixth element of the CDT model is *Telling Purposeful Stories*.

People are social animals. And as much as managers like to believe that their team members are rational creatures, studies show that 70 percent of our decisions are based on emotional factors, not ration and data. They respond when they can identify with what they see and hear. If you're trying to transform your organization, the best thing you can do is tell the success stories of the people who are doing it well. If certain team members have embraced the changes and are showing great results, celebrate them. If you're still early in the process, find another organization that went through a similar transformation successfully and tell their story.

These stories help connect the team on an emotional level and give each team member a way to visualize what success looks like. In later chapters we will talk more about how storytelling plays an impactful role in communicating quick wins that keep the team energized, combats change battle fatigue, keeps them connected to the long-term vision and brings the naysayers on board.

Telling Purposeful Stories shouldn't just happen in a monthly or quarterly company-wide meeting. Leaders, managers and members of the transformation task force should find informal opportunities every day to weave in stories about transformation progress being made. And it isn't always about happy talk. Communicate the good with the bad and allow the team networks and evangelists to help spread the word.

For example:

"Hey, did you hear that we exceeded our goal timeline for the selection of the new software platform by six weeks? This puts us way ahead of the implementation timetable! Here's what happened . . ."

You also want to maintain a sense of urgency by not always keeping it all about the positive stuff. For example:

"We did achieve our goal of being up 5 percent year over year, which is awesome, but we are still losing market share to our main competitor. Let's keep at it."

Telling Purposeful Stories is easy and should be done with the intent of delivering aligned communication throughout the entire organization. Again, the CDT model isn't a "first step" but rather a process that must be utilized throughout the entire transformation journey. And you'll see how all this starts to come together in the following chapters.

STORIES FROM THE FRONT LINES

To give you some real-life insight on how CDT works, let me tell you some stories about how it has been developed.

In December of 2012, I got an email from—let's call him Jason—the president of the Asia-Pacific region of a global bank. He had just read the first column I wrote for *Forbes*—"From the Battlefield to the Boardroom: A Navy SEAL's Guide to Business Leadership Success."

Jason was a young, energetic banking prodigy who had risen quickly in the ranks from Goldman Sachs to UBS and then to his current position at this global bank. He told me how much he admired the Naval Special Warfare culture, and how I have applied it to the world of business. He went on to explain that the massive merger they had recently gone through was still causing some culture growing pains, and he was hoping I could help him find some solutions. Like other large mergers, such as HP's acquisition of Compaq (a culture of quality mixing with a culture of being a low-cost provider), combining vastly different cultures can cause significant long-term issues that must be addressed aggressively.

For this global bank—two organizations, really—plenty of cultural assimilation issues arose immediately and lasted for years, which is by no means unusual. At the end of his email, Jason invited me to come do a series of keynote presentations and workshops during their global leadership conference in Hong Kong. We both knew I could not single-handedly provide the solutions they needed, but this would be the catalyst for ongoing efforts for improvement.

When I started working with Jason and his team at their offices in Hong Kong, he gave me a detailed background on the cultural challenges that both companies were facing. And not just from a geo-locational standpoint but from a wide variance in culture between the two organizations—a sophisticated high-end investment and wealth management firm and a global bank known at the time as "the Walmart of banks." But the economic downturn made the acquisition an attractive opportunity.

Naturally, a global company of this size had been putting an extraordinary amount of time and resources toward addressing these challenges in all of the traditional ways a large corporation would. But they were running into significant obstacles, and change was happening slowly.

Jason is a great leader, and he understood that the organization needed to be brought together using more unconventional methods—but the way it had been done thus far was very corporate and traditional. They did it very rigidly, through human resource mechanisms, newsletters, more meetings and digital resources like an intranet site—which pretty much guaranteed the rank-and-file team members wouldn't truly connect with what they were trying to accomplish.

This is where the inception of the CDT model began. I started to realize that for any organization to make major changes and overcome certain change obstacles—in this case a large merger—culture misalignment has to be addressed aggressively. This is true for any size company that acquires another and a key driver in whether a merger will be successful or if it should even happen at all. I've seen smart business owners walk away from what seems to be a very lucrative move that will double the value of their organization because the variance between the cultures of their company and the potential acquisition will be too difficult to overcome. And ultimately result in failure.

So for this event in Hong Kong, I used the keynote presentation, workshops, and breakout sessions to start real conversations about how to merge the cultures, keeping the positive aspects of both that compliment one another and eliminating the negative aspects.

These presentations and initiated discussions gained so much momentum that I was asked to go to Singapore and Australia to meet with other senior leaders the next month—and I've made a circuit around their Asia-Pacific offices every year since, presenting on topics ranging from leadership and culture to improving communication, trust, and accountability. The regular feedback I receive from Jason is that things are improving and leading to amazing measurable results. Primarily because they are taking ownership over the transformation process.

I wouldn't feel comfortable advising a client (or you!) to use the CDT model if I wasn't willing to use it myself, in my own companies. By 2013, our marketing agency had been in business for almost five years. We had seen plenty of success—doubling in head count and revenue growth each year since the company's inception. We had landed on the prestigious Inc. 500 list of fastest growing private companies three years in a row and had seen 1,700 percent growth over a three-year period. The first year we made the list we were the 187th fastest-growing business in the United States. Not bad.

We had built a great team, had amazing clients, and had just moved into a new 17,000-square-foot office building in San Diego. We clearly weren't in a crisis.

But still, the warning signs had started to pop up.

That year, we started to see a gradual uptick in client turnover, and we noticed that our net margin was steadily decreasing. The processes we were using just weren't working as well.

This is by no means unusual for growing companies. The maturation process can be uncomfortable when you realize you have been drinking your own Kool-Aid and blinding yourself to challenges that may be coming down the road.

When I was a budding entrepreneur in business school, I read just about every business book I could get my hands on. One of my favorites was Marshall Goldsmith's *What Got You Here Won't Get You There: How Successful People Become Even More Successful*. The book focuses on fundamental career success factors and the mindset and behaviors required to go to the next level. It's a book about transformation. I went on to read books like Jim Collins' *Good to Great: Why Some Companies Take the Leap . . . and Others Don't* and *Built to Last*. The combined and tested theories in these books explain that the tools and behaviors that take a person or company to a certain level are not necessarily the same for going the distance.

Growing businesses face inevitable challenges as they reach certain barriers they must overcome. The people, systems, processes, and even cultures that take a business to a certain level of growth aren't necessarily the same that will take it past a certain point. Businesses must adapt and mature as they grow.

I was starting to see the light. We had made significant adjustments to our processes and business model to grow to more than one hundred employees. But now, like many organizations, we were confronted by problems for which we didn't necessarily have the answers.

One thing we did know, however, was that we had taken great care in building a strong culture and that we could leverage it to drive necessary changes. It was time for culture-driven transformation.

Our internal research pointed to the fact that we needed new systems, new software, a new sales and marketing strategy, new departments, and a laundry list of clients we needed to part ways with. Basically, it would be a full transformation and rebranding effort from the inside out. Using the CDT model, we *Defined the High-Level Vision for Transformation* and performed the *Culture Diagnostic Analysis* to gather data. Using that data, we *Defined the Mindsets and Behaviors That Get the Desired Results*.

For example, the diagnostic uncovered that a strong part of our culture was the passion team members had for doing great work for their clients—for improving their businesses. That contrasted a bit with the declining client satisfaction ratings we were getting on communication—which pointed to a serious disconnect. And we soon found that the solution was easy. We just hadn't been addressing it.

Our mission became using that passion as a driver for better client communication—and it was that message we hammered home time after time with our teams.

But it wasn't just words on a PowerPoint slide. We took action to reinforce those words. We completely restructured our divisions, pairing account managers with project managers and giving them five to ten clients each to personally "own." We also changed the metrics by which we measured our teams, so that they were rewarded by achieving the same goals we had established as a part of this transformation. We found alignment.

Senior leadership was very much involved in every step of this process—and I can say this with conviction because I was one of those senior leaders. I sat down and thought about the company's culture and our existing core values. When a company is going through a complete restructuring from the inside out, culture, values and brand play a big role. Who are we and more important, who do we want to become? Revisiting these questions is not a bad thing. It's imperative. We had great core values and mission and vision statements—although they needed some tweaking to align with our renewed vision. We did not, however, have a culture statement or a defined "purpose." A big no-no when the majority of your workforce is made up of millennials!

When I reflected on the vision of who we wanted to become, what we had didn't align with where we wanted to go. It was time to get feedback and bring the team together in an effort to define our "why." It had to be about more than just one or two senior leaders writing on a whiteboard and developing what they think sounds good. Team feedback would be crucial and ensure buy-in.

I learned about the importance of transparent feedback in the SEAL Teams and implemented this as part of the company culture. When we began, we had raised about $1 million in Series "A" angel capital round and were experiencing great growth. But as we grew and continued to recruit great talent, questions started arising about the company's direction, values, and mission. I wanted to know not just what managers felt about the people on their teams, but what the team members thought about how they were being led—myself included. So we launched an anonymous 360-degree review process.

The entire team filled out the surveys anonymously, and I got on a San Diego–to–New York flight, excited to read the pile of them and find out how great our company really was—and how great *I* was doing as their leader.

What I read astonished me.

I read that some people didn't understand what I did every day. Others had no idea what our overall strategy was. Some of the feedback was good, but the negative stuff was a real gut punch—and as the CEO, I knew what I had to do about it.

I called a meeting and laid out everything I had read, good and bad. I owned the bad parts, and emphasized that it was important that everybody on the team felt free to speak up if they saw something they thought needed to be changed. It was a lesson I had learned my first week on SEAL Team 5, but it had gotten away from me when I transitioned into the civilian world.

From that day forward, we did the same 360-degree review every six months. Transparency became ingrained in our culture. It made me more accountable as a leader—and it reinforced within the culture that *everyone has a voice* (which became one of our core values). And it was a fundamental part of the transformation we were now going through.

Did the transformation work perfectly? No. It took longer than we expected, and conflicting priorities caused distractions. But in the end, the CDT model—a foundational principle in the *TakingPoint* process— was successful in transforming the company into a more efficient, profitable, and scalable company. The company recently landed on the *Inc.* 500 list for its seventh year in a row, and has continued the upward trend.

The CDT model doesn't work in a vacuum, nor is it just a "first step." It must permeate the entire *TakingPoint* process. And just because you're doing it doesn't mean you abandon the traditional transformation strategies and tactics that any consulting firm would recommend. What CDT does is *enhance* those other tools—and it gives you the best chance to make your transformation work.

If you commit to the six steps of the CDT model, you'll see something amazing happen. Teams start to band together and get even tighter in the face of adversity. In SEAL speak, they "get comfortable being uncomfortable."

By describing the vision and explaining the strategy behind the transformation completely (and repeatedly), you can shift the prime emotion associated with change from fear to excitement.

Culture becomes the chief enabler. Then, almost anything is possible.

2

TRUST: FUELING THE CHANGE ENGINE

Uncompromising integrity is my standard.
My character and honor are steadfast.
My word is my bond.
—NAVY SEAL ETHOS

How important is trust in the workplace, especially as it relates to organizations facing the need for significant transformation? Is trust a nice-to-have social variable, or is it a critical component that sets mediocre teams apart from winning teams that generate great financial returns?

According to the Human Capital Institute (HCI), trust can be defined as "the willingness to put oneself at risk based on another individual's actions." Organizations composed of aligned teams that trust each other outperform those that are lacking in trust—plain and simple. HCI performed a study called *Building Trust 2013: Workforce Trends Defining High Performance*, which was based on a survey of business professionals. One fundamental takeaway was that employees working in high-performance organizations view their leaders as—highly trustworthy—those who lead by example and live the values on and off the battlefield. Trust starts at the top.

The two factors that trust affects the most? *Productivity* and *Engagement*.

And since we have already established that engagement is low in today's workforce, one could theorize that trust is often either not valued or not measured and managed. As I referenced previously, Gallup research points to the fact that employee disengagement costs the U.S. between $450 and $550 billion per year. So it seems that trust is not a nice-to-have social variable but rather it drives financial performance—or nonperformance.

So what drives engagement? In his book *The Speed of Trust*, Stephen M. R. Covey explains that employee retention and engagement increase when there is a high degree of trust. High-trust organizations earn loyalty both inside and outside the company, from employees and shareholders to customers and partners. So you can imagine how imperative trust is to successfully leading change in volatile, uncertain environments.

Seems obvious, right?

Trust is an essential component within a SEAL Team, and you start learning it's important from day one. And every SEAL remembers Hell Week like it happened yesterday. The days and nights blur together, but there are specific evolutions you will never forget.

Once you've been through about a month of indoctrination and a couple weeks of the first phase of the BUD/S program, you get to Hell Week. And it is exactly what it sounds like. At this point, about half the class has already quit. And many more will ring the bell during the first couple days of Hell Week.

It isn't like the first two or three weeks leading up to Hell Week are a picnic, but at least you get to sleep for a few hours a night. But when the pain is getting ready to start on a Sunday afternoon, you're already miserable with anticipation. The class reports to the main classroom Sunday morning with only a few required items in their possession. The beauty of that first day is that you have no idea when Hell Week will commence. The stress and the anxiety are eating you up, and all of a sudden "breakout" starts. It's a whirlwind of explosions, and the instructors are all around you, firing M60 machine guns—using blanks, but still. You're getting sprayed with fire hoses, and smoke grenades are going off everywhere. The instructors are shouting orders.

"Bear crawl to the surf zone—get wet and sandy!"

"Boat crew leaders, give me a head count! Where is your boat crew, sir?!"

"One hundred burpees! Bust 'em out!"

It is total chaos. And after a couple of hours of insanity, the class heads to the beach for some nice, long "surf torture." You link arms with your classmates and walk into the ocean and lie down. The instructors want to make sure they keep you cold, wet, and sandy all week. My class had the privilege of doing Hell Week in the winter, when water temps in Coronado can be in the fifties.

And you know what? Good. The Lord wants hard SEALs—and SEALs can only be "forged in adversity."

But guys will quit even in the first few hours. I enjoyed watching others quit, because I knew it meant my chances kept improving, statistically speaking. On Sunday night, there is no light at the end of the tunnel. Not even a glimmer. For the next six days, you won't have more than a couple hours of rest. Even when you get it, it's not exactly restful. Whenever you stop moving, your muscles clench up uncontrollably—so much so that the pain is overwhelming and you can't even fathom being able to move again.

But you do.

Everything about Hell Week is designed to test your physical and mental fortitude. You're running and crawling everywhere, covered in sand, sweating during the day and freezing at night. It's nonstop intense physical activity, and the instructors are whispering in your ear every minute, trying to get you to quit. You only stop moving to eat. That could mean running over to the chow hall or eating MREs (Meals Ready to Eat) in the surf zone.

What gets you through is your mindset, your relationship with the other guys in your boat crew, and the leadership of the officers in the class. Our class leader—the highest-ranking officer in the class—was the ideal combination of tough, principled, and compassionate. We all gravitated toward John. He had a positive mental attitude and was able to get us fired up about the misery we would face each day leading up to Hell Week. On Sunday afternoon, a couple hours before Hell Week started, he read us the St. Crispin's Day speech from William Shakespeare's *Henry V*. This speech has a lot of meaning to me. I was the captain of our rugby team my junior and senior years at SMU and we actually had it on the back of our team T-shirts.

John read aloud:

"From this day to the ending of the world, but we in it shall be remembered. We few, we happy few, we band of brothers; For he today that sheds his blood with me shall be my brother."

John died four days later.

It was early Thursday morning—basically the middle of the night. Those of us who had survived the week so far were with our boat crews, doing relay races in the Olympic-size swimming pool across the street at the Naval Amphibious Base. One of the evolutions was called a caterpillar race, and there's nothing cute about it. All the guys in your boat crew—six or seven—jump into the water while wearing cammies and gear belts. Each guy is on his back with his legs wrapped around the waist of the person in front of him. Everybody is exhausted, and you're all trying to stay just coordinated enough to keep your head above water. But you're also trying to beat the other boat crews. If you do, there is a small chance you might get to sit out the next race. The instructors would shout "It pays to be a winner, gentlemen!" When the caterpillar breaks up—which it always eventually does—everybody has to tread water and get back into position.

It is truly exhausting.

In the middle of it, the instructors yelled at us to all get out of the pool, go sit by the fence and put our heads down. Nobody thought anything of it, because you've been given orders relentlessly and you're delirious with exhaustion at that point. You're literally hallucinating constantly and just trying to make it to the end.

But something was different this time. Something was off.

They had us run back across the street to the Naval Special Warfare Center and assemble in the classroom. We noticed John wasn't there but weren't sure why. A couple of hours later, the door to the room opened and the instructor staff entered. The commanding officer of BUD/S was with them. He walked to the front of the room.

He didn't waste any time.

He told us that John was pronounced dead at 1 a.m., apparently from heart failure, but nobody was sure yet.

After pausing for a second to let it sink in, he said something that sticks with me to this day. "Get used to this feeling, gentlemen. In the Teams, you're going to lose guys. That's one of the unfortunate aspects of the job."

He looked to the second-highest-ranking officer and said, "You're in charge now." The exhaustion of the moment and time that has passed have made me forget his exact words, but I do recall him talking to us about the importance of team trust, especially in the face of adversity.

The instructors walked out and left us to process what had happened. Some cried. Others just stared off into the abyss.

We would have a new leader for the rest of BUD/S. At first, we weren't sure we trusted him the way we did John. He had a very different leadership style that we would have to get used to. Before John's passing during Hell Week, the class had become very strong. The crucible of Hell Week forged a bond that you can't describe. Simply put, we were brothers who trusted each other. But things would be different now.

Leaning on each other was the only way we were going to survive training—and the missions we would eventually go on as SEALs. It would become even more important than we realized at the time, too.

This was just a few months before the 9/11 attacks, and the things we would face as SEAL operators would be incredibly intense. We had no idea what was in store for us—and that we would be going to war.

As a class, we rallied around our new leader, and it drew us even closer together. As a young lieutenant, he was still developing as a leader himself and worked hard to develop a style that worked well with the culture of the class. Well before graduation day, he had earned the respect and trust of the twenty-three of us who made it through.

He had led us to victory.

THE TAKINGPOINT PRINCIPLE

All my experiences and research have led me to the conclusion that building a culture of trust is a game-changing strategy. People are happier, experience lower levels of stress, collaborate better, produce a higher quality of work, and stick around longer. But trust cannot be established without consistent action that matches leadership's spoken words—and of course, accountability, which we will discuss in detail in Chapter 3. Without high levels of trust, an organization can't thrive and grow—and it certainly will not navigate change successfully.

Despite some of the language you hear, business isn't combat. People aren't usually going to die if you make a mistake. But the trust element that was such an important component of BUD/S training and combat is equally important in the business world. Like culture, trust is not an irrelevant social variable that has little to no impact on the financial performance of a business. It is one of the most important elements of any high-performing team that is driven to do great work, achieve great financial results, and fulfill the vision of the organization.

It is the foundation of everything we're going to talk about in the rest of this book. If you can build trust with the people on your team—whether you're an executive on the senior leadership team or the point person for a group on the front lines—you're going to be more prepared for the challenges ahead of you.

In its 2016 global CEO survey, PwC reported that 55 percent of CEOs concur that a lack of trust is a threat to their company's growth. But it seems that many have done little to learn how to measure, manage, and improve trust. This chapter will give you the framework for doing just that.

Being able to measure internal and external trust levels within an organization and then implement systems for improving trust will ensure that the business is ready for change. The pillars that you will be learning in this chapter will help you focus on the most important *trust factors* and provide you the tools necessary for creating a high-trust environment.

APPLICATIONS FROM THE BATTLEFIELD TO THE BOARDROOM

As we've been talking about, even though SEALs are a part of the military, the culture is not one of command-and-control. Hierarchies exist, and there is a chain of command like any other branch of the military, but the trust and confidence team members have in each other is strong because of the decentralized environment and empowered teams. And it starts at the top. In other words, the leaders have to earn the trust of their teams. It isn't something that happens by command, rank, or because regulations say so.

Unfortunately, many, many civilian organizations don't operate this way. Leadership expects trust and loyalty to work from the bottom up. It's a blind and inauthentic "trust." In fact, the first article I wrote for my *Inc.* column many years ago was on this exact topic—and it's still one of the most viewed and shared pieces I've written. The article talked about trust and loyalty as a top-down strategy—not bottom-up. Simply assuming that trust exists is an enticing way to operate, because it gives leaders a sense that they're controlling something, and, frankly, it's easier—especially when you start dealing with larger organizations with multiple divisions, departments, and silos.

Trust cannot be assumed.

I've seen it happen in my own companies and companies I have worked with.

Here's an example. When the CEO gets a call directly from a senior executive of a client firm—bypassing his or her regular point of contact to go straight to the top—what happens next will set the tone for the team's trust level. Let's say that client has a complaint about the quality of work being done. The client executive says, "We've spent all this money with you and we're not getting what we expected. What are you going to do about it?"

The natural inclination might be to react to that information by calling in your team and blistering them—saying the client called us and is complaining, and we'd better get things straightened out or we'll lose a huge piece of business. It starts a whirlwind of activity—teams frantically being called together to patch up some problem in a poorly directed fire drill. Promises are being made to the client and endless freebies being given.

This type of behavior from senior leaders shows inexperience and immaturity—and it certainly does not exhibit trust. Trust must first be given in order to get it in return.

The client executive probably got his or her information filtered upward from an operational team. The problem could be the result of a variety of factors—many of which are out of your team's control. You could come down hard to save the business, or you could ask your team for a report on what's going on.

"This is the information I'm getting. How does it match with what you see on your end? Are we dropping the ball, or do we have problems on the client end? Or both? What can we do to sort this out?"

By showing your team you trust them, you're giving them reasons to trust *you*. And by showing them you back them, you're transforming mindsets, and then they will want to run through a wall for you—instead of resenting you for giving them endless hours of additional work to fix something that may or may not have been their fault. At the end of the day, accountability matters and the team has to *own* the outcome. But trust is built when that outcome is earned together.

If you damage internal trust in your organization, it takes a long time to rebuild. Unless something radical happens with the behavior of the leadership team—or a change in leadership occurs—it often *can't* be rebuilt. Especially, when things like this happen frequently.

Those problems can certainly be solved with the right kind of shift in mindset, but it's obviously better to create a system that sustains the right kind of culture in the first place.

If trust is to be the foundational element of a high-performance team, it must be built on something. In the time I've spent after the Teams working within my own organizations and helping others, I have distilled that growth platform into what I call the *Seven Pillars of Trust*. Building these pillars into an organization's culture is imperative for change. Without these trust factors as a foundation, transformation efforts always fail.

PILLAR 1
Integrity of Leadership On and Off the Battlefield

Life on a SEAL Team tends to expose who you are at your core pretty quickly. You're living in close quarters when you travel or deploy, and you're going into life-and-death situations where trust is obviously at an absolute premium. If the person next to you isn't trustworthy, that is something you discover—and address—right away. It's extremely rare that an untrustworthy person even makes it out of BUD/S, much less through the rigors of advanced training. But if for whatever reason it happens, they won't last long in the Teams.

It might not be so clear-cut in the business world, but that integrity piece is still a huge part of what creates a culture of trust. At the most basic level, what leaders in an organization say needs to square with what they do. And consistency is key. If you're a senior leader and you're hammering home the concepts of trust and integrity while simultaneously being dishonest in your dealings with your staff, customers, strategic partners—or even at home—you're establishing that words don't really matter.

Integrity matters on and off the battlefield.

And as much as we like to think of our private lives as private, how you operate in your personal life *does* impact the trust component when you're on the job. If you're the head of a division and you work closely with your team, you're going to be judged by your actions both inside and outside the office. One of the many burdens of command. If words and actions don't align, trust deteriorates quickly. If you desire to be trusted by your team but you lose control when you're out at a company function, or you're cheating on your spouse and everyone at work knows it, you're compromising the trust your team will have in you. And, more important, they're going to believe that dishonesty isn't something that gets punished. That it's allowed.

The examples don't even have to be big and gaudy—like infidelity. Say you're running a small shop with twenty employees, and you have the chance to take on a huge new client. But that client has a bad reputation, and a quick Google search turns up a bunch of articles about negative dealings they've had. You can rationalize taking them on by saying that the firm needs the business, but if you're simultaneously trying to spread the message that integrity and trust are important, your team is going to see it for what it is—that integrity is not valued by the organization or its leaders. Like all culture elements, trust and integrity starts at the top. It must be constantly demonstrated.

If integrity is valued, managers need to reward team members who show it—even if acting with integrity hurts the bottom line in the short term. In a conversation with one of my clients during preparation for a leadership off-site meeting, the topic of integrity came up. The senior leaders were working on developing the vision for their transformation. They had recently gone through a series of acquisitions, and they had been working diligently to get aligned (and stay aligned) with the vision for the "new" company. They were experiencing a lot of change. They assembled a culture task force. One of their initiatives was a renewed focus on improving morale. Fatigue was setting in and everyone was feeling the growing pains of change.

The CEO kept mentioning one of their clients by name. In fact, it was the company's largest client representing 20 percent of their revenue. But the client was running the team ragged, racking up hundreds of hours of unpaid-for work. The main point of contact on the client side kept throwing my client's project team under the bus to her boss, trying to save face due to many mistakes and misalignments on her end. On top of that, she was verbally abusive to his team.

The CEO had people with one foot out the door and ready to quit. They couldn't take it anymore, especially with all of the other new initiatives the company was taking on. But what could they do? It was their largest client!

I asked him what he was going to do. This couldn't continue. His team was losing trust and felt unprotected. Past attempts to reason with the client had failed. At the risk of sending him into a tirade, I told him it was time to cut bait. Based on the financials, their largest client was also their most unprofitable client, due to all the extra work. So in reality, it would just mean a temporary top-line hit.

A few days later, he called me and told me he had made the decision to fire the client. The following week, he assembled the project team and told them the news, following that with a company-wide announcement. What happened next was astounding.

His bold move sent morale soaring to unprecedented heights. The company was literally a different place to work. Resources shifted to other great (and much more profitable) clients, and nobody quit. The CEO's integrity and passion for looking out for his team strengthened trust, resulting in a more efficient and profitable business.

PILLAR 2
Creating and Communicating a Winning Vision

If you want a team to pull together and trust each other in pursuit of a common goal—especially during times of change—you need to create trust *in* the common goal. When a group is aligned, it gets everybody excited and willing to do the work. You're not twisting arms and making threats.

Creating that vision starts with consistency and communication. You can't just put a sign up on the wall with your vision statement and mention it in a meeting once a quarter. Trust and alignment come from the message matching actions, every day—both formally and informally. A formal way? Reinforcing the message by rewarding behaviors that support it. We will be talking more about creating a powerful vision for change later on, but it's important to emphasize its impact on building trust. If you're building a one-team-one-fight mentality, what that fight is and *why* you're fighting it must be crystal clear.

But the most effective way to expand trust is to be consistent in actions *informally*. When people see that you're sharing a consistent message and doing the same things even when you're not "on the clock" or getting measured, it shows authenticity.

This came up in a conversation I had with one of the VPs at a client company—a large healthcare organization that employs thousands of veterans. They brought me out to do the keynote at their Veterans Day event. I had just finished my presentation, and we were walking over to their athletic field where they were going to have an Army-Navy flag football game. He mentioned that one of their newest culture change initiatives was a renewed focus on employee wellness. This was part of their vision for transformation. Apparently, the CEO believed so fully in this new initiative that he adopted a new daily routine in order to lead by example. He didn't just talk about it. He showed his company that he would lead from the front.

Every day, he would put on his running shoes and jog throughout the company's massive campus. He didn't hide away on the treadmill in the company's amazing gym, but rather showed his company that wellness was part of the new vision. His actions spoke much louder than words. He also made a point to interact with more people—especially those he didn't know—to casually talk about the new vision for wellness and why it was important. Purposeful storytelling. Gradually, more and more behaviors changed with him. The quad became a battleground for fitness! He had created a winning vision and lived it every day.

PILLAR 3
Building and Investing in Respect

At some point most organizations will have people with tenure and high levels of subject matter expertise in a given field—but who are also toxic. People who make cracks about management, about the direction of the company, about co-workers—you name it. But they are also intelligent and great at what they do. That's makes them "A" players, right?

Wrong.

When you're around such a person, you're probably thinking the same thing as the person next to you: Why isn't somebody doing something about this? The longer this person is allowed to remain in his position without his behaviors being addressed, the more the poison spreads. Leaders get the behaviors they tolerate.

If this person keeps getting ahead—or doesn't get confronted for the negativity—how do other team members even know that their *good* behaviors will be evaluated objectively?

When you're building an organization or a team, you can create systems from scratch that reinforce the idea of trust and respect—and literally invest in them. The mission of every manager and human resource asset should be rooting out disrespectful conflict and disrespectful employees.

Notice that I didn't say root out conflict altogether.

You don't want to confuse conflict with disrespect. *Respectful conflict* is a crucial part of any high-performance organization. It's how a company grows. If you build a team culture where people are afraid to speak up or offer constructive criticism, you'll be missing out on valuable input. Input that could lead to critical course correction or new lucrative opportunities. Not encouraging the team to have a voice is just as damaging to trust—leading to complacency and lack of connection to the mission.

One of my clients is a global food company based in Germany and expanding rapidly across the United States. They have a very formal culture with command-and-control leadership mechanisms. Everyone's office looks almost identical, and freely speaking your mind isn't really part of the culture. You had to choose from a database of artwork for decorating your office. Special permission had to be granted to hang a whiteboard in your office! That said, they are actively working to transform their culture as they expand.

The company has plans to triple in size over the next five years while adding hundreds of new store locations. Change! They brought me in for their two-day managers' retreat to do the morning keynote presentation, followed by an all-day workshop. The director of HR and professional development wanted us to focus on getting people out of their comfort zones and engaging in respectful conflict so they could produce a wider array of actionable solutions.

Based on our planning sessions, I created five topic categories: leading change, improving culture, improving internal and external communication, improving supplier relationships, and capitalizing on growth. The managers were divided into teams, and I facilitated discussions on how to implement changes in these areas. This requires a little bit of respectful conflict and for the managers to understand that voicing their opinions transparently was fine as long as communication was respectful. It took them some time to break out of their shells, but they did. And that's where the magic started happening—engaged in respectful conflict. They were simultaneously getting aligned and building trust. They had successfully invested in respect—and leveraged it to develop actionable solutions for each of the five categories.

PILLAR 4
Authentic Empowerment at All Levels

I was more than a little worried about using a word like "empower" here, because it has become such a faddish business buzzword, but it really is the word that works the best for what we're trying to accomplish. Many leaders and managers use this term, but in many companies it is inauthentic. Teams will be empowered with an important project, but then micromanaged to death. Or a team will be empowered with work that doesn't matter. Both cause problems.

Today's business environment is volatile, uncertain, and ambiguous. If you're going to survive, you're going to have to be a part of a team where the members of that team have the power and autonomy to participate in the transformation process—and frankly all aspects of the business.

With the proper training and resources, employees have to be given the power to manage people and execute projects how they see fit. Being trusted to be creative and problem solve in their own way is a huge motivation. A 2014 Citigroup and LinkedIn survey found that nearly half of employees would give up a 20 percent raise for greater control over how they work. That speaks volumes about the importance of empowerment and autonomy.

Autonomy also promotes innovation, because people will naturally try different approaches in different situations. Oversight and risk management procedures can help minimize disaster when mistakes are made. And of course, the after-action review allows for those mistakes to be coaching moments in which lessons learned are applied to future projects.

Within the SEAL Teams, this is a basic element of our functionality. Every mission has a purpose, but when a team goes out into the field, things are changing minute to minute. We're trained to respond to those changes by using the tools we spent years developing. The goal is stationary, but the tactics are adaptable. Every member of a platoon or troop is empowered with extremely large amounts of responsibility. Some of your teammates might only be twenty-one years old yet be a sniper and a JTAC (Joint Tactical Air Controller—the radio operators who control air support—a HUGE job). But we can empower them with these jobs because they know the mission and have the best possible training and appropriate resources to get the job done.

The idea of truly empowering a business team gives some leaders hives, but even ones who embrace the concept often get it wrong. They offer the idea of empowerment, but it's really a fake gesture. Members of the team can make decisions, but the decisions are routinely overridden—or the decisions are about things that don't really matter.

Again, that's hollow. It doesn't take long for people to realize that their input is being very specifically restricted. Either they'll stop worrying about things outside their lane, so to speak, or they'll get resentful and stop trying. The most talented ones will often leave the organization and look for a place where they can participate in a more meaning-ful way.

Let's say your organization is going to choose a new project manage-ment software system or a piece of expensive equipment for the ware-house. Getting input from the frontline troops who will be using that system day to day is obviously a great idea. You might even assemble a team and task them with making the decision about which system to choose. Leadership obviously needs to establish the big-picture param-eters in terms of cost and functionality, but that team needs to have the freedom to do its job—and pick the system or machinery that will work best for their needs.

An entire generation of organizations is finding out the hard way that ignoring advice from the front lines has painful consequences. It's hard to generalize, but one commonality many millennial workers share is the desire to do meaningful work. They want to feel connected to the cause. They are inspired and motivated by the trust and responsibility that comes with being empowered. Take it away and make it just about the paycheck, and you'll turn your team into a group of mercenaries. That is an expensive and stressful way to do business. Eventually, turn-over will skyrocket, morale will plummet, and efficiency is destroyed.

Like trust, empowerment isn't just a cultural nice-to-have. Struc-tures have to be put in place that allow true empowerment. With a clearly defined mission and vision, specific boundaries put in place, and the right resources, empowerment can be more easily enacted. This piece is important. It's really hard to generate authentic empowerment without providing proper training and resources. If I tell a direct report that I am empowering them to lead an important new initiative but don't provide them the resources to get it done, I have set them up to fail. And they will figure it out really quickly. This also damages trust.

Does this always work perfectly? Of course not. Mistakes will be made, and you'll go down some dead ends. But the benefit to overall pro-ductivity, engagement, trust and morale is measurable and significant.

PILLAR 5
Embracing the Suck and Owning the Sacrifices

As we say in the Teams, "Embrace the suck!" Like a lot of important things, sacrifice can be real, and it can be symbolic. When you're talking about an organization in a state of change—and establishing trust within that organization—it has to be both. And it has to be done together.

The first thing everybody in the organization has to understand is that at the individual level, change is an intense sacrifice. Let's say you're undertaking a large, multifaceted transition at your firm, and a big part of that vision is to become more efficient and increase net margin by 7 percent. To the person on the front line, that translates into doing his or her job differently, and spending more time—usually long after they would usually go home—figuring out new systems, new rules, and new goals. They're really doing two things in tandem. They're doing the job they get measured on while also performing the new functions related to the transformation. They're venturing out of their comfort zone, and they're probably not going to get a pay raise or bonus for those ten or twenty extra hours a week they're working to get it all done—at least not immediately. They are told that everyone just has to dig in for a while and suck it up—that the sacrifice won't last long and that raises and bonuses can come once the company is more profitable.

It is easy for leadership teams to get lost in the clouds and believe their own hype. The transformation is going to be great! We're all going to be so much more efficient and make so much more money! Maybe true, but the people on the front line still have to get the job done while learning the "new way of doing things."

So imagine how those frontline teams feel when the metrics they're measured on aren't adjusted to account for the new reality. And think about what all frontline people immediately understand when an organization starts talking about efficiency and profit as it relates to change.

It could mean some people are going to lose their jobs. That's certainly a reality, but you can't forget the human toll on the people who are worried about losing their jobs—or worried about the work they're going to have to carry when there aren't as many people around to do it.

Those realities need to be addressed and discussed—not hidden away in a spreadsheet somewhere—although it's tempting. As we've been discussing, you can have hard conversations within the team when you have established trust and the team knows it can count on honesty. Sacrifice is easier when the team knows that integrity exists in the leadership team and that respect matters, regardless of the discomfort that lays ahead.

This is where the symbolic part of that sacrifice comes in. If the leadership group is preaching the idea of change, efficiency, and profit, it quickly becomes disconnected if the members of the leadership group aren't living the change. If folks are losing jobs and spending long hours figuring out how to handle new systems, resentment will spread like wildfire if the leadership group is still flying private and parking their Ferraris in their personal parking spots. Does this mean they have to sell the mahogany desk and downgrade to a Toyota Camry? Not necessarily, but visible sacrifice should exist. The frontline people know what is real and what is excessive. If short-term sacrifices must be made, they must be made by all.

Everyone has to embrace the suck.

When one of my companies was taking a bit of a hit to the bottom line one year, the senior leaders changed our compensation model so that we wouldn't take a single bonus or dollar over our base pay until things were back on track. Why would I take a bonus and then tell others, "Sorry, guys, no bonuses this year." I wouldn't be sacrificing with the team, and I'd be rewarding myself for subpar performance.

During BUD/S, the officers in the class suffer just as much as the enlisted students. Sometimes more. When the class shows up late to an evolution or isn't performing well, who pays the man? The leaders. They'll receive extra remediation in the form of burpees, push-ups, and getting wet and sandy. I recall one officer in my class being buried up to his neck in the hot desert sand.

The symbolism also takes some subtle forms. If a leadership team calls everyone together and talks about the grave threats to the business and the big changes that are coming, that needs to be backed up with visuals supporting the "sacrifice." Where is the sense of urgency? With change must come calculated urgency. Where are the war rooms set up to strategize about those big changes? Those kinds of things create a unity amidst the sacrifice. In the SEAL Teams, we were all in the dirt and grime and danger together, no matter what our rank was. We embraced the sacrifice together. And many made the ultimate sacrifice for his brothers next to him.

PILLAR 6
Transparency in Communication

Many organizations and their leaders talk about the need for greater transparency. Transparency between team members. Transparency with customers. But not every detail of a business needs to be shared with everyone at all times. Certain strategic decisions and big-picture financial details often need to be held close to the vest, for obvious reasons.

But if the default setting in your organization is one of secrecy—or of dishonesty—you're going to struggle to ever build trust.

In the SEAL Teams, the flatter management structure meant that we had very transparent communication about the operational details of the missions we did. When preparing for a mission, we had to rely heavily on our agency partners for intelligence and then rehearse relentlessly for each operation—because if we weren't prepared, we wouldn't be able to adapt to changing circumstances.

But having a flatter structure and transparent communication didn't mean each of us had *all* the information. Every high-performing organization still has a chain of command but works tirelessly to ensure vertical and horizontal silos aren't impeding the flow of information—delivering the most relevant transparent information to the people who need it. But it must be the right communication to the right people at the right time. Otherwise, you risk overwhelming people with information they don't need to do their job. There is a time and place for delivering transparent communication.

The goal here is to streamline communication and make sure every member of the team feels that what is being communicated is honest and in the right context. It's fine for a leader to tell a team member that a certain part of a plan or strategy isn't ready to be shared, but the information that *is* shared needs to be truthful and consistent with the mission's goal.

This means sharing information that is good, bad, *and* ugly. Because leaving out the bad and ugly will just cause bigger problems later. If you don't own the bad news and give it the proper context, the people who don't know what is going on will often draw their own conclusions—and the conclusions they draw will often be worse than the reality! A business setback that is relatively minor can bounce around the rumor mill and turn into something that has people updating their resumes and LinkedIn profiles.

Organizations fumble this in a variety of ways. One important one is how they handle removing a person from the team. Letting people go is a part of business. It's never fun, and it's stressful for everybody involved. But what often gets overlooked is how the separation impacts the rest of the people who remain. This magnitude grows exponentially during more sizable layoffs.

For example, in one of my companies, we had to let a longtime employee go because he wasn't meeting his goals and wasn't effectively communicating with his team. When the time came, we sat down with him and he was dumbfounded. He had no idea it was coming, because *his* manager hadn't effectively communicated with him over the preceding months. If you don't have transparent communication and well-defined performance metrics, you're going to cause frustration with your people—and you're going to cause distrust when people are removed from the team for reasons that aren't immediately apparent, or that seem arbitrary or cruel. And feedback can't come in the form of an annual performance review. Highly functioning teams that invest in respect, provide ongoing feedback and support to their team members who are in a constant state of self-correction and improvement. And there are plenty of tools and apps out there to help perform this function.

The most important aspect of having transparent communication as part of the culture is for learning and making improvements. In SEAL training and after every real-world mission we perform the after-action review, which I mentioned earlier. Rank and emotion are left at the door (usually) and we do a deep dive into what went right, what went wrong, and how we can do it better next time. And we don't just get into the weeds on generalities. Individual performance is on the table. Everybody is encouraged to engage in respectful conflict. It's part of our learning culture and how we hold each other to high standards.

One of my earliest experiences with the AAR was during a land-warfare training trip with my platoon in Arkansas. We had just completed a full night of ambush drills. Usually, we do everything with live ammo, but for a nighttime evolution like this we transition to using blanks. We use the same weapons but with different barrels. During land warfare, I was an M60 machine gunner. It's a heavy weapon, and you're carrying about one thousand rounds of belt-fed 7.62 mm ammo. New guy gets to carry the heavy crap, remember?

We had already completed a full day of running and gunning in one-hundred-degree heat and humidity. I was tired and lost focus. I failed to swap out my live barrel for the blank barrel for that night's training evolution. But no excuses. I screwed up. This meant that my M60 wouldn't fire the blanks. Yes, it was just training, and yes, it was only blanks. But what if I made the opposite mistake on a real mission?

Needless to say, I realized my mistake early on and was not looking forward to the AAR.

I was hoping our platoon chief would let it slide, but I knew he wouldn't. It would be irresponsible not to bring it up. I will spare you the flurry of expletives that came my way and paraphrase his comments. The bottom line is that I messed up, and it doesn't matter to us how seemingly small a mistake is. It must be addressed and fixed immediately. I never made that mistake again. We obviously can't execute that type of harsh AAR process—in the civilian world the same way we do in the Teams, but a calmer version—with fewer swear words—is an important trust-building exercise.

With transparency, good communication, and respectful conflict, any organization can build trust and be in a constant state of improvement.

PILLAR 7
Total Team Accountability

The last pillar, accountability, is really an accumulation of all the previous ones—and a preview of what we're going to discuss in Chapter 3. It's important to talk about it here first, because I want to stress a point now that will be a recurring one throughout the book.

The term "accountability" is just like the term "change" in that it has often become code for something negative. My goal is to dispel that misconception. Accountability handled correctly translates into trust and teamwork. It eliminates excuses and finger pointing while simultaneously improving performance at the team and individual level.

When a SEAL team is out on patrol or setting a perimeter, every single member of the team is responsible for owning a particular "field of fire" should an enemy attack. If you picture a 360-degree circle around you, a field of fire is the section of that circle you are responsible for covering. It is drilled into you from the moment you start training that you are accountable for that field of fire and for more. Overlapping fields of fire make the team even stronger. Accountability and ownership are how we build teams that are stronger than the sum of their parts.

This piece of our culture helps the entire team function more efficiently. Effort isn't duplicated or wasted—and you aren't running the risk of shooting one of your own guys because you went outside your field. The best sports teams (and business units) work in a similar way. The coaches establish responsibilities for each player, and the player is accountable for doing his or her job.

If somebody makes a mistake and doesn't do their job, there's a mechanism in place to fix the problem. That's another kind of accountability that gives people the freedom to concentrate completely on what they need to do without extra worry.

How does it usually go wrong for a business team? Usually, it's when the "A" players in the group are getting their jobs done and are willing and accountable, while the "B" players act with complacency or waste time on activities that don't align with mission and goals.

When those people aren't held accountable for what they do (or don't do), the concept of accountability starts to erode for the whole team. The "A" players are often most affected by this, because they feel like their efforts are being wasted, that they aren't being supported or that leadership tolerates underperformance. They're also the most likely to leave for another organization—because they have tons of opportunities. The unfortunate reality is that the disengaged and actively disengaged demand the majority of a manager's time.

Accountability can't exist—or be built—in an organization that is inconsistent in how and who is held accountable. As it develops over time, people will hold themselves accountable, own mistakes, and get their jobs done because it's part of the culture. It's what is expected. But trust deteriorates when people are held to different standards. Like the toxic subject matter expert mentioned earlier. If they aren't dealt with because management is afraid of ruffling their feathers or even losing that employee, two things happen. One, other good employees notice that favoritism exists and poor behavior is allowed. And they know exactly why. Therefore, trust for management erodes. Two, that employee thinks they can get away with treating others disrespectfully and will continue that behavior.

With a consistent standard for accountability, it becomes one with the culture.

TALES FROM THE FRONT LINES

When I come in to work with an organization on some of these issues, one of the first questions I get is usually about "measuring" trust. Leaders often think of it as a "social variable" that isn't easily measured or quantified on a financial report. And while it may not be a line item on the P&L, it is there. Which we established earlier based on the HCI report, *Building Trust 2013: Workforce Trends Defining High Performance*. Trust impacts engagement and engagement has a direct economic impact on an organization.

The first thing I tell them is the stark truth. Like the saying goes, anything important must be managed and measured. You can measure anything you want, but probably the single most important cultural aspect of *any* high-performance team is trust. And yes, it can be measured using some of the culture sentiment tools I mentioned in the previous chapter as well as through detailed employee surveys. Leaders and managers should take it a step further and build trust metrics into these surveys so that *they* can individually be scored on trust.

The simplest way to think about trust is to look at it as an account. If your trust account is low, speed goes down and costs go up. You don't have to talk to an accountant to know that those things directly affect an organization's performance—both financial and otherwise.

When the trust account is high, speed goes up, costs go down, and efficiencies are unlocked. This increases profitability (obviously) and satisfaction—both for people on the team and for external groups like customers and strategic partners.

To measure this trust account, I break it into three distinct categories, with the goal being a determination of the economic impact on the business:

- Internal trust levels

- External trust levels

- Behaviors that build or damage trust

INTERNAL TRUST

To judge the first variable, an organization needs to start by asking the most basic questions.

Does the team trust leadership?

Is the culture collaborative, or do people function in silos?

Do people compete against each other or work as a team?

Is there a flow of information between team members and across departments?

Are the behaviors of managers and leaders consistent with their words?

How thick are the walls of the silos and are they a result of a lack of trust?

Are our engagement issues due to a lack of internal trust?

Measuring internal trust isn't rocket science. When the trust account is low, everyone knows it. Every now and then you have poor leaders or managers who are so blinded by their own selfish desires or who score really low in emotional intelligence that they won't be aware that trust is lacking. But studies actually show that productivity, income, and profits are directly negatively or positively impacted depending on the levels of trust within an organization.

EXTERNAL TRUST

The second trust factor affects customers, clients, and partners. The questions associated with this component are:

Do our customers trust that we have their best interests in mind?

Do our partners, suppliers, or distributors believe we have a trusting relationship?

How openly and frequently do we communicate with them?

Do we openly request and apply customer feedback for making our products and services better?

Are these relationships purely transactional or is there something more real that exists?

External trust can be more visible in the financials than internal trust, because it directly relates to customer and partner loyalty. If trust is low, turnover will be high and retention low; and that's a very easy financial piece to measure—because you're losing business and building a poor reputation that precludes you from gaining new customers.

BEHAVIORS THAT BUILD OR DAMAGE TRUST

The third component is a laundry list of all the behaviors and actions that build or hurt trust. If you want a high-performing team that has a high level of trust, you have to *behave* your way there, not think or talk your way there. Only when you measure areas like credibility, accountability, consistency of action, and transparency do you get the real answers.

The economic factors are usually the most important to the leadership teams that bring me in as a consultant. All of this talk about culture is nice, and trust is a great thing, but how does it actually impact the bottom line?

It would be really cool if trust was an actual line item on a financial statement, but it takes a little bit more work. In my organizations, I used 360-degree anonymous feedback surveys like the one I described earlier to parse out behaviors that were both building and damaging trust. When I found behaviors that were damaging it—including my own—I began rebuilding them immediately.

What does that mean in real dollars? Billions of dollars, remember?

Low-trust organizations suffer much higher employee turnover and customer churn. If you're losing employees due to low trust levels—something you can ascertain easily during an exit interview—it will cost you almost double that employee's salary to replace them, and that's on top of the lost productivity. It's too expensive *not* to think about. Similarly, a large array of studies has shown that replacing a customer costs up to five times as much as retaining a customer you already have.

Let's go back to the example of the global food company. One of the most important strategies for capitalizing on their unprecedented growth was to improve their relationships with food suppliers. They needed to improve trust and build more meaningful relationships. Where would a food company be without its suppliers? Nowhere. They needed a renewed focus on external trust.

We started with a detailed analysis of a supplier survey. In general, the survey focused on what the company could be doing better with supplier relationships. The data pointed to a few common themes mostly centered around communication and developing less-transactional relationships. The suppliers wanted more feedback on their products, and for the food company to be accepting of their feedback. They wanted longer-term contracts as a show of good faith that they were all in it together. And they wanted the company to take more risks with them so that they could grow together—instead of being told to test new products with Walmart and then they might be considered after being vetted. None of these would be overly complicated to fix, but it meant a major shift in approach and mindset—and consistent action.

The outcome of the survey showed that external trust with suppliers needed some work. But they knew that tripling in size over the next five years while adding hundreds of new store locations would be impossible to execute if trust with the suppliers wasn't at peak levels. So they got to work.

Again, it's as simple as asking the question: What can we be doing better? This question can be asked of customers, employees, partners and between peers. But in order to build trust, just asking isn't enough. Action must be taken. Trust is very delicate, but it's the most powerful tool for building a high-performance organization. And like marriage, it isn't a 50/50 relationship—it's 100/100.

It's also the best culture weapon for leading change.

3

ACCOUNTABILITY:
OWNERSHIP AT ALL LEVELS

In the absence of orders I will take charge, lead my teammates and accomplish the mission. I lead by example in all situations.
—NAVY SEAL ETHOS

In any high-performance organization, the concept of accountability isn't just something that's talked about when things are going wrong. It is the bedrock of a culture where tasks get done and everyone exhibits true ownership over failures and successes. Beyond trust, accountability has the most significant impact on morale and the financial health of any company. It is the single most important ingredient in a culture poised for change.

I must emphasize the importance of engagement as it relates to building a culture where accountability thrives. And while many companies spend a considerable amount of time measuring "employee satisfaction," it's not necessarily a great indicator of high performance. Gallup research shows that while measuring and managing satisfaction can create a great workplace, satisfaction and happiness levels alone are not sufficient for successfully leading change, retaining top talent and positively impacting the bottom line. Because many of the satisfied employees fall into the disengaged category—team members who are relatively happy but doing the bare minimum. Engaged employees are found to be the most accountable.

The notion of accountability as it relates to a set of organizational expectations and behavioral norms isn't new. Early Greek philosophers like Plato and Aristotle include the concept of accountability in their discussions around the topics of duty, justice, social order, and punishment. And it can be viewed at two levels: (1) individual-level accountability and (2) organization-level accountability. Individual-level accountability can be broken down to *task performance* and *contextual performance* (activities contributing to the social and psychological core of an organization).

The study of organizational accountability and its link to the financial success of an organization is becoming more and more popular both at the academic and practitioner levels. During the major transformation at my last company, we performed a research study on this concept. As we grew and matured—and faced the need for more change—we realized that we could not sustain without having authentically empowered teams that had control over how and when work got done. The result was clear. When teams—and individuals—are given more ownership over tasks, they will invest more time, talent, and energy and produce better work. In command-and-control environments, the opposite is true. Organizations that thrive are made up of teams that feel they have a voice that's heard and real influence over important decisions.

Imagine an environment where people literally fight over the scraps of fault when the mission fails. Where everyone knows without a doubt that each team member will execute their duties to the best of their ability. What would that look like? What kind of results could be attained? And what experiences create an authentic environment of accountability?

In BUD/S, the concept of accountability begins day one, and as we say, "our training is never complete."

Starting from the very first week, throughout the entire training cycle, we perform an anonymous peer review process. You anonymously rank the top and bottom performers and have the opportunity to share your reasoning.

The instructors weigh this data heavily when deciding to keep or drop students. Those who receive poor ratings from their peers are usually brought in for a board review. The instructors aren't just looking for the "right" answers when calling a student out about why they feel their peers are concerned about their performance. They are also examining a candidate's demeanor during that inquiry. Anything but humility and a sincere desire to improve will usually "seal" that student's fate.

For the person who is otherwise a star performer, getting identified as one of the bottom performers can be an incredible motivator—a career-saving wake-up call. It might mean that you have the skill set to potentially be a superior operator, but the other members of the class don't currently trust you. Or you're rubbing people the wrong way with your ego and attitude, and that needs an adjustment. For a candidate in the middle of the pack, it can be the push that ultimately gets him through training.

But if a candidate can't put the team before himself or has a bad attitude and lacks humility, it will often come through during the review. And if it does, and that student is defensive and unwilling to look in the mirror, that is usually their last day at the command.

It brings together all of the best elements of a team—trust, character, transparency, and most of all, accountability. And again, this process is part of our culture—a ritual that guides expectations and social norms. It's no surprise to anyone and most importantly, it keeps everyone focused on excellence.

You have to perform at the peak of your abilities, because that's what is expected by the team. If you can't do it—or if your peak performance isn't good enough—you're endangering the lives of the other people on your team, and you have to go. But more often than not, those ranked toward the bottom have something missing. Whether it's a moral compass that is a bit off, or the lack of ability to go above and beyond for the guy next to you, everyone sees it.

It is a very important part of the SEAL training and selection process, and the lessons you learn carry you all the way through to when you join a Team and are deployed to some of the most dangerous places in the world. Even the way SEALs move, shoot, and communicate in a war zone speaks to this concept. Every choreographed movement, every communication passed between team members to the way we engage the enemy—it's all by design. The cultural experiences every SEAL goes through in training exist as part of an overarching strategy: to create the best warfighters in the world. I've heard it said that even other conventional forces on the battlefield can identify a SEAL element engaged in a firefight with the enemy, simply by listening to the rhythm and aggressiveness of their attack.

A conference room in an office park is definitely not the same as a hot spot in central Ar-Ramadi. But the lesson of ultimate accountability is one that translates extremely well from its military application to the business world. Without accountability woven into the fabric of the organizational culture, no change effort can be successful.

THE TAKINGPOINT PRINCIPLE

Trust and accountability are the two most important cultural pillars for any organization facing significant transformation. Trust brings the team together with a shared sense of purpose: To achieve an aligned vision. Accountability ensures that the mission is executed properly and that the vision is realized. Learning to measure and improve both is a key part of the *TakingPoint* program. But remember, culture change that really sticks becomes a reality toward the end of a transformation process, not the beginning. It must be done in tandem while implementing the other principles.

One of my clients, a San Diego–based medical device company, achieved one of the biggest transformations in their space and knows this concept well—and has the battle scars to prove it. The company—currently one of the largest publically traded medical device suppliers in the world—brought me in for a keynote presentation and a series of leadership development programs. In preparation, I started researching the history of the company to better understand their culture. I also interviewed some of the key executives who had survived the numerous mergers and acquisitions the company had been through.

What I discovered proves that a model and strategy for improving accountability drives great financial results.

Before their transformation, the original brand was on the brink of extinction and was one of the most-leveraged companies in the sector. Their reputation on Wall Street was that they had good ideas and good intentions, but they couldn't execute. And the company culture was where many of these problems stemmed from. They lacked the needed sense of urgency to remain competitive. They lacked overall accountability throughout the organization. In a last-ditch effort to save the company, the board brought in a new CEO—a man with an incredible track record for turning around failing companies.

For the first couple of years, he implemented his tried-and-tested method of sifting through the financial data looking for inefficiencies—areas where cash could be generated to pay down debt and opportunities for reinvesting in research and development. Old systems were replaced with new approaches and more efficient processes were rolled out. And all of this change only further strained an already failing business.

The company's stock price continued to fall. He couldn't understand what was going on. One day, during a conversation with one of the company's marketing directors, the concept of accountability came up. She was telling a story about how some of the people in their research division were "go to" people. She went on and on about how they always got the job done, they always followed through, communicated effectively, and owned mistakes when they dropped the ball. And more important, if that did happen—and it was rare—not only did they own it, but they quickly developed a plan to ensure that mistake didn't happen again. They were the epitome of accountable team members.

"Imagine if every division in the company was like this?!" she said.

The CEO's mind started racing. Maybe he had been going about this all wrong. He hadn't even thought about the cultural elements at play. What was holding them back? What beliefs and experiences were pushing them further toward bankruptcy? And even worse, where would they be if they didn't have such talented and accountable people—and what could they accomplish if everyone in the organization behaved this way?

From that day forward, he shifted his time and attention away from the financials to the culture. He developed a strategy for leveraging the strengths of the existing culture while working toward improving the areas where accountability was lacking—a modified version of my CDT model. Over the next three years, the stock price soared and the company went from highly leveraged to extremely profitable.

Like trust, organization-level accountability is reflective of leadership. And there are *Six Fundamental Leadership Accountability Skills* that all should master. Especially, for leading change.

- **RESULTS-DRIVEN MESSAGING:** Accountability starts with providing crystal-clear expectations as to the exact result that needs to be achieved. Then leaders need to allow autonomy over the "how" of that achievement.

- **COURAGE TO TAKE OWNERSHIP:** This goes both ways. When leaders publicly take ownership over mistakes or failures, the team will be more likely to do the same.

- **CLEAR DIRECTION:** If a dog is chasing two squirrels, he is likely to fail at catching either. When priorities are clear and leadership's messaging is consistent, the team can be more accountable. Constantly shifting directives causes confusion and chaos.

- **TRAINING FOR SKILLS:** Without the training for specific skills that the team needs to execute their duties, accountability becomes irrelevant. Set the team up for success by investing in training and development.

- **WILLINGNESS TO CHANGE:** When leaders are accepting of transparent feedback and acknowledge the changes they are willing to make, others on the team see that as part of the culture—and will follow suit.

- **RESPECTFUL CONFLICT RESOLUTION:** Similar to the trust pillar of *respectful conflict*, leaders can build a culture around accountability when they demonstrate the ability to engage in respectful conflict and encourage the team to do the same.

Again, accountability shouldn't be a set of consequences for when things go wrong. Is that part of it? Sure. But it should be the smallest part. Accountability sets the stage for great organizations to accomplish even greater things. It lets you navigate change with confidence.

APPLICATIONS FROM THE BATTLEFIELD
TO THE BOARDROOM

One of the primary ways the SEALs reinforce the idea of accountability is to live by a code of transparent communication. It can happen during the more formal AAR process we have discussed or just in casual conversation. We have a learning culture, and much of that learning is from peer to peer.

Checking into your first SEAL Team is quite a milestone. You couldn't possibly feel more "new." You have survived the most arduous military training in the world, but none of that matters. Now it's time to prove you have what it takes to really be a SEAL. I remember the day that I checked into SEAL Team 5 with a few other members of my BUD/S class. We were already assigned to our respective platoons. The command didn't have the fancy buildings that it does now. Our platoon huts were still small, one-story shacks along the back fence that led to the beach. Our gear was stored in milvans—large military shipping containers. I remember this distinctly because one of my first important duties as a new guy at the Team was to repaint those suckers. My first weapon at the Team was a paintbrush. It's not all glitz and glam!

After checking in at the front desk, I walked back to our platoon space to meet the guys. One of the first guys I met was Mark. This was his second platoon, so he was part of the "E5 Mafia"—middle management, so to speak. He was a cool, laid-back guy from Alaska who went to college in Orange County, California, before joining the Teams. He was well respected and known to be an accountable "go-to" team member.

He invited me to join him for a light run during lunch. I quickly learned that life in the Teams would be a much higher tempo than BUD/S or SQT. We ran seven miles at a leisurely six-minute pace while maintaining casual conversation. At least he did, anyway. Mark talked about how things are done, what's expected of a Team guy and how important accountability is.

Mark became a mentor, and he's a good friend to this day. He later wrote the #1 *New York Times* bestselling book *No Easy Day*, about being a part of the mission to capture or kill Osama bin Laden.

During a workup (months of intense training to prepare the platoon or troop for deployment), the complexity of the exercises and missions is far greater than when you're in SQT. Accountability and ownership at all levels is crucial to success. At this point, we were a year into our engagement in Afghanistan and getting ready to turn our attention to Iraq. My platoon got word that we would in fact be some of the first SEALs going in-country, so everything we did mattered. It mattered more than ever.

During workup, you do a series of FTXs (final training exercises) to close out a block of training. You are putting all the moving parts together. For example, after a block of combat diving and maritime operations, we would develop a mission profile for what is called a "multiple ship attack" (destroying or capturing enemy vessels). It starts with the entire platoon doing a static line jump out of the back of a C-130 transport plane. Before we exit the plane, we push out four black Zodiac boats rigged with parachutes—and in them is all of our weapons and dive gear. We land in the water a couple miles from the mouth of San Diego Bay just before sundown, ditch our chutes, and quickly assemble the boats (while treading water), climb in, and start heading to our designated drop-off point. We "jock up" in our dive gear while in transit. By this time the sun has gone down and it is dark and cold. We arrive at a predesignated location, where we slide into the water and swim at a twenty-foot depth for about a mile to our targets. We plant explosive limpet mines on two of the ships and perform a hook-and-climb assault on the third. This requires us to use heavy magnets that we attach to the hull and to clip dive rigs to the magnets with carabiners before ascending to the surface.

Using a long, expandable pole, we hook the cable ladder to the top edge of the ship and climb up. Accountability is critical for bringing all of these pieces together for a successful mission. And it's better to work out the kinks in training than on the battlefield. The more you sweat in training the less you bleed in battle.

And as always, when the training exercise is complete, we perform an after-action review. I remember one particular AAR in Iraq, when a teammate who had called me out for something later pulled me aside as we walked back to our tents. He had been an experienced Marine scout sniper before becoming a corpsman in the Teams. He just wanted to make sure that there was no love lost between us—that what was said in the meeting was meant with respect and purely for learning purposes.

The concepts of accountability and transparent communication were ones I took with me from the SEALs and implemented in the companies I built. One of the core values I established—"Everyone has a voice"—is a direct offshoot of the transparent communication I was talking about. It is the cornerstone of a culture focused on accountability.

If you build a team that is empowered to hold you accountable, you will operate at a different standard. It's that simple.

This level of accountability and communication is unfortunately rare in the business world. Plenty of companies perform 360-degree reviews—where each employee is responsible for reviewing his or her supervisor, peers, and subordinates. And while that is certainly an effective tool, it's wasted if the information collected from those reviews isn't used productively.

▲

Accountability and transparency doesn't mean a license to complain without offering a solution. The goal is to create a mechanism that identifies problem areas and offers potential solutions. It isn't a stage for people to unload their grudges and perform for the group. If you're going to gripe, you'd better bring some solutions.

Describing the way SEALs are trained to be accountable makes for a colorful sound bite, but how do you actually create those systems in your organization? It begins at the most basic level, with how you hire and reward people and what leadership tolerates from the team. And it's up to the leaders to create the right culture—one of accountability—that is designed to achieve specific results.

One of my favorite books about organizational change, *Change the Culture, Change the Game: The Breakthrough Strategy for Energizing Your Organization and Creating Accountability for Results*—by Roger Connors and Tom Smith—focuses on improving accountability for driving successful change. I want to take an excerpt from the first page of the introduction which reinforces my theory:

> Creating an organizational culture where people embrace their accountability toward one another and toward the organization should occupy center stage in any effort to create successful organizational change. Without accountability the change process breaks down quickly. When it does, people externalize the need to change, resist initiatives designed to move them forward, and even sabotage efforts to transform the organization. With accountability, people at every level of the organization embrace their role in facilitating the change and demonstrate the ownership needed for making true progress, both for themselves and their organization.

Their four-tiered "Results Pyramid" lays the foundation for how organizations can ingrain accountability into the culture and successfully lead to lasting change. The tiers include (1) defining the *results* the organization needs to achieve for transformation, (2) the *actions* that must be taken to achieve those results, (3) the *beliefs* that must be closely held by all in order for everyone to take those actions, and (4) the *cultural experiences* that must be implemented and leveraged to instill those beliefs.

In an organization where accountability thrives—like the SEAL Teams, everyone's beliefs and actions are aligned behind a clear mission narrative. And those beliefs and actions are designed to achieve very specific results: purging the world of evil.

Think about the hiring and compensation mechanisms you have in place in your organization. Are you hiring and rewarding people for actions and behaviors that are aligned with the organization's goals? Are those things aligned with what you're trying to accomplish in a transformation?

In one of my companies we had been showing exponential growth during the first few years in operation, but some of the metrics we were tracking started to throw off some warning signs. Our customer satisfaction and retention numbers began to deteriorate, and our customer turnover began to increase.

We decided to transform the way we did business so that we could provide better quality work to our customers and ensure scalability. We changed the way we rewarded our account and project management teams so that they were incentivized to work more collaboratively with the service departments in delivering for clients. There had been too much finger pointing and not enough "team" ownership over driving results. I had failed to ensure that our culture promoted that belief.

Under the new structure, not only did we improve our customer retention numbers, but we also attracted *much better clients*. Instead of scrambling to find clients who met the minimum budget requirements, the comprehensive case studies we were able to build with better marketing and research integration (the result of better collaboration) converted much larger and more profitable clients. Knowing that we could provide great service gave us the confidence to hunt the "whales."

It certainly caused some short-term pain in the sense that multiple departments needed to learn new ways to operate, but in the end, we achieved two goals. Financial performance improved and job satisfaction—and morale—among staff increased. All of which was the result of improving accountability.

When I start spending time consulting with an organization that is facing some serious transition challenges, lack of accountability among frontline troops often comes up. This is used as an explanation for not hitting established goals.

But whose fault is that? If team members aren't acting with accountability, then accountability is clearly not part of the culture nor embodied by senior leaders. And none of that is surprising, especially in a crisis.

When smart people are looking for answers, they're often very ready (and very relieved) to assign the blame to something or somebody else. But I can tell you from personal and professional experience that accountability starts at the top of the organization—not the bottom. I've seen amazing SEAL commanders and experienced executives take ownership over catastrophic failures, even though there was plenty of blame to go around. Accountability can only become a cultural bedrock if it is embodied, every day, in every situation, from the top. Whether it's the very top of the company or the top of a department or division, that's where it has to start.

If you're counting on your team to help you turn things around in a transformation, but you don't provide the right resources, remove obstacles in their path, or give them a workable plan, what exactly are you doing to be accountable to *them*?

If those pieces aren't in place, you're setting the team up for failure, and you're damaging the trust you've worked so hard to establish. You're going to send your people into a protective hole, where they go inward and try to simply accomplish the basic day-to-day tasks that keep them employed. Or, as Roger Connors and Tom Smith put it—in their book *Change the Culture, Change the Game*—some will even actively work against the transformation initiative. This does nothing to drive change. It only ensures that change initiatives will fail.

You will have turned yourself into a manager instead of a leader capable of inspiring lasting change. You must master the *Six Fundamental Leadership Accountability* skills.

It isn't surprising this happens so frequently, because so much of the focus in business in the last fifty years has been on the mechanics of management—not the essentials of leadership.

When a crisis hits, management teams come together, crunch the numbers and analyze inefficiencies. They cut bodies, cut costs, and move line items on spreadsheets—all of which might ultimately be necessary in a transition environment—but they don't do anything to solve many of the other systemic problems they're facing. These activities don't help clearly define the vision for what needs to happen, either. It becomes a conglomeration of messy tactical moves that aren't aligned to an overarching strategy and vision. And certainly not aligned with the positive aspects of the culture that can be leveraged to drive change.

Think about the basic issues facing a sales manager at any given organization. What happens when the sales staff starts missing quotas?

The knee-jerk response? More reports. More communication about what kinds of customer calls frontline troops are doing, and an analysis of how those people are spending their time day to day. Call tracking. Time tracking. More time spent on entering data into the CRM software instead of taking actions designed to deliver specific results that align with a strategy.

I'm not saying those actions are necessarily wrong—measurement and data collection are imperative, especially if goals are being missed. But the peak performers in the group are going to look at the new reporting requirements and say to themselves, "I'm spending three more hours per week doing these reports—which gives me less time to spend working the phones and meeting clients."

Are those directives really driving more productivity, or are they just creating more work?

A core function of leadership is to create *alignment* on the vision. Then and only then can tactics be applied to the strategy.

Instead of imposing arbitrary rules and command-and-control functions to achieve accountability, leaders create systems that build alignment—and establish accountability in ways that directly benefit the team and the organization. They transform mindsets and rid the team of those who stand in the way of progress.

In BUD/S, each individual boat crew was made up of seven guys. How well the crew did was totally dependent on the efforts and achievements of everybody on the crew—not the greatest or the strongest, toughest person in the group. But it also came down to leadership and the team culture created by the boat crew leader. During the early weeks of BUD/S, instructors would swap boat crew leaders from boat to boat as a leadership experiment. High-performing crews would be assigned a leader from a low-performance crew and vice versa. Oftentimes, under new leadership, underperforming crews would excel. Similarly, high-performing crews under new leadership from an underperforming crew would still win. Why? Because they already had a winning culture of teamwork and accountability that was strong enough to sustain under a lesser leader.

This is where true leadership comes into play. Managerial tasks only get you so far when preparing a company culture for change. Improving accountability is a leadership function and can only be attained when evangelized from the top. Every day, leaders create experiences that define the culture—for better or for worse. As discussed previously, a culture will exist and evolve either way. Haphazardly or by design. These experiences can be anything from company meetings and off-site events to how internal communication and collaboration are executed. Each experience either supports, detracts from, or has no real impact on supporting the culture.

A great way to discover if those experiences are influential in achieving accountability and the desired results of the organization is to diagnose them. Similar to the first step in the CDT model, assessing your organization's level of accountability requires some research.

In the Teams, we started with the big picture and worked backward. What are we trying to achieve? What actions will get those results? What mindsets and beliefs will drive people to proactively take those actions? What cultural experiences do we have or need to implement to ensure people believe and act in that manner? Our training and structures answer all these questions clearly.

For example, one imperative "result" we needed in the Teams was to be ever vigilant and prepared for anything at a moment's notice. Readiness. That meant that all of our gear and equipment had to be clean, prepped, and ready at all times. And that meant that nothing superseded preparedness. Take care of your gear and your gear will take care of you—as our saying goes.

Another one of our many mantras is related to the prioritization of this process. After any training scenario or mission, we focused on cleaning and preparing the Team equipment, then the troop or platoon equipment, then our own equipment. Then and only then—after checking with everyone to make sure everything is done—do you head to the showers or to get a bite to eat. You put yourself last. That process is a cultural experience that instills that belief. That belief drives the actions that result in us always being prepared for anything at a moment's notice.

One night in San Diego, after my platoon had just finished hours of open-ocean navigation in our Zodiacs, we were back at the team cleaning the boats. Team gear first. We were exhausted, the sea state had been ridiculous (twelve-foot swells), and as luck would have it, one of our outboard motors kept crapping out on us.

My platoon chief told me to make sure all the Zodiacs had a freshwater rinse before we stowed them for the night. The boats were on trailers behind our big white Ford F-150 pickup trucks. A couple of the other guys had the hoses ready so I hopped into the truck and started backing the trailer up so we could spray the boat down. If you've ever tried to back up a large trailer behind a truck, you know that it requires some concentration. And practice.

I immediately realized this was a bit more tricky than I had anticipated, but no worries, all was clear. I just had to back up the truck about twenty yards to get it close enough to the hoses. I started jerking the wheel left, then right. I went from reverse to drive several times trying to get the trailer lined up. Once that was established, easy day. All I needed was to give it a bit of gas.

I did, and the truck surged backward.

BAM! It came to a screeching halt, and all I heard was my platoon mates screaming swear words at me.

I had just run over one of the poles supporting the net for the legendary Team 5 volleyball court! Imagine some idiot driving onto the volleyball court during the epic scene in the movie *Top Gun*. Luckily it was 2 a.m. and no game was under way. These poles had been cemented into the ground since the Team was built. It was so badly damaged that nobody ever made an effort to rebuild it. Our legendary volleyball court would no longer be a part of Team 5 culture—but rather Team 5 history. Let's just say that my platoon mates held me accountable that night! As I recall, two rolls of duct tape were involved.

TALES FROM THE FRONT LINES

Early in my time in the Teams, we were tasked with capturing a high-value target in a rural area about an hour outside of Baghdad. Improvised explosive devices (IEDs) were a regular part of the enemy's strategy, so we routinely used UH-60 Black Hawk helicopters to get us close to the insertion point.

On this night, the moon was out and we had good visibility. The property we would be assaulting had two buildings, so we divided the platoon into a collection of four-man squads, or fire teams. My squad was responsible for taking the smaller building on the southeast corner of the property, while the rest of the platoon would take down the main house.

My squad's Black Hawk came to a steady hover fifteen feet above the ground just north of the building, and the four of us slid down the fast rope and quickly moved to the main door. We stacked on it and tested the handle.

Unlocked.

Slowing opening it, we looked for threats and went inside—each man scanning his assigned corner. A frightened, agitated man came out of the back room followed closely by his two-year-old son. They clearly weren't a threat, so we called out to them in Arabic as we cleared the room. *"Imshi, imshi!"*

After quickly placing some black plastic cuffs on the man and sitting him in a corner, I heard a voice come over the radio. It was the platoon commander, telling us to collapse back to the helicopters. The pilots had gotten the coordinates wrong, and landed us on the wrong target.

I cut the cuffs off the man and we ran back to our helicopter. A few minutes later, we were sliding down our ropes again at the correct target about a mile away.

As we moved across that yard, we started taking fire from a tree line across a small field on the west side of the property. It was ineffective fire so we kept moving while one of the AC-130 gunships accompanying us kept an eye on it.

After grabbing our guy quickly, with limited resistance, our exfil plan was to move out through a dense palm grove on the south end of the target location. We had two predesignated LZs (landing zones) in a field on the other side of the grove. Two Black Hawks would pick up the platoon while the other would extract our prisoner handlers, agency partners, and hostage. As we moved through the grove, we started taking heavy fire—again—from the same tree line. We started to return fire but quickly called a cease-fire, realizing that the enemy couldn't see us. We were all wearing night-vision goggles and they weren't. Our JTAC got on the radio, called the gunship and passed the coordinates of the tree line. A few seconds later we heard over the radio, "Rounds away."

Ten seconds passed. We knelt in silence in the concealment of the grove. Then all of a sudden—*BOOM! BOOM! BOOM!*—a series of perfectly placed explosions, one after the other, annihilated the tree line in rapid succession—fire and smoke shooting into the night sky. We called the helo pilots, making sure they knew it was a "hot" landing zone. We sprinted across the open field toward the helos. Running across tilled farmland, wearing sixty pounds of gear and NVGs isn't easy. I rolled my ankle on one of the raised rows of dirt and went smashing to the ground. Literally, the first thought that crossed my mind was, crap—I hope nobody saw that! We made it to the helos, piled in and got the hell out of there.

This was one of those nights where teamwork, trust, and accountability kept the mission together and allowed us the ability to quickly adapt to the circumstances. Without accountability and ownership, it would have fallen into chaos.

The need for 100 percent accountability in combat situations may seem self-evident.

In a corporate setting, however, you have to develop team alignment and mechanisms that drive it into the culture. Just talking about it with no prescriptive process or systems in place to ensure that behaviors shift toward accountability doesn't work. The environment must breed accountability through consistent action and those behaviors must be rewarded and celebrated. That's when it starts becoming part of the culture.

To do it right, any organization can follow a series of simple steps. They work whether the accountability you're trying to establish is internal—among the people on the team—or external, with clients, strategic partners, or others outside the organization. We've talked plenty about the importance of building great internal teams, but the best organizations know that customers, clients, partners, and vendors can be the most powerful source for keeping an organization moving in the right direction. One of my clients makes a regular point to collect external feedback from suppliers because they know if they help each other run better businesses, develop better products, and lean on each other to achieve success, everyone wins. The relationships are real, not simply transactional. Trust exists and accountability is a known element of their interactions. It's expected.

To achieve true accountability you must:

1. **RECOGNIZE REALITY.** You can't be accountable if you don't see and acknowledge what is going on around you. Whether it's the management team or the front-line troops, all must have complete situational awareness, understand the problems at hand and the slate of desired outcomes. If you can't get into alignment about those details, you won't be able to move off of step one.

2. **OWN IT.** Until everybody involved personally invests in the mission, you can't develop the overlapping web of performance that makes a team stronger than its parts. Internally, that means open, honest feedback that goes toward the goal of aligning processes, behaviors, beliefs, and actions with the desired results. Externally, that means acknowledging shortcomings quickly and honestly and enlisting as much feedback as possible to build solutions.

3. **ENGINEER SOLUTIONS.** When you accomplish the first two goals and are able to proactively assemble information from reliable tools and data sources, you're in position to tailor a solution. The key to the engineer mindset? Understanding that problems will *always* come up, and building contingencies and redundancy into your plan. Resiliency as part of the strategy.

4. **MOVE BOLDLY.** Here's where many teams either execute or get consumed with second-guessing. The best teams put their faith in the process, and when they get to an aligned decision with the full cooperation of an accountable team, they go for it. Own the outcomes and make adjustments as needed.

Ultimately, what you're creating is a culture where teamwork, accountability, and trust are rewarded. It isn't a culture of fear, where people see "accountability" in the most pejorative way—where they're required to follow a set of rigid rules or face these dire consequences. In a real environment of accountability, everyone takes ownership. Everyone is always asking themselves what else they could be doing to help the team accomplish the mission. Mediocrity is not tolerated. All of my experiences as well as many studies show that accountability—like trust—has a positive economic impact on the financial health of any organization. It improves morale. It improves efficiency. And it improves speed of execution.

Any organization can leverage its culture to simultaneously drive change and transform mindsets. But building a culture—whatever that culture is—takes a long time, as does transforming a culture.

The San Diego–based medical device company focused on redesigning their culture to align with the specific business result they needed to survive. During a three-year period after shifting toward fixing the culture and focusing on improving accountability, their stock price went from $0.31 per share to $22.35 per share growing revenue at about 15 percent per year, in an industry where 3 percent was average. They were later purchased by a Fortune 20 company for a 1,700 percent return on equity investment and then spun off to become the medical device giant they are today. All due to clearly defining the results they needed to achieve and working backwards to create a culture founded on the principle of ultimate accountability.

PART 2

PREPARING FOR THE CHANGE BATTLE

nce an organization has taken the initial steps for redesigning the culture to fit the new vision, it's time to start shifting mindsets, gathering valuable information from as many people as possible across the organization, planning the change mission, and communicating the intent. It's time to start *preparing for the change battle*.

To successfully lead change, senior leaders must first transform their mindset and embrace the fact that they will be pushed outside of their comfort zone. Then their words and actions become authentic. Authenticity and belief are what inspire the team to come together and achieve lasting change. As mindsets shift, it will be easier to engage the team in the mission planning process.

The planning and execution of your transformation mission will only be as good as your preparedness and the intelligence you gather from inside and outside of the organization. Without the proper tools and organizational structures in place, this will be a daunting task to say the least. But this stage of the transformation offers the perfect opportunity to bring as many people as possible together to provide feedback and ideas and to plan the mission. Once the initial components of the mission plan have come together and alignment has been achieved, the timing and consistency of communication become one of the most vital pieces of success or failure.

In Part 2, I will provide the tools and methodologies necessary for shifting mindsets, engaging the workforce in the intelligence gathering process, planning the mission, and successfully communicating its intent. Using these tools, your team will be well prepared for the change battle.

4

MINDSET: BELIEF IN THE MISSION

*I serve with honor on and off the battlefield. The ability
to control my emotions and my actions, regardless of
circumstance, sets me apart from other men.*
—NAVY SEAL ETHOS

Successful transformations begin with the leaders embodying the appropriate mindset that aligns with the mission narrative. Having the right mindset separates leaders who achieve their transformation goals from those who don't. In their *Harvard Business Review* article, "What Separates Goals We Achieve from Goals We Don't," Kaitlin Wooley and Ayelet Fishbach explore the concept of delayed gratification and its benefits when setting both near- and long-term goals. Their research also supports the notion that a little immediate gratification also goes a long way and keeps people energized and emotionally connected to fulfilling the long-term goals. For example, students who were surveyed cited how important it was for their study materials to be interesting. Students who enjoyed the material spent more time studying and earned better grades. Imagine that!

We will talk more about the importance of Telling Purposeful Stories and celebrating quick wins in later chapters—especially as it relates to diminishing change battle fatigue and keeping the team energetically focused on mission success.

In their article, Wooley and Fishbach provide three strategies for harnessing immediate benefits for increasing persistence—a quality that is imperative for successful transformations. Their study focused on students, gymgoers and museumgoers, but I am presenting these strategies as they relate to organizational change.

1. Factor in enjoyment when selecting the activities associated with goal achievement. As we know, change comes with a little bit of discomfort, so make a concerted effort to weave in some enjoyable activities that engage the team, reduce fear and keep the team excited about change.

2. Include some immediate benefits in the plan. You will have more success transforming the disengaged into the engaged—employees who drive change—when tangible near-term benefits are enjoyed by all.

3. Reflect on those immediate benefits while working toward the long-term transformation goal. Use Telling Purposeful Stories from the CDT model to ensure everyone realizes those benefits and their relation to mission success.

A core reason why most transformational change efforts fail is because the leaders do not have the mindset required to envision the necessary path for success. Their existing beliefs, views, and assumptions about their people, customers, and their organization as a whole keep them from accurately perceiving and understanding the dynamic challenges they face. Consequently, they respond with strategies and tactics that do not match the transformational reality in front of them. They make unsound decisions and rush headfirst into the abyss, skipping key foundational change steps.

Some of the traditional leadership beliefs and assumptions actually inhibit change—not accelerate it. And the belief that speed is critical causes leaders to tackle the transformation effort too quickly using disorganized tactical moves that don't align with what they are really trying to accomplish. And some don't really know what that is in the first place. Identifying early benefits and celebrating them doesn't mean inappropriate levels of speed are necessary.

We have a saying in the Teams: *Don't run to your death.*

Simply put, take it slow, move through the target, mitigate risk, and use aggression as needed.

In these situations, when leaders don't embrace the proper mindset, they skimp on resource investment and take a mediocre approach to change—when they should be going "all in." Without the mindset, proper vision and aligned narrative supporting that vision, leaders and managers race for the finish line protecting their own departments or divisions. Communication across departments is fragmented—if it happens at all—and chaos ensues. When leaders don't advance with a holistic approach it keeps them from integrating their change initiatives properly, causing redundancies and confusion that waste enterprise resources and slow the change process.

This might sound familiar to you!

Research shows that most leaders score relatively low in two areas: *self-reflection* and *requesting feedback from others*. A leader's mindset—the way they perceive the world around them and process concrete information—is determined by the lens through which they are looking. This of course is largely unconscious behavior causing leaders to improperly deduce the change battle challenges they face. This is why emotional intelligence is so critically important for leading transformations successfully. We will touch more on this in later chapters.

In an article on ChangeLeadersNetwork.com titled "Why Leading Transformation Successfully Requires a Shift in Leadership Mindset," by Dean Anderson and Linda Ackerman Anderson, they explain a leadership style called "co-creating." It is the antithesis of the most common leadership style we have already determined does not work during transformations: command and control.

They explain that a "co-creative" change leadership style often catalyzes these conditions for successful transformation:

- Organizational alignment with local control of local decisions

- Massive information dissemination in all directions so the entire organization can participate intelligently

- Easy integration of change plans across hierarchical and functional boundaries

- Common and aligned change goals throughout the organization

- Constant learning and course correcting change plans

- Credible leaders people trust as they march into the unknown (VUCA)

Transforming an organization and its culture requires a broader viewpoint—attention to variables and dynamics many leaders overlook. Most focus on the systems, processes, technology, products, and service, while neglecting to transform mindsets, behaviors, and culture. And that is a painful path to failure.

▲

You go through plenty of changes during BUD/S. But more than anything, your mindset evolves. Those who thrive during the worst, most unpleasant parts learn to channel all the pain, shivering, and misery into aggression—an aggression so powerful that it drives you relentlessly to the end of training. It's aggression that fuels the metamorphosis from a young, scared tadpole into a bold, confident, dangerous frogman. Embracing the suck requires a dramatic shift in how you view your current reality.

During Hell Week, your legs are so swollen that there is basically no definition between your calves and thighs. Wet, sandy clothes strip away your flesh until you have hardly any skin between your legs, around your waist, and under your arms. Relentless running with two-hundred-pound boats on your head leaves your scalp a scabby mess. Flesh-eating bacteria attacks some students so badly that they have to be dropped from training—some come close to losing limbs.

One of the guys in my class finished Hell Week with two fractured shins—but he kept his mouth shut and fought through the pain so he wouldn't get rolled back to another class and have to repeat the misery again. I had severe ITBS (iliotibial band syndrome)—an overuse injury from running—a fractured left elbow, and a bad case of bursitis. My elbow was so swollen, it looked like I had a baseball under my skin. But I forged ahead—and yes, it sucked.

On one of the evolutions, we spent the night in the mudflats in the southern part of San Diego Bay—a place you don't see on any of the postcards. What's it like? It's like crawling around for hours in black semifrozen yogurt.

Your boat crew is engaged in various races and competitions, and the instructors clearly take pleasure in expanding the torture. After a couple of hours, everybody is covered in cold, thick mud. The only thing you can see is a bunch of white eyeballs looking out from a sad, dirty mess. We're all exhausted, beaten, and shivering uncontrollably. The instructors have us turn over our boats and set them up as diving platforms, and order us to make running leaps and flips onto and off the platforms, while they judge us for form and creativity.

The boat crew with the highest scores (a bit of a subjective point system) gets to stand by the fire for a few minutes. It seems like an unbelievably awesome reward—a early-stage benefit!—until you earn it—and you spend five minutes getting your face roasted while the back part of your body freezes.

It sucks, but you have to push through. You have to develop an unbreakable mind.

How is it possible for people to survive this kind of punishment? One of the classic lines from the SEAL Ethos is *"A common man with an uncommon desire to succeed."* None of us are exceptionally extraordinary individuals, but the relentless desire to succeed sets those who finish apart from those who fail.

Mindset transformation is what leads to success.

By the time a SEAL class reaches the third phase of BUD/S—which begins in the fifth month of training—it is a collection of men in peak physical and mental condition. They know they will graduate and move on to advanced training, and there is nothing the instructors can do to break them. We would laugh and yell "hooyah!" when the instructors would punish us with a beat-down session of getting wet and sandy followed by endless burpees and push-ups. Nothing they did at this point would damage our spirits. You smile and say to yourself, "Thanks for making me even stronger."

We embraced the suck and laughed in the face of pain.

The mental fortitude required to finish the most challenging special operations training in the world is what defines us in battle. Another impactful line from our ethos says "My nation expects me to be physically harder and mentally stronger than my enemies." That belief is what ensures that we *will* be more prepared than the enemy. It's what allows us the ability to adapt amidst adversity.

Navy SEAL training is designed to create operators who can adapt to changing conditions, and self-aware nimble leaders who can process complicated information in real time and make decisions with the ultimate consequences—human lives—on the line. It's a developmental process that starts the first day of training. And we never stop training.

In a SEAL platoon or task unit, senior leaders provide the vision and context for the given mission. They define it, and deliver the message to the rest of the team. They reinforce their belief in the mission—which is infectious and emotionally connects everyone to the cause. They remove obstacles, provide the necessary resources and training and—maybe most important—they *engage* the rest of the team in the planning and preparation for the mission, which we will talk about in later chapters.

They also do this by delegating many of the most important tasks all the way down the chain of command. The seemingly endless investment of time and resources in training and preparedness is of course by design. Overlapping skill sets and subject matter expertise in many areas is imperative. By diffusing training, responsibility, and leadership throughout the team, you create small groups of warfighters stronger than the sum of their parts.

As I have touched on already, any high-performance team that has a desire to develop networks of empowered teams and leaders must invest heavily in their training and development. Without the skills and resources necessary to tackle transformation obstacles, the efforts will always fall short. This often first requires a leadership mindset shift, because time and budget must be transitioned away from other initiatives. Embracing that reality is the first step.

Mentally preparing for battle requires reflection and focus. The same applies to the change battle. A strong, accountable team who trust each other will rally around leaders that embody the warrior mindset—and they will all step onto the battlefield as one.

In this chapter, we're going to talk about how to achieve mindset shift and widespread belief in the mission.

THE TAKINGPOINT PRINCIPLE

To achieve success on the battlefield, there must be belief in the mission. The commander must show a passionate connection to the cause—and to the strategies and tactics that will drive mission success. The same applies on the business battlefield.

To successfully lead change, senior leaders must first transform their mindset and embrace the fact that they will be pushed outside of their comfort zone. Then their words and actions become authentic. Authenticity and belief are what inspire the team to come together and achieve lasting change.

In many organizations I visit, many people in the boardroom don't understand the time, commitment, and investment it takes to make real changes. They're in denial, or they're scared, or they simply don't have the vision to see the organization as something greater than it is at that moment. They fail to ask "What if?"

Or, I'll see that there's a consensus on the destination, but nobody is aligned on the path to get there. It's not uncommon that leaders and managers want to put more effort toward the systems and processes they already have in place—because that's comfortable and "safe." There is a dip in revenue—sell more. We have more work than the team can handle—

work harder, stay later. Our product mix no longer seems to mesh with customer needs—find new distributors and enter new markets.

But isn't doing things the same way expecting a different outcome the definition of insanity? Nobody wants to look at what the data reflects—because facing reality usually equates with discomfort.

One of my clients, a major Italian restaurant chain based in the Northeast, is a great example of successful mindset transformation. During many discussions preparing for their annual leadership conference (where I would be speaking about leading organizational change), the CEO shared details about the history of this thirty-year-old business. In their inception, they built a beloved brand based on the principles of quality and a customer-first mentality. Nothing mattered more.

But as they grew and notoriety spread, the brand earned the attention of larger restaurant groups as a potential acquisition. Eventually, they were acquired. But the acquisition partner's senior team was made up primarily of financially minded leaders—CFOs and VPs of finance. They devised plans for rapid growth that included straying away from what had originally made the brand what it was—an extreme focus on quality. Fresh food products that were sourced locally each day were replaced with mass-produced frozen products. Speed and simplicity replaced time and care. The list goes on. And these aren't unusual tactics for positioning a chain for expansion. But it can destroy the relationship with a brand's most important asset—the customer. When making decisions based purely on a set of current and historical financial data, you will miss fundamental opportunities that make any organization thrive—the people and culture.

The CEO jokingly said, "They did their best to kill the brand, but they failed."

When he took over, he instituted a new vision for getting back to the basics. Quality and customer would once again come first, and everyone in the organization had to embody that new mindset—and were thrilled to do so. They reinvested heavily in training and new technology for real-time customer feedback and sentiment analysis. They provided the tools necessary for their newly empowered teams to lead and win.

This would be a significant organizational transformation effort, but the light at the end of the tunnel burned bright. The CEO's mindset and passion for the mission infected everyone. Droves of store managers and leaders across the company were reinvigorated by the new vision. They knew it wouldn't be easy—but they believed.

The definitive question to ask, then, is how to flourish in that environment of uncertainty. How do you create a compelling vision and mindset for a team that acknowledges the real uncertainties that exist but still inspires people at all points on the compass to bring forth their best efforts and "embrace the suck"?

By addressing the core areas that are affected by transformation:

- Mindset—an authentic belief in the mission.

- Behavior—attitudes and thinking that supports the culture.

- Culture—an environment that instills these beliefs.

- Strategy—a plan that aligns with the vision.

- Tactics—the actions that drive results.

As shown in the beginning of this chapter, the *TakingPoint* principle of mindset shift is a crucial step that first starts with senior leaders—ensuring that they are viewing the change battlefield through the proper lens. Doing so allows them to step onto that battlefield with the right approach and a team that is aligned behind a clear vision for success.

APPLICATIONS FROM THE BATTLEFIELD
TO THE BOARDROOM

Donald Rumsfeld was appointed for his second stint as secretary of defense in January 2001 by President George W. Bush. Rumsfeld was one of the key individuals responsible for the restructuring of the military in the new twenty-first century. He knew change was coming, and he wanted the military to be ready for it.

Rumsfeld was crucial in planning the United States' response to the September 11 attacks—which included two wars: one in Afghanistan and one in Iraq. One of his biggest initiatives was to grow the ranks of the Navy SEAL Teams by 15 percent. So all we needed to do was make the training easier so we could graduate more students, right?

Of course not.

If you think about it from a sales and marketing perspective, one of the things we really needed to do was fill the top of the "funnel" with better leads—SEAL candidates who were well prepared for the rigors of training and had a better chance to make it through. In order to do that, we needed to showcase what the Teams are all about to a wider audience. This meant more marketing, which would require a dramatic shift away from the old "silent warrior" mindset.

Many in the upper echelons of leadership in the Naval Special Warfare community were against this. It took some time to find alignment. But eventually, most realized that this was fundamental to better recruiting. The movie *Act of Valor* was in a sense part of that strategy. The 2012 film about Navy SEALs was directed by Mike McCoy and Scott Waugh and written by Kurt Johnstad. It starred active-duty U.S. Navy SEALs and U.S. Navy Special Warfare Combatant-Craft Crewmen—

and was designed to essentially showcase what the NSW community was all about.

Needless to say, this was a far cry from what our community was used to, but it was a necessary piece of the strategy to turn the Teams into a modern, and hopefully larger, twenty-first-century organization. We had to go where the candidates were, and in order to do that, we needed a shift in mindset. To move past the old way of doing things. It was a bold move, but it led to a significant uptick in recruiting capability.

But change isn't always about bold, dramatic leaps by some visionary, once-in-a-lifetime leader. This concept is at odds with a good bit of the "heroic" origin stories you read about great executives, sports coaches or even military leaders. The myth that often surrounds those folks is that they had a special combination of insight, charisma, and determination that let them accomplish things "normal" people could not have achieved. And that they did it single-handedly.

I'm not downplaying greatness or saying bold leaders don't matter. They obviously do. But the reality today is that a visionary CEO is nice to have, but the mission will be accomplished only within an organization that goes out of its way to transmit leadership, creative thought, and initiative *down* the org chart. Instead of obsessively studying how to manage people and capital more efficiently, it needs to grow leadership through the ranks—especially in times of transformation—and those leaders need to believe in the mission.

During a full-day leadership development workshop I led for a large global healthcare company, I had an interesting conversation with the director of training and development. She was telling me about a major turnaround that occurred at her last company, also a healthcare giant.

On the surface, things didn't look so bad. Revenue was relatively stable, but the organization's rapport with customers and physicians was deteriorating at an alarming rate. On top of all that, they were actually losing $1 million per day! As is usually the case, many of the company's issues could be traced to its culture.

For more than 150 years, the organization had forged a very conservative culture that forced employees to be so steadfast that they had become almost totally risk-averse and intolerant of change.

They were essentially shooting for non-controversial mediocrity—they just didn't realize it.

In the late 1990s, the company had merged with another large healthcare company with a much more progressive and risk-tolerant culture. Unfortunately, this only reinforced the existing rigid culture, and the new, merged company wasn't able to generate any momentum with innovation. Two cultures were clashing against one another, driving a significant rift between many divisions that were designed to work closely together.

As a last-ditch effort, the company brought in a new CEO—the fourth in five years. My client recounted exactly how the employees reacted:

"Here we go again . . ."

"Another initiative that will fail."

"Get ready for more change stuff piled on our already-full plates."

But that's not what happened. This CEO brought with him a new mindset. A positive new approach that would be contagious. His vision was aligned with reality. Instead of laying out a new strategy and culture-shift plan that was conceived behind closed doors with no input from the troops, he did the opposite. He took time to visit the employees, get their take on things, and engage them in the planning process. He developed team networks of well-respected and influential employees from across the organization to help lead the transformation. These employees were also sensitive to the realities of the company culture.

What did all of this activity accomplish?

He was gathering great ground intelligence that would be used to develop a sound mission plan. This data uncovered the misalignments in both the strategy and culture. It also brought the positive aspects of the culture to the surface, highlighting elements that could be used to drive the transformation. And last but not least, it gave employees across the entire organization a voice by being involved in the process.

He was gaining buy-in and shifting mindsets.

If you're a leader, how do you establish a new mindset? How do you figure out *what* mindset, and *how* to get that buy-in? And if you're on the front line, how do you embrace it to become a leader yourself? In my experience, I have identified six basic tenets for beginning to develop an aligned leadership mindset.

1. Made, not born

Volumes and volumes of new research on children shows that kids who believe that they're naturally gifted don't achieve at the same rate as kids who have been taught to work hard. Why? Because when confronted with something they didn't know how to do, the gifted kids tended to feel threatened and uncomfortable, while the worker kids just saw it as another problem to solve.

In my experience, leadership works the same way. Are there people with amazing natural charisma, intelligence, and broad vocabularies that let them command a room? Sure. But those gifts don't guarantee anything—and they certainly don't prepare somebody for combat or a stressful corporate transformation.

Great leaders are lifelong learners. They're good listeners. They are good at asking for, collecting, reflecting on, and acting on transparent feedback from those they lead. Whether you're a young entrepreneur, an emerging leader within an organization or somebody who has been successfully leading an organization for three decades, you're the one at the workshop or keynote address sitting in the front, taking notes, constantly trying to absorb new ways to get better. As I have mentioned before, as SEALs we believe that our training is never complete. Leaders who will inspire change hold this same belief. They learn, apply, self-correct and then learn some more.

2. Lead by example

One thing there's no shortage of in the SEAL Teams is gear. We have warehouses and warehouses of it, all of it specialized for particular job functions.

But virtually every SEAL cared so much about his performance that he would spend his own money on various pieces of equipment that would help do the job better. Maybe it was a plate carrier that was lighter and had pouches in the right place, or a different sidearm that you were more comfortable using than the standard-issue model.

The same kind of mindset held true in physical training. Almost by definition, every SEAL is in peak physical health. But many guys would take jujitsu classes on the side, or do crazy stuff like ultra-marathon running to make sure they were the elite of the elite. David Goggins, one of the guys from my BUD/S class who came with me to SEAL Team 5, embodies the elite "lead by example" mindset better than anyone I have ever met.

After our first deployment, when everyone cycled back into training mode, he opted to attend Army Ranger School—another brutal crucible that transforms basic soldiers into special operations professionals. He wasn't required to go, he volunteered. And after he came back from his successful stint at Ranger School, he decided to take it up a notch—if that's even possible at that point.

David sat down and did a Google search for "hardest ultra-marathons in the world." He found a race called the Badwater, a 135-mile race through California's Death Valley. Having never run more than 20 miles, he couldn't qualify. So he signed up for a 24-hour race in San Diego that was two days later. He had no training. He ran the race in 18 hours and 56 minutes, which qualified him to run a 100-mile race in Hawaii called the HURT. Those two race times got him a place in the next Badwater race— which was only six months away.

David is now known as one of the world's most elite athletes. He broke the Guinness record for pull-ups, live on the *Today Show*. The most pull-ups anyone has ever done in twenty-four hours. You didn't even know that was a thing, did you?

We can't all be David Goggins. After all, he's the only person ever to make it through SEAL training, Ranger School, *and* the Air Force's tactical air controller training. Oh, and he did BUD/S Hell Week three times!

But in the civilian world, I've seen plenty of leaders and frontline people built in a similar mold. Employees go out of their way to learn other roles during their off time so they can be more useful. They'll attend webinars or read white papers to expand their knowledge base. They do whatever they can to expand themselves and bring value. This is the definition of an "emerging leader."

As a leader at my first company, I wanted to show that I was passionate about building high-performance teams, so I constantly studied and wrote about these practices. And then I would share those articles with the team. I engaged on the subject every day, instead of staying in my office and covering it over a twenty-minute PowerPoint presentation at a quarterly off-site meeting. Leading by example transforms mindsets because words and actions are real—and everyone sees it.

3. Define the win

Watching the Rio Summer Olympics in 2016, I saw an interview Michael Phelps gave at the pool after winning one of the many Gold medals. His goggles had filled with water halfway through the race and he had fallen behind, only to come charging back to win by a fingernail.

The interviewer was breathlessly asking him how he could have possibly won, with all that adversity. He answered very matter-of-factly that he had visualized himself winning that race over and over in his mind hundreds of times, and that he didn't need his goggles to be able to see what he needed to do.

The truly visionary leaders are able to do that not just for themselves, but for the entire team—give them the visual blueprint that they follow for the win. Within the stress and uncertainty of a transformation, they define not just what the long-term vision of the organization is, but what each of the moves mean and why they're happening.

A great exercise is to take the team through the process of picturing what the company will be like after the transformation is successful. What will we look like as an organization? What will it feel like to work here? How will our culture drive results? What will people in the community say about us? What positive things will competitors have to admit about us? What physical and visual transformations will we experience?

Attempting to answer these questions together is fun and helps everyone see what winning will look like. Not to dive down the neuroscience rabbit hole, but studies show that when we visualize ourselves accomplishing a goal, our brains will start to work backwards and find a path to get us there. Defining the win changes mindsets because people can start to work backwards to find a path to success.

4. Expand the toolbox

Think about the last time you were in a work situation where you could see that things needed to dramatically change (maybe that's today!). If you're heading for a transformation or are in the middle of one, it's a dynamic, changing situation. People are coming and going on the team, positions are being switched around. There can be a ton of confusion and stress. Resources and training are critical.

Sounds like a great time to pile on some "extra" homework, right?

It's all fine to say nice things like "push leadership deeper into the organization," but if you don't come up with a systematic way to do that *within* the day-to-day responsibilities of somebody's job, you're putting a pretty stiff barrier in the way.

If you've committed to buying and reading this book, you're obviously serious about improving performance and interested in thriving in a change culture. But if you're spending the majority of your waking hours working at the office and what little time you have left trying to be there for your family, where are you going to find the "extra" time to develop as a leader—whether you're doing it on your own or as a mentor or mentee?

Many organizations try to hack this process by sending team members to the occasional workshop or keynote address from somebody like me. I do what I can, but if the only commitment to growing leaders is an hour or two a quarter, the results will be reflective of that.

Whether you're somebody in charge of a team or a team member interested in growing in your role, you need to be expanding your toolbox day-to-day and week-to-week. That means setting up the actual structures of the organization in ways that empower true leadership development. Structures that provide proper resources for ongoing training that employees can take ownership of.

When my organizations were going through transformations, I did that in a variety of ways. One of the simplest and most successful was to start a book club. We were interested in having a culture that rewarded creativity and innovation. So we asked the leadership team (directors and above) to come together for an optional meeting once a week during lunch to read and discuss a variety of leadership, management, and peak-performance books. The company sprung for lunch, and attendance was voluntary for everybody. The goal was for attendance by the management team, but the club was open to anybody in the organization who wanted to come and learn. The frontline people who came picked up some great information from the books and had a chance to interact on a personal basis with the leadership team. Everybody learned something— both from the books and from the conversations the books inspired.

Another popular and productive tactic came from an idea we borrowed from the tech sector. We designated a large workspace as the "innovation lab," and every team member had the autonomy to spend as much time there during the week as they liked in between their "official" work assignments. The goal of the lab was very specific—and described very explicitly. We wanted people to work together in teams across departments to come up with out-of-the-box ideas to improve the quality of our services, create a new service line or product, or devise a way to improve the workplace experience.

Like the book club, it was optional—which can cut both ways. Participation from senior leaders is imperative. This goes back to how the leaders' behaviors have cultural implications. The frontline people won't take it as seriously if they don't think anybody at the top of the org chart believes in the process or cares what comes out of it.

Initiatives like these need to be a real part of the day-to-day operation, not tacked on after hours or done as an afterthought. They need to be seriously conceived and budgeted appropriately, both in terms of time and money.

By investing time and resources in the expansion of everyone's toolbox, job satisfaction increases, as does retention. Trust improves, thereby opening the floodgates for easier mindset transformation.

5. Embrace feedback

Feedback can terrify even those with the thickest skin. It is much easier to assume you have a solid understanding of your own performance and other's perceptions about your performance. Anonymous feedback and a peer review process will solve that misunderstanding quickly. I've experienced this firsthand—and the negative feedback can shake your self-confidence.

But if you don't have a handle on reality, you won't ever be in a position to make substantive decisions about the direction you're going to go, and how you're going to get there. When a football team starts losing games, the best coaches don't start making random changes and hope something sticks. They listen to feedback and evaluate what's been happening.

I spent some time with my buddy Mark Owen during a series of meetings in Los Angeles, and we were talking about some of the interactions we'd had as consultants in the business world. One of the common points we reached in our talks was that, for the most part, civilians in the corporate world are terrible communicators—especially when it comes to being accepting of feedback.

Sounds harsh, but it's true—for the most part.

We're going to cover communication more in later chapters, but it makes sense to mention it in passing here because it is so intertwined with feedback.

In the corporate world, communication either barely happens or if it does happen it's peppered with passive-aggressive attempts to avoid respectful conflict. During times of change, so many people not only don't have a good handle on what they're supposed to be doing, but they also don't get open, honest and productive feedback about *how* they're doing. If they do, it doesn't come frequently enough.

You're trained from your first day at BUD/S to be an effective communicator, because it's a flat-out necessity in a chaotic, dangerous environment like an urban firefight. If your team doesn't communicate, people die. We are successful in battle because we can move, shoot, and communicate seamlessly.

The consequences obviously aren't that dire in the corporate setting, but an organization can *figuratively* die if feedback can't be communicated effectively—and embraced appropriately.

The first way to do this is to embrace and enforce more frequent feedback. And these can't just be perfunctory "we all did great!" meetings. Have the courage to be open and leave the politics and rank aside. This is where you learn powerful and productive things about your organization and the people in it.

It's a powerful thing when the senior management team brings everybody together and says with openness, "What are we doing wrong? What can we do to improve? How can I make your life easier? What resources do you need?" Leaders who embrace that feedback can reform new mindsets—their own, and the team's.

The best organizations take that feedback and instead of being threatened by it, they take action on it. That doesn't mean you just blindly adopt everything mentioned as new best practices. But when leadership teams listen to feedback and incorporate the most productive elements of what they hear into new practices, they build trust and buy-in from their teams.

It means they're listening.

6. Celebrate the wins

No organization—not even NSW—has 100 percent buy-in all the time.

There are always going to be naysayers. They could be longtime employees who are resistant to change. It could be a business partner or a board member. It could be a mid-level manager who is going to have a significant increase in workload under the new plan—so he or she is either going to sit and stew in quiet discontent or be an active agitator against the new initiative.

When things change, you're always going to hear murmurs. We tried this before, and it didn't work. That idea doesn't make sense. Why are we wasting our time with this?

If you're waiting for full buy-in, you're going to be waiting forever.

And if you're judging the success or failure of your transformation by the voices of people who are pushing against it, you're going to get discouraged quickly.

Instead of focusing on those discordant voices—or trying to push them into submission—the goal should be to continue to show the vision and preach the new mindset to the group as a whole by showing what the real wins have been.

That means offering more than a basic recitation of the previous quarter's numbers, or a vague "We're doing better this month." When you can communicate the step-by-step way the new mindset and new approach has been producing positive results, you're reducing that resistance from the naysayers.

We will go into more detail on this when we talk about maintaining focus and treating change battle fatigue, but it's important to note now that the best way to quiet the negative insurgency is to *show*—and celebrate—the quick wins.

By offering real information—and a real "face" to the change process—you're taking ammunition away from the naysayers. There's less uncertainty to fuel the negativity.

Mindset transformation doesn't happen without a conscious effort from leadership and each individual. It will not always be achieved, unfortunately, but it's more likely to permeate the majority of an organization as a leader-first model.

TALES FROM THE FRONT LINES

One of my favorite quotes, actually from a WWI German field marshal, is "no plan survives first contact with the enemy." By definition, that forces SEALs to be an adaptive organization.

A SEAL Team has access to the full power of the United States' military intelligence community, and even we had to deal with "gray" intel.

How many enemies will we have to face on target? Not sure.

How certain are we that the guy we're after is there? Pretty certain, but not sure. How sure are we that this source is reliable? We think so, but it's not 100 percent.

A fascinating book called *Top Secret America: The Rise of the New American Security State*, by Dana Priest and William Arkin, details the overlapping web of agencies in the post-9/11 intelligence community. The org chart in the book where all of those agencies fit is mind-boggling—including more than 1,300 government facilities, 2,000 government contract companies, and more than 850,000 people with "Top Secret" security clearance. Their theories point to the fact that our transformation in the intelligence community in response to 9/11 may have created more redundancy, waste and confusion than we had before.

In the early years of this conflict, we worked closely with many of those agencies to get our intelligence, but that caused some issues and uncertainty over time. One of our many transformations since 9/11 was to bring that intelligence capability in-house so we would have the ability to not just vet the intel, but hold ourselves accountable for getting the best information possible. If your own guys are the ones going out on the basis of this information, you're going to be fully committed to proper data analysis and deriving actionable insights. It also let us work backwards and judge the quality of intelligence we were getting after the fact—which improved our data gathering process and helped us modify mission tactics. We were able to match our tactics with our level of confidence in the data.

Once the intel is gathered, senior leaders bring in other team members to analyze the information and use it to develop the mission plan.

What do you think is the best way to infil on the target?

Do we come right in and land on the roof, or drop a couple miles out and hump in?

Once you have your mission plan, it goes back up the chain of command for final approvals—and of course, those leaders are going to have an opinion. Then it comes back down for a final mission brief, and you begin working with the support assets you need for the mission—traditional Army forces for blocking off areas of operation, air support, whatever you might need.

Does everybody love every mission plan? Hell, no. There are tons of moving parts, and plenty of decisions made that don't always make sense to everyone. But everybody on the Team was a part of the process, and we're knitted together—even if we're sure it has the potential to become a bit chaotic once on target.

After the mission, as you've read, we're brutally transparent in how we evaluate it afterward. If something didn't work well, we talk about it and learn from the mistakes. We improve and evolve.

This is the critical point where so many civilian organizations—and their leaders—*lose* buy-in and fail to shift mindsets. They pass directives down the chain of command having gathered no information from key people in the organization. They don't utilize a co-creator transformation leadership style.

That causes two very serious kinds of cancer in the organization. One, it sends the message that there's no value or connection between buying in and moving forward. If I commit my time and energy to the mission but my manager doesn't bother to get my feedback about the plan, why would I ever stick my neck out again? I'm going to put my head down and just try to get along—or, if I'm a high achiever, I'm going to find another job. Next, it can cause even further rigidity and zero room for course correction—which will be needed many times throughout the change process.

This isn't abstract theory, but something I believe in and act on. In one of the companies, we had a major initiative to consolidate five software programs under one new system. We picked a new software program that ended up being far more complicated than what we needed. I compounded the mistake by putting the wrong person in charge of implementing the new software. We gave him an office and a budget, and basically said, "Go create this new system for us."

The leadership team didn't help lead that process nor had we taken the time to evaluate "reality" and the landscape of the change battlefield challenges we might face. We didn't stay involved. And we didn't check in often enough. We made a decision, handed it off to someone to "execute" and *ran to our death*.

This wasn't true empowerment, it was misguided and ill-conceived.

And it was my fault.

The person we put in charge saw the issues and decided to replace the software program *again*. The new one was even more elaborate and complicated. We basically had a Ferrari parked in the driveway, when a plain old Toyota would have worked just fine.

The director overseeing the project rolled out yet another training program and hired ten new employees—which we approved—to implement it and then we shortchanged that process because we were smack in the middle of a transformation and were feeling the financial strain that it was causing. The training provided was the bare minimum. Exactly what I mentioned earlier as the wrong thing to do.

As our frontline teams lost out on training and struggled to use the software, they didn't get the support they needed. They ended up doing what any rational person would do in that situation. They basically abandoned the software and went back to what they knew worked. So we had time and money invested in a vestigial software program everybody hated, nobody implemented and was just sitting there collecting digital dust.

The flip side?

When leaders can communicate what needs to happen and show the frontline people that resources are in place to help them win, those people will stay calm and on point because they know they're set up for success, not failure. They will believe in the mission.

They'll push in the same direction as leadership. They've bought in.

When the CEO of the healthcare company I mentioned earlier started the transformation with a new mindset, everyone followed him into battle. Why? Because they knew he believed in the mission, and he was fully committed—so they became committed, too.

Over the following years after the new CEO began leading this effort, it became clear through surveys, conversations and observation that most of the employees felt rejuvenated and proud to be a part of the "new" organization. And the best part? The company's financial performance reflected the changes. In a few years, the company went from losing $1 million a day to earning $5 million a day. Operating income went from a $300 million loss to a $1.7 billion gain—and the stock price jumped from $5.84 to $48.40.

It didn't come from some kind of miraculous, elaborate rebuild. It came from gathering and focusing the collective mindset of the team.

Something any organization can accomplish.

5

PREPARATION: GATHERING INTELLIGENCE AND PLANNING THE MISSION

The lives of my teammates and the success of our mission depend
on me—my technical skill, tactical proficiency, and attention to detail.
—NAVY SEAL ETHOS

As I previously touched on, in the immediate aftermath of the 9/11 attacks, the American military quickly realized that transformation of mindset and culture would be necessary to sustain the fight and defeat a dangerous, dynamic, and vastly decentralized enemy. We had the best warriors, intelligence specialists, and civilian support at our disposal, yet weren't nimble enough to move at the speed these wars required. And even though we had a vast proliferation of data and intelligence, much of it was redundant, conflicting, or trapped in silos.

This is not so different from what we face in today's global business environment.

We have access to the most comprehensive data-collection tools and diagnostic information in the history of business. But if we don't adapt our tactics so that data is actually useful for the "war" as it is being fought today, those advantages aren't advantages at all.

The opportunity?

Leveraging big data to gain the necessary intelligence for transformation decision making.

The challenge?

In order to properly utilize big data for transformation decision making, an organization must first become *data-driven*—which also requires a shift in mindset and culture.

At every level in the SEAL Teams, we train for and embrace a decentralized approach to leadership, collaboration, and communication. We're ready for the unconventional fight. But when you pile on everything else that comes with modern warfare—the intelligence assets that filter in from around the globe, the political ramifications of the missions we undertake, the actions other organizations are undertaking at the same time to solve the same problems—it's easy to see how chaos can reign. Without a holistic approach to data analysis and integration, the intelligence that can be applied to the overarching strategy becomes too complex and difficult to decipher.

The traditional hierarchical structures, cross-branch subcultures, and information sharing methods often made us have to fight against ourselves before we could fight the enemy. Senior leaders finally realized that the military in general and various task forces at the tip of the spear had to transform into modern twenty-first-century organizations that were aligned behind a single narrative. To do that, we had to be better positioned to gather and share information and share that information seamlessly. Rigid structures not only inhibit the ability to collect data, but also to communicate an aligned vision, which we'll talk more about in Chapter 6.

What the special operations communities understood in those first years after 9/11 applies directly to today's business world—from startups to regional organizations to global corporations.

In a 2015 report by KPMG titled *Data-Driven Business Transformation: Driving Performance, Strategy and Decision Making,* they point to the fact that the phenomenon of big data has changed the business world like never before. Organizations now have the opportunity to use data and analytics to become less process-centric and more data-centric—and therefore data-driven when it comes to strategy and decision making.

Data-driven organizations are seeing upwards of 20 to 30 percent improvements in EBITDA due to unlocked efficiencies and more granular financial insight. But many organizations have yet to put the proper systems and subject matter experts in place to reach their full business intelligence potential. And even though big data has crept to the top of the corporate agenda (similar to culture), most companies need to vastly improve in several key areas:

- The ability to combine, organize and manage multiple internal and external data sources.

- The skill set required for building analytics models and dashboards for predicting and optimizing the outcomes that transformation will achieve.

- The discipline senior leaders must have to transform the culture to be more data-driven.

For example, Amazon Prime uses data to ensure on-time delivery of their products. Similarly, SEAL Teams use data and intelligence to ensure the on-time delivery of "hot lead" to terrorists' bodies. It's basically the same thing!

Data matters. Intelligence matters. Alignment matters.

And so does establishing the competence and *freedom* to use data in order to adapt and respond to challenges in real time. SEAL Teams have to do it to stay alive and defeat the enemy.

So do you, and so does your organization.

In KPMG's biannual global CFO survey (which they reference in this report), respondents saw big data and analytics as critical for implementing "lean finance" strategies (optimizing finance processes for minimizing inefficiencies, reducing unnecessary costs, and improving speed, flexibility, and quality). This is the core reason that we replaced the CFO and our entire finance team during one of my company's transformations. We needed to gather and organize business intelligence and the skill to extract actionable insights. We lacked the ability for our finance function to play a proactive strategic role. And even though people and culture must maintain a position of priority in any high-performance organization, so too must financial and operational data.

Forty-one percent of the high-performing survey respondents also cited big data and analytics as "extremely important" as an enabler of lean finance and decision-making mechanisms. SEAL Teams act on intelligence—literally and figuratively. Information comes in from sources that have been developed, local assets, allied forces, agency partners, and civilian organizations. Intelligence forms the basis of the mission SEAL Teams are assigned to complete, and it is the raw material of which those missions are constructed.

But no matter how high-quality the intelligence is, no SEAL Team ever expects a mission to run according to a script. Even if all the intelligence pieces are right on, people change, situations change—and enemies react in unpredictable ways. So the basis of SEAL training and preparation is to practice for a seemingly endless variety of contingencies.

Dealing with the Inevitable Ambush

Every SEAL mission—whether we're talking about an offensive action in Iraq or a training mission in BUD/S, SQT or platoon training—had built into it a variety of contingency plans that counted on the team's ability to adapt when faced with adversity. In one training scenario, my platoon was assigned to develop a complex mission plan for an assault on an "enemy" village on San Clemente Island, off the coast of San Diego. We were given the intelligence brief and used that data to plan our mission.

At 10 a.m., we boarded a nuclear submarine at the sub base in Point Loma for transportation to the island. That's the only time I have ever been in a submarine, and let me tell you that the interior is much smaller than it looks in the movies. The only space they had for us during the twelve-hour journey (they would be doing maneuvers all day before our insert) was the torpedo room. So I took a nap on top of a torpedo—which is exactly as comfortable as it sounds.

At about 11 p.m., the submarine surfaced, and we brought our gear and Zodiac boats to the top of the sub. We assembled the boats, slid them off the side of the sub, piled in, and started our insert under the cover of darkness. About half a mile offshore, the assault team slipped into the water in our dry suits and fins, and pushed our weapons and gear in front of us in waterproof bags. We came over the beach, regrouped, and began the four-mile hump to the location of the village. About five hundred meters from the target, we got hit with a massive ambush from the ridgeline above us. The opposing force was in a dominant and elevated position, but the SEAL philosophy doesn't say anything about shrinking from a fight. Our ambush credo is to react with *violence of action*. That means a counterattack with overwhelming firepower or calling in air support to annihilate the enemy position.

The ridgeline ambush was a contingency we had planned for before the mission using the data provided and the actionable intelligence we derived from it. We were ready to adapt, and we did. Predicting a set of outcomes is a core function of successful data analysis and application.

What You Do When the Hood Comes Off

Another example comes through an exercise we call the Hooded Box Drill. You stand in a room in the middle of a square that's been taped off on the floor. Over your head is a hood that is connected to a pulley on the ceiling with a wire. An instructor is controlling the wire, and he feeds you a scenario while you're standing in the room blinded by the hood. You'll hear some basics about what is unfolding, but you don't learn anything about the configuration of the room, or the number of people you will encounter—or if they're friends or foes.

After letting you stand there for a while wondering what will happen, the instructor pulls the hood, and your job is to deal with whatever scenario comes your way in the simulation. For example, you might first see a pretty girl standing ten feet away waving to you, but you have three military-age males screaming at you from behind.

You have to quickly assess the situation.

The girl might not be a threat. But when you quickly turn and train your weapon on the belligerent men and go through your engagement checklist, you might all of a sudden feel a pistol against the back of your neck.

The girl? Maybe she wasn't such a non-threat after all.

The point of this training is to get you in the mindset that conditions and variables are constantly changing, and it is up to each individual SEAL to be able to both make a judgment about a particular scenario, calibrate his response, and have informed intuition about what fellow team members are going to do around him. It's how the best NFL quarterbacks seem to be able to find their most important receiver when a play breaks down. They've practiced what to do when it all goes wrong hundreds of times, so there's calmness instead of panic and disarray. Real-time data assimilation is as important in these situations as it is during any business transformation. Without real-time data (and the consistent and rapid sharing of that data) it is difficult to understand when course correction is needed.

Contrast this to what happens in many civilian organizations—which often have, at best, practices that are diametrically opposed to this concept of broad, shared responsibility and information dissemination. A typical command-and-control organization with vertical and horizontal silos will have a challenging time disseminating valuable intelligence to frontline managers. Information they need to make decisions in VUCA environments. And the same applies up the chain of command.

By building a data-driven mindset and culture—and the proper models associated with the strategy—any organization will have a greater propensity for success in the areas of transformation and business performance as a whole.

THE TAKINGPOINT PRINCIPLE

The planning and execution of your transformation mission will only be as good as your preparedness and the intelligence you gather from inside and outside of the organization. Without the proper tools and organizational structures in place, this will be a daunting task, to say the least.

I can't think of many organizations out there that don't want to be more collaborative, more aligned, communicate better, and improve trust and accountability. You don't have to be a CEO or have an MBA to understand how all of those things—when executed well and ingrained in the culture—would lead to better financial returns. But many organizations struggle with their legacy systems and structures. They can't—or won't—move away from them and toward something better, because they worry about the unknown or about losing control. Or they lack the confidence to invest in more appropriate data-gathering tools—and the people skilled enough to use them.

Say you work for a decent-sized accounting firm that has both individual and corporate clients. At a big annual meeting, the leadership team shares a plan to increase the organization's corporate business by devoting more time and energy to soliciting big regional clients. The organization's marketing team could be fully on board with the goal, and develop big plans to attract those clients, but if the frontline representatives who actually work those accounts aren't a part of the planning, they can't contribute intelligence about what actually makes those relationships work—and what kind of structures, systems, tools, and data sources need to be in place to support data-driven decision making for those clients.

In that case, there's horizontal alignment on the new direction, but no alignment *between* the silos vertically. Of course, it's very easy to be out of alignment both vertically and horizontally at the same time. It happens when senior leaders don't have enough access to important ground intelligence from their frontline troops while directives and information from the top gets lost in translation on its way down.

A March 2013 McKinsey & Company article by Dominic Barton and David Court titled "The Keys to Building a Data-driven Strategy" outlines this TakingPoint principle well. They detail three action steps that organizations can take to make progress toward becoming more data-driven. The first step is to develop business-relevant analytics models that can be understood and put to use. The best way to do this is to gather intel from frontline managers so the tools mesh well with existing decision-making processes (although some of those process will have to change). The next step is to embed analytics into simple tools for the frontline troops. The key word here being *simple*. The goal is to provide intuitive tools and models that will improve their job functions and decision-making capability. And third, to develop capabilities to exploit big data. To achieve this, it usually requires a multifaceted approach involving championing by senior leaders, training and rewarding new behaviors.

Common Features of a Data-Driven Organization

There isn't necessarily a singular path to becoming a data-driven company, but there are some features that are shared by those who get it right:

- Data-driven companies value the ongoing sharing of information. Collaboration is a core tenet of the culture and it's understood that ALL appropriate data should be accessible to anyone in an organization.

- Data-driven companies believe the right shared data should be made available to all employees. This lends itself to improved situational awareness and performance at the individual and team level. The key term is "made available"—not shoved down their throats.

- They have the tools and skills to make sense of vast amounts of structured (data gathered in formal databases) and unstructured (information from emails or presentations, for example) data to inform decisions and make transformation predictions.

- Data-driven companies make data collection a primary activity across departments—a behavior to be measured and rewarded.

- They have the ability to provide real-time insights as to where course correction may be needed or new opportunities seized.

- Senior leaders not only buy in to building a data-driven culture, they evangelize it from the mountaintops.

- They use data to constantly diagnose existing systems and processes. When a business case for change is made— it's backed by data.

- They value transparency and encourage upward management and communication.

In 2012, the Economist Intelligence Unit performed a survey that was sponsored by Tableau Software (a vendor partner of my last company). They surveyed 530 senior executives from North America, Asia-Pacific, Western Europe, and Latin America across a wide range of industries. A key insight was that "the most successful companies have adopted a data-driven culture in which they maximize the use of data by providing necessary training and promoting the sharing of data across all levels of employees and departments."

In all, 76 percent of executives from top-performing organizations cited data collection as essential, compared with only 42 percent from companies that fall behind their peers in performance. That said, like many of the principles in this book, they seem simple but are often difficult to execute, especially in larger companies that have seen relative success using legacy systems—or not using the advantages of big data at all.

My marketing agency, for example, prided itself on being data-driven. It was part of our culture and strategic advantage. But it didn't happen overnight. It took time to first identify the opportunity as a core differentiator and begin implementation. This transformation could be broken down into two parts: *internal data sourcing* for marketing, operations, and human resources, and *external data sourcing* to improve products, services, and client relationships. This required a total shift in mindset, brand marketing, resources investment, talent acquisition, training necessity, and how we approached the marketplace in general. And it wasn't easy. The outcome, however, was a massive internal and external transformation. Internal efficiencies improved, and our ability to make strategic decisions for client campaigns went through the roof.

Leading companies understand the importance of data and analytics and invest heavily in the tools and people required to leverage this opportunity. By building a data-driven culture, the entire organization understands the importance of data and base all decisions on actionable insights. This improves speed, efficiency, ability to predict outcomes, and maneuverability during transformation.

All of which have a positive impact on the bottom line and shareholder value.

APPLICATIONS FROM THE BATTLEFIELD TO THE BOARDROOM

One of my good friends and mentors, Jeff Campbell, had a long and successful career as an executive in the restaurant business. We met when we were both speakers at a senior executive training event in San Diego, and Jeff later began bringing me in to lecture at his MBA leadership development program at San Diego State University. Jeff became the president and CEO of Burger King in 1982, when the company was in the depths of a protracted business slump. It was losing heavily in its head-to-head war with McDonald's, and the Burger King franchisees were on the verge of revolting.

Jeff came into the company with a unique set of credentials. In addition to the standard academic ones—a bachelor's degree in psychology and master's degrees in marketing and history—Jeff had been an officer in the Army's elite 82nd Airborne Division. When Jeff took over at Burger King, the temptation was strong to blow things up and reorganize from the ground up. After all, nothing was working—and he had been promoted up the ranks as a *change agent*.

But Jeff went the other way.

"We had to turn around a company with 4,000 restaurants and 1,000 franchisees who didn't like doing what they were told—and they were already angry at how things were going," he said. "The answer was not to tell them what I intended to do. That meeting would have lasted ten minutes."

Data gathering doesn't always have to require a million-dollar investment in new software applications and a dedicated team of data scientists. The process should involve a little human interaction as well (a lot, actually)—and as I have pointed out, this accomplishes two things: You gain valuable insight from the front lines and build buy-in because their voice is being heard.

Similar to the CEO of the healthcare company I referenced in the previous chapter, Jeff went on a nationwide "listening" tour. He booked conference rooms in various cities and asked franchisees to come in and tell him all of their problems and frustrations. Once they had the chance to vent, he asked them what they would do to change the direction of the company.

Using a good bit of their advice—as well as plenty of his own turnaround plan—Jeff was able to get the company headed in the right direction. He would later go on to work in brand development for Pepsi and become the CEO of the Johnny Rockets and Catalina restaurant groups before moving to his current role as a mentor and program director for San Diego State University's School of Hospitality and Tourism.

Jeff's approach came in part because of what he learned from *his* mentor, world-famous restaurateur Norman Brinker, who was president of Jack in the Box and founder of Steak and Ale.

"Norman led by asking questions," Jeff said. "By definition, you get better ideas when you talk to people who are closer to the customers. In the best organizations, leadership and data are moving up the chain of command, not just down."

With this free flow of information, organizations are better able to plot out a realistic picture of where they stand—and where they want to go. Their risks and challenges are more clearly delineated and more completely understood. And they are in a better position to predict transformation outcomes.

Planning the Mission

In the SEAL Teams, we followed a straightforward intel gathering and mission planning process:

- Analyze intelligence and overall mission detail to understand the battlefield commander's intent and how it relates to the big picture. This intelligence comes from both internal and external resources.

- Identify resources, assets, personnel, and time available for planning.

- Plan the mission in an inclusive, decentralized way by bringing in key members of the team and various subject matter experts.

- Determine the high-level plan.

- Empower key leaders to collaborate on the details and course of action.

- Plan for contingencies.

- Understand what risks can be controlled or mitigated and plan accordingly.

- Continually check the plan and contingencies against emerging information and changing landscapes. Adjust accordingly.

- Brief the whole team on the plan and gather input from those not involved in the planning process. Apply their feedback as needed. Gain buy-in.

Sounds good, right?

But when I spend time with my corporate clients and hear how they describe their operational process in rosy terms—and compare it to what I see with my own eyes—it often doesn't match.

You can have the best plan in the world, but as the saying goes, "No plan survives first contact with the enemy." Or the marketplace. Many, many organizations go through the effort to build a strategic plan and "implement" it, but when the first major thing goes wrong, they go into crisis mode. Everything becomes a triage—lurching from one problem to the next and throwing people and resources around with abandon.

That strategic plan? In this case, it isn't worth much beyond the paper it's printed on.

My goal for you is to change your mindset from focusing strictly on *planning* to embracing *preparation*. Those are two fundamentally different things.

Planning is certainly a part of preparation, but it's much more than that. Preparation means you know the plan, but you also have the functionality and skill to pivot when things don't go according to that plan—which they rarely do! And you have the capability to leverage big data, extract insights for the mission planning process, and use that data for course correction as needed. Going with your "gut instinct" usually isn't enough in today's VUCA environments.

So much of the business literature and self-help space is consumed with helping people make better and more comprehensive plans for what they want to do personally or professionally, but none of it addresses the stark reality that situations are fluid.

A sports metaphor is useful here. My friend and client Dwane Casey, head coach for the NBA's Toronto Raptors, explained his approach to me. Basketball coaches routinely research their opponents for the coming week. They spend lots of time figuring out the strengths and weaknesses of the opposing team, and they come up with their plan for how to exploit the weaknesses they find—just like a military unit does for a mission.

But the best coaches don't simply follow the plan doggedly no matter what happens. A key part of the preparation for the week is a series of *if-then* questions. If the other team responds with this, what will we do then? If we don't function efficiently with this part of our plan, what is option B or option C?

The best way to describe it is to say that the best coaches—and the best military and organizational leaders—are not coming up with better ways to plan. They're coming up with better ways to *be*. They combine real-time data and transparent team feedback to make informed decisions.

You want to be a part of an organization that expects change and is prepared for it—not in a constant state of triage. If you're a dynamic group with that kind of preparation, you're actually looking forward to change—because you know you're much better positioned for it than your competitors.

This kind of nimble organization requires responsibility and authority to be diffused down the chain of command—which we've already talked about—but it also requires a significant shift in how various team members are measured and judged. Like trust and accountability, if you want a team that values and uses data, you must provide the proper tools and training and reward data-driven behaviors.

The Zero-Defects Mentality

Throughout the 1980s and 1990s, the U.S. military was mired in a mindset analysts have called "zero-defects." The culture of advancement became one where the officers who were able to present the "cleanest" record—no friction, no casualties, answers to all the right questions— were the ones who moved up. This mindset promoted an extreme risk-avoidance streak throughout the leadership class. If you tried something different or promoted a strategy that wasn't widely understood or accepted, you ran the risk of getting passed over and eventually downsized right out of the military.

This is clearly a leadership problem, but think about it from the perspective of junior people in an organization. If you see a problem—or an opportunity to offer intelligence that could improve the way something is done—and have no confidence that information would be accepted and acted upon by your leadership, how long will it take for you to put your head down and just "do your job"? Worse, what would happen if you were actively discouraged from even *raising* a point that could be considered counter to the status quo? As one mid-level manager at a law firm once told me, "Senior leaders say they want transparent feedback, but when we give it or fill out their surveys, that's where it ends. The information seems to flow up into a black hole and is never addressed. And nothing ever changes."

Even if that "zero-defect" culture produced exactly what it intended— a fighting group that eliminated risk and operated with "efficiency"—it would still fall far short of being successful at achieving the ultimate goal of any military group. Missions would fail—and sometimes they did—because many leaders in the various branches of the service lost their ability and willingness to encourage creative thought and weigh risks and rewards appropriately.

Heavy on Management and Light on Leadership

John Kotter and James Heskett offer a great explanation of how these environments inhibit information sharing and this zero-defects mindset in their book *Corporate Culture and Performance*. They describe the process at overmanaged and under-led organizations as follows:

A combination of visionary entrepreneurship and a little bit of luck creates an initially successful business strategy.

⊿

A dominant position is established in the marketplace.

⊿

The company experiences revenue and profitability growth for some time.

⊿

The company grows and promotes managers, not leaders, with little experience and minimal training.

> These managers are allowed to create silos and adopt subculture tribal behaviors, as do the people beneath them. Senior leaders do nothing to stop this or don't see it.
>
> ▲
>
> An arrogant divided culture develops with many tribes that don't collaborate or share information. These managers fail to acknowledge the value of true leadership and those among the ranks who can provide it. They stifle innovation and behave in centralized bureaucratic ways.

Many, many civilian organizations unconsciously promote a zero-defects model with their frontline troops with the way they respond to new information—or their ability to share it across silos. If frontline people feel like they're going to be judged harshly for being "wrong," they will be very cautious in what they share. That makes sense for, say, a brain surgeon—who holds human life in his or her hands.

But what if you're a part of a software company that produces B-to-B solutions, and a big customer comes to one of your salespeople with a new problem he or she is trying to solve? Leadership could insist on that salesperson focusing on the bottom line—selling more stuff from the current line. Or, it could be open to hearing this market intelligence and potentially create a new and lucrative line of business. Could the new line turn out to be a dry hole? Sure. But as they say in the NBA, you miss 100 percent of the shots you don't take. A leadership group hamstrings itself when it doesn't have a free flow of information to at least consider, nor the tools and processes to obtain that information.

TALES FROM THE FRONT LINES

When I started my first company after leaving the SEAL Teams and finishing graduate school, I figured I would be able to use what I learned about preparation and planning in both places to create a system that would keep data flowing both up and down that chain of command.

It didn't quite work out that way at first.

In one company, we developed a renewed vision to be in a better position to design and deploy truly integrated solutions for our clients. But to actually achieve this, it went way beyond better data analysis, creative thinking, and piling more services on top of one another. Custom strategies required a new approach to talent acquisition, departmental structure, and most of our existing processes. The first action we took was intelligence gathering to support our mission plan for transformation. Using focus groups, survey tools, round table discussions, stop-start-continue exercises, and a series of polls and interviews, we gathered as much data as we could. But we didn't just do this internally, we did it externally. We surveyed clients with the simple position based on two questions:

Question 1: "Here's what we are trying to achieve. How do you think we currently do this well, and what do we need to change to achieve this goal and serve you better?"

Question 2: "Would you currently recommend us to other clients right now? If not, would you if we achieved this new vision successfully?"

I was on the executive board of the San Diego Ad Club, so I had many friends and colleagues who worked for our direct competitors. I would schedule lunches or have casual conversations and ask them how they would tackle certain objectives. I was developing "intel" sources! I was transparent about the reason for my questions because we were all friendly competitors.

THE INTELLIGENCE GATHERING TOOLS:

- Surveys

- Focus Groups

- Interviews

- Round Table Discussions

- Finance, Accounting and Project Management Software

- Time-Tracking, Sentiment and Customer Feedback apps

- Stop-Start-Continue Exercises

- In-Person Meetings with Friendly Competitors

Using the information we gathered, we went through the mission planning process I outlined earlier. We merged teams for better collaboration, implemented new reward mechanisms, reworked reporting structures, redesigned the whole office, and knocked down walls— literally and figuratively. By using good data from internal and external resources, we were able to develop a successful mission plan with solid contingencies.

Even with the diverse background I have brought to my companies over the years, my experience wasn't so different than that of many entrepreneurs. A flight path through graduate school is a common one— but most of the time you don't really learn everything you need to know in school. Nor do you learn everything you need to know in the SEAL training pipeline. In combat, things change at the pace of war and there is no *training time-out*.

Sure, getting a handle on the principles of accounting, finance, marketing, and management are helpful. But running a real business means dealing with uncertainty, risk, and almost constant change—now more than ever. Theories and ideals only go so far.

But most entrepreneurs, for example, start small and build out a staff person by person in the beginning. You have a close-knit team of people you really know well, and you see an almost seamless flow of information. After all, you're probably all sitting in the same room! This applies equally to leaders and managers in a division of a larger organization.

As the bus gets larger and more people get on, you don't have the same personal connection with everybody on that team, and you can lose that intelligence flow as silos begin to form. But again, great intelligence can come from outside the organization as well. Either from friendly competitors you respect or new hires who have previously worked at competing companies.

Let's say your sales manager has "acquired" a salesperson from your direct competitor (although I don't encourage poaching). This is a coup, because you have a person who is very familiar with the competitive landscape and can often bring access to new customers from their existing database.

How did your last company do this? Where did they fall short? When they went through this type of transformation, how did it affect the culture? What worked and what didn't? How is this organization perceived by your last company?

In essence, you're also getting a scouting report on *your* organization as seen through the eyes of a competitor. It's a free source of information about what your team is already doing right and what they're missing— and it's something that few organizations actively try to discover.

This happens for a lot of reasons, but the most common one is overconfidence.

If an organization has historically had success using legacy systems and processes, you'll see a culture where the leaders are very comfortable doing things the way they have always worked. It's a low-risk strategy that prevents a lot of second-guessing and uncertainty. If the leaders of those kinds of organizations face a crisis, the most common response is what seems like a sensible one: We've faced this before, and this is how we beat it. So we'll handle it the same way again. Unfortunately, organizations today are facing obstacles they have never encountered before. So there is no battle plan to fall back on.

You don't have to look very far to see how dangerously out-of-date that mindset is. Giant companies are getting disrupted in the span of a few months or a few years, and they're disappearing because they tried to confront problems the same way they had always been addressed.

Sears opened for business in 1886 and was a dominant retailer for more than a hundred years, through depressions and dramatic changes in consumer tastes—until it was passed by Walmart in 1989. By 2005, it had been bought out by Kmart and had shrunk from 3,500 stores to less than 700, because it wasn't able to operate in a similar low-cost, wide-distribution model. In 2000, Yahoo was valued at $120 billion and was the undisputed leader of the digital world. By 2008, it had shriveled to the point where Microsoft offered $50 billion in an unsuccessful takeover. In 2017, Yahoo disappeared as an independent brand when it was purchased by Verizon for $4.5 billion.

It's just as dangerous (if you don't know what you're doing) to immerse yourself in the modern world of big data analytics as it is to hold on blindly to the strategies that might have been safe in 1990. Jeff Campbell talks often about how corporate America is being strangled by the "financialization" of the workplace. Leaders of people are being replaced by accountants, finance experts, and lawyers who make decisions purely based on a set of financials. When people are dehumanized and converted into data points, it goes without saying that leadership groups are going to have trouble connecting with and motivating those people.

There is a balance. As I stated before, financial modeling must also align with the strategic vision for transformation. Data and insights must converge with transparent intel from frontline troops.

As I mentioned previously, this happened to one of my clients, the large restaurant group based in the Northeast. The acquisition strategy was essentially run by financially minded individuals who didn't make decisions based on brand, quality, feedback from store managers or even the customer.

"They were basically doing everything they could to kill the brand!" the CEO told me. "But they failed. The brand was already so strong that it survived. I was brought in to bring us back to what we do best."

I completely agree with his approach, which is similar to Jeff Campbell's. I've always led organizations by prioritizing the three most important assets in this order: employees, customers, shareholders. As long as you're being fiscally responsible, putting the team and customers first will almost always result in happy shareholders.

But analytics and data visualization are equally important. You need to have a dashboard and understand your business's key performance indicators (KPIs). Poring over financial data, using executive dashboards and exploring ways to increase efficiencies are always going to be a part of a leader's portfolio. But if a team leader believes he or she is going to be able to sit above the fray and say, "Hey, I did it this way at my last company so I'll just apply these standard tools"—there are some unpleasant surprises coming.

You think the numbers don't lie, but of course sometimes they can. There are all kinds of soft costs that don't show up on a profit and loss statement. For example, how do you value trust? How do you value buy-in? Loyalty? Morale? What are the economic indicators for each of these?

The goal is to use information and a new, inclusive mindset to align your people with the mission. To get the best information to make decisions, and then deliver the data the frontline troops need to make *their* decisions. Top down, bottom up, and horizontally.

When you compile just to compile, you have a stockpile of information and a thick strategic plan, but you're flying blind. You can do that for a long time if you have some luck and disorganized competitors, but you're putting pressure on so many places in the organization, and it's only a matter of time before one of those seams breaks.

When Good Data Doesn't Lead to Good Results

One particular SEAL mission had us going to a rural area outside Ar-Ramadi, Iraq, to capture a high-value target. The source providing the ground intelligence told us we would find the leader and financier of a strong anti-coalition force there.

At about 2:15 a.m., we left the staging area that was a few miles from the target location, where we had stopped to meet with the Army assets that would be acting as a quick reaction force if needed. We stopped briefly about one click (1,000 meters) out from the target to reconfigure ourselves in the Humvees, and then we headed to the house where the target was supposed to be located. Slipping out of the Humvees, we approached the property silently, on foot.

At the front of the house, the breacher set the explosive charge. *"Three, two, one. Execute. Execute. Execute."* BOOM! Then something happened that we had never encountered. The high-value target himself rushed us as we entered. We were running with two point men. The first three guys in the stack lit him up. As we moved into the house, we got a second surprise.

The layout was nothing like the source had described. Instead of a traditional Iraqi home, it was two stories with a large open courtyard in the middle. It had open doors everywhere—which translated into "threats." With shots fired already, it was now a hot target.

We spread out in our traditional formations, addressing the threats as we moved. But the nontraditional floor plan spread our team thin. Almost immediately, I found myself standing at a doorway to a room with four military-age males who were not happy to see me. But I had nobody behind me ready to give my shoulder the squeeze (the sign that we give each other to move into the room—the signal that says "right behind you, brother"). In a close-quarters battle situation, the doorway is what we call the "fatal funnel." I had to make a decision. I moved closer into the doorway to scan as many corners as I could without fully entering. One of the first rules of our fight club? You never enter a room alone if possible. You always go with a buddy. One of the men in the room was extremely agitated and immediately raised his AK-47. So I took immediate action.

Based on our intelligence, we had anticipated none of this and had to adapt to new circumstances on the fly. The intelligence we were given seemed solid, but sometimes data can be deceiving. Or it can be good data that is quickly tested by unforeseen circumstances.

Who's Getting It Right?

It's easy to look at case studies or tell stories about massive business failures, but we need to be spending just as much time (if not more) learning from companies that are getting this stuff right. I was recently chatting with one of my clients about the company's history and how they have been able to lead change in their organization. The company, MBX Systems, has defied the odds in an extremely competitive space by making dynamic moves proactively, not reactively, and engaging its team in the intel-gathering and mission-planning process.

MBX designs and manufactures server appliances for some of the world's largest and most demanding independent software vendors and service providers. But they didn't start out that way. Founded in 1995, the company used to develop computer motherboards—and their clients were mostly small businesses. As the company entered the early 2000s, motherboards became obsolete and the custom server business became more commoditized. Selling to end users no longer made sense. Change was coming!

Knowing that they were going to have to make some fairly bold moves in order to survive, the senior leadership team surveyed key team members from across the entire organization to gather as much input as possible. They had always been diligent about protecting the company culture and had a good track record of leveraging cultural strengths when faced with unique challenges. One of those strengths was their frontline troops' deep appreciation for customers. But one thing became apparent very quickly. They were going to have to move away from small business customers and replace that revenue with larger OEM (original equipment manufacturer) clients.

At the time, about 30 percent of their revenue came from these small business accounts. After going through an in-depth planning process, they gradually parted ways with those customers, finding them new homes with trusted partners, and replaced that revenue as they went. Employees understood why they needed to make this move because they had been involved in the decision and mission planning process. They took time and care in moving their customers to other providers and were able to protect the company's great reputation.

We went through a similar process at my last company. It feels strange to walk away from millions in revenue in order to restructure how you do business, but that can often mean the difference between winning and losing in the long run. Downsizing its client list allowed MBX to increase efficiencies and work with fewer but more profitable customers. It freed up resources to focus on other core areas of the business.

When the recession hit in 2008, MBX did the opposite of what many companies did. Instead of slashing costs and cutting heads, they invested in growth. While many of their competitors went out of business, they actually increased revenue and market share. They had successfully shifted into the OEM space and dramatically reduced their number of customers while doubling revenue. Key team members from across the organization had been part of the planning and execution of this strategy. The buy-in allowed them to manage fear and cultivate a culture accepting of risk. And it prepared them for the changes they would face down the road.

In 2011, the senior leadership team determined that the company would need to go through another transformation to stay ahead of the competition. Again, they put a transformation task force together and dove into the data collected from a number of sources. The data showed 82 percent of their revenue was coming from only 15 percent of their customers. This was a risky position to be in. But one of the lasting benefits from their previous transformation—and their historical culture—was a tradition of transparency in communicating the financial realities of the organization. They let everyone know what was happening and what needed to change. By showing everyone the numbers, they immediately supported the "why" behind the new strategy.

The plan? Eliminate 65 percent of their customer base and focus on the most profitable ones. You'd think that people's heads would spin right off their shoulders when seeing the plan. But they didn't, because inclusion and transparent communication were a fundamental part of the intelligence gathering and planning process. They removed those customers but only decreased revenue by 15 percent. The result? A dramatic increase in efficiencies and revenue per employee. Quality and on-time delivery improved, as did average revenue per customer.

Our conversation turned to culture and values, and I asked my client how her team had managed these things during these major transformation efforts. What she told me reinforced my theories about culture-driven transformation. MBX intentionally created cultural experiences designed to help execute their change strategies. They leveraged the positive elements while simultaneously fixing the negative aspects. They led book clubs and set goals for being ranked one of the best places to work. They shifted away from referring to their core values as "values." They renamed them "habits."

Why?

Because great leaders know that values are only as good as the behaviors everyone in the company embodies every day. Values only matter if people actually live them. They only become part of the culture when the values-driven actions become habits. And those habits are openly rewarded. Financial data transparency and collaboration at all levels was part of this culture.

By creating a culture that accepts risk, embraces transparency, and includes everyone in the planning process, MBX continues to dominate their market and increase in value. And what's more, they have never used layoffs as part of their transformation strategy. In 2016, they achieved their goal of landing on the Great Places to Work list. By planning for change now and empowering everyone in the organization, they continue to be a role model for successful—and lasting—transformation.

If you find that your organization is lacking in the areas of data collection, deriving insight and decision-making application, there are some initial steps that can get you moving in the right direction. Most organizations understand the importance of big data and intelligence but still lack the tools, processes, and people required for proper data usage. Once the strategic vision is defined and the business case built, you have the foundation to invest in becoming a data-driven organization. Businesses must either build or acquire the appropriate business intelligence tools that align with their goals. And again, obtain only the tools you need—keep it simple, especially in the early stages of transformation.

Like the SEAL Teams, our agency partners, or leading organizations, when we transform culture to be accepting of data usage, we can move at the speed of war by making better decisions based on better information.

6

TRANSMISSION: COMMUNICATING THE VISION

*Brave men have fought and died building the proud
tradition and feared reputation that I am bound to uphold.
In the worst of conditions, the legacy of my teammates
steadies my resolve and silently guides my every deed.*
—NAVY SEAL ETHOS

In the SEAL Teams, our mission narrative is clear because it has been defined and redefined by brave men that forged the path ahead of us. A powerful vision for change is most effective when understood and embraced by most of the people within an organization. Sharing a common sense of what the new future will look like energizes the team and helps them deal with the pains of change—it steadies their resolve, even in the worst of conditions.

But effectively communicating the new vision and gaining commitment across the organization can be a monumental task, especially in large corporations. Managers and leaders too often under-communicate a great vision, or they overcommunicate a weak vision. And sometimes messaging is misaligned. The result is the same in any of those cases.

Mission failure.

Read a Fortune 500 company's glossy annual report and the first few pages will usually be wallpapered with credos, promises, and philosophies. GE's 2016 edition starts with big headlines like "Leading a Digital Industrial Era," and "Executing a Pivot," and mines the deep well of business verbiage to talk about "positioning GE to win" by undertaking change versus merely "managing momentum." An entire brand messaging and communications strategy team with a dozen professionals was probably responsible for putting all of that together, but what does all this visionary language mean to the masses? It depends on how the details are communicated day-to-day within the organization.

One of the fundamental jobs of every person in an organization—or a family, or a sports team—is to be able to communicate effectively. It's obviously important to be able to share information that matters both up and down the chain of command. But it doesn't stop there. Every member of the organization needs the tools to be able to both communicate and understand the context surrounding the information being communicated.

That's where leadership comes in.

When you watch a basic offensive play take place in an NFL game, it's easy to miss just how sophisticated the symphony of movement and decision-making you're witnessing really is. Months before, the coaching staff created a playbook with the full variety of formations and plays the team could conceivably use. The playbook gets distributed among the players and it's their responsibility to learn it. As they do, the coaching staff works to perfect the plays during practice, so that when each one is called everybody knows what to do.

That's all pretty straightforward, but think about it within the context of a real game. The offensive coordinator calls a particular play based on the situation, relays it to the quarterback through an earpiece in the helmet, and the quarterback goes into the huddle and tells the rest of the offense what's coming. The quarterback walks up to the line of scrimmage before the play and surveys the defense. Does the play still make sense? He has only a few seconds to decide to run the play that's been called or call an audible—changing the play to something else. Real-time course correction. Everybody on the team needs to be in alignment. If they aren't, the wide receivers run the wrong routes, the linemen block the wrong people (or no people) and the play gets blown up.

Watching a great drive is to see communication in its perfect form. The leadership team has communicated the playbook and the players have internalized it. The correct plays are getting called, and the information is getting out to the frontline people exactly when they need it. When the players come off the field, they communicate to the leadership team what tendencies they're seeing and that information is used to refine the play calling to create a smarter plan going forward.

It's amazing to watch.

And as we have been discussing, communication in today's dynamic, volatile, and uncertain global business environment is more challenging than ever before—despite dramatic technological advancements that let us interact in real time with people in the next cubicle or across the world.

Nowhere are the stakes for good communication higher than in the dangerous missions SEALs undertake every day. On one particular mission, we were tasked with performing a direct action (DA) assault on a two-story apartment building in central Baghdad. Intelligence reports showed that approximately fifteen to twenty military-age males would be on target, and five of them were high-value targets we wanted to capture.

We would be using three teams to perform this mission, and we would be coordinating with other traditional military forces in the area, air assets, and our Army Ranger quick-reaction force. The assault teams included two platoons of SEALs and a platoon of Polish GROM— the elite Polish special forces operators I mentioned in the Preface. My platoon was the primary assault team divided into three UH-60 Black Hawk helicopters. The other SEAL platoon was providing "mobility" support for the Polish team, which would be assaulting from the ground using Humvees as their insert platform.

The SEAL mobility team and GROM team would approach the target in four Humvees and perform an explosive breach on the main door at ground level. Simultaneously, we would fast rope onto the roof and breach the rooftop door. Timing was critical, because only one helicopter could deliver an assault team to the small roof at a time. We would clear the second floor while they cleared the first floor, and we would "de-conflict" on the stairs that ran down the center section between the two floors.

Simply put, we'd meet in the middle.

Despite all of the moving parts, the mission was a success. We got our guys without a single shot fired. All pieces worked perfectly together.

This is a powerful way to overwhelm a substantial enemy force barricaded in close quarters, but it has some drawbacks if communication isn't seamless—namely, the potential for a "blue on blue" situation (taking friendly fire). When we first started working with the Polish special forces, we had to work hard to break down the cultural and literal silos that existed between our teams.

Tactics had to be combined to ensure we functioned seamlessly as one team. Language barriers caused communication to be slow at first until we developed some standard operating procedures around what would be communicated and between which parties. During the first few months, it was like a company that had just formally finished a merger with another organization and then taken on the most important mission either company had ever faced. Without an aligned vision for the mission and seamless communication in chaotic environments, missions like this could have never been successful.

THE TAKINGPOINT PRINCIPLE

That improved communication is crucial during any component of a transformation effort seems obvious, but after spending hundreds of hours with clients struggling in this area, I can tell you that many or-ganizations fall short. It's a fundamental reason so many transformation efforts fail to fulfill their ultimate objective.

They aren't using the six principles I outline later in this chapter. They aren't keeping the message simple and authentic, using multiple channels and tools, being repetitious, maintaining consistent behavior among managers and leaders, nor gathering feedback along the way.

In order to better define the TakingPoint communication principles, we need to define the barriers that stand in the way of properly communicating a vision for change within an organization. They can be both behavioral and structural.

Structural Barriers

SILOS

In the previous chapter, we talked about vertical and horizontal silos and their effect on gathering data and passing aligned communication throughout an organization. Eliminating silos altogether in most companies is very difficult. But creating a culture where teams are empowered to work across departments and create cross-functional groups with the autonomy to make real-time decisions (based on good data) is when great organizations can move at a faster pace in this ever-changing business landscape.

Working across these organizational silos was revolutionary in the 1980s, when it was first being championed by Jack Welch during his time as CEO of GE. His philosophy was to embrace the speed of globalization and technological innovation, and challenge his people to think and work differently—with shorter decision cycles, more employee engagement, and stronger collaboration than had previously been required to compete.

Fast-forward to 2017. Communications technologies have dramatically improved, and we have instantaneous access to massive amounts of information. Welch's vision seems like it should be the new reality, but it's quite the contrary. Most organizations still have hierarchical, siloed, and fragmented processes and cultures. In fact, in an attempt to cope with this new environment, many companies have inadvertently created even greater internal complexities that make it harder to communicate and get the right people together to make decisions quickly.

WEAK TRANSFORMATION TASK FORCE

The transformation task force I have been referring to is by design an eclectic group of leaders, middle managers, and frontline workers from key areas of the organization. Their job is to understand the full scope of the transformation and spearhead the communication function.

But another structural barrier can actually be a weak transformation task force that either has the wrong people, little to no senior leadership involvement, or no real autonomy for taking point and making things happen—or all of the above. In this situation, there isn't the right mix of subject matter experts, influential change agents, nor senior leaders involved. Therefore, they are lacking in leadership, skill, and the respect necessary to lead change.

NO SOPS (STANDARD OPERATING PROCEDURES) FOR TOOL USAGE

One of the major problems organizations have when rolling out transformation strategies is alignment on what to communicate and how and when to do it. Many organizations fail at this because the communication is too infrequent and confined to company-wide emails, newsletters, and intranets. The issue here is that we live in an age of utter disruption! People are constantly being pulled and pushed in different directions by different priorities, and assaulted by notifications from any number of different devices—computers, smartphones, tablets, and even smart watches.

In an independent study by Atos Origin, a France-based IT services company, employees were found to be spending approximately 40 percent of their workweek reading and sending internal emails that added no value to the company. The study was part of the CEO's vision for becoming an email-free organization. In another study, the University of Glasgow and Modeuro Limited followed the email patterns of a large London-based power company. It found that senior executives spent 1.5 hours a day sending, on average, fifty-six emails. Beyond that, the study pinpointed that about 80 percent of all email traffic was deemed useless or irrelevant.

Things quickly get buried amid all this "information" flow. In one of my companies, we did an anonymous survey to find out how many employees actually even read company-wide emails and newsletters. We couldn't rely solely on open-rate analytics because that didn't provide insight into how the information was being absorbed, if at all. We encouraged transparency and honesty so the results would be authentic. We also asked team members to leave comments supporting their answers. Twenty-five percent of respondents admitted to not reading newsletters at all. They said the content was confusing, misaligned with the company vision or current initiatives, just another executive's pet project, or something they felt wouldn't be followed up on.

So they did the sensible thing. They stopped reading them.

Fifty percent of the respondents said that they only gave company-wide communications a cursory glance. They said they were too busy, and already had dozens of "real" emails to go through every day because the company suffered from a "reply all" email culture.

The other 25 percent said they found the communication to be useful.

This kind of disconnect is only becoming more prevalent, because a new generation of employees (the Generation Y folks born closer to

2000) don't even use email much anymore outside of the workplace. They communicate using tools like social media, FaceTime and Google Chat. Getting an email is like getting a letter from somebody born in the 1970s or 1980s. You want to really confuse a millennial? Respond to their text message with a phone call—from a land line!

Behavioral Barriers

LOW SENSE OF URGENCY

Complacency plagues many organizations, especially ones that have significant silo issues. When senior leaders don't create the appropriate amount of urgency behind new initiatives, employees tend to be slow to adapt. They are already busy, so if it doesn't really seem like a high priority to the people at the top, why should they break their backs taking on the additional work?

MISALIGNMENT IN ACTIONS AND MESSAGING

This is another big killer when it comes to transformation messaging. When the narrative supporting the vision is misaligned and people in different areas of the company—or in different ranks—are hearing different stories, many people will stop paying attention. It gets too confusing, and the message becomes a buffet of truth and accuracy mixed with messaging about competing priorities and other agendas.

LOW LEVELS OF TRUST AND ACCOUNTABILITY

When trust and accountability don't exist as the bedrock of an organization's culture, you will have a very hard time getting people to pay attention to messaging about a major new change effort, regardless of how aligned that message is. If vertical and horizontal silos exist, senior leaders are doing and saying different things, and information doesn't flow seamlessly throughout the company—then the message becomes too fragmented.

The unfortunate reality is that most organizations understand the need (and the benefit) to being able to communicate as effectively and efficiently as a SEAL platoon or professional sports team, but they can't execute. As self-evident as good communication would seem to be, not many organizations (or people) are able to do it well. They suffer from the barriers I just described, and they fall into three very common traps.

1. The Content Trap

2. The Execution Trap

3. The Unintended Consequences Trap

THE CONTENT TRAP

As we've been talking about for five chapters now, the content of the change message an organization is sharing is vitally important. If an aligned narrative for the change vision doesn't exist in its purest form, the validity of that message withers or is lost in translation.

This is something I see a lot in organizations that are dealing with a crisis. A quarterly earnings report is dismal or a massive problem in the marketplace emerges overnight, and they go into triage mode. It's almost like there's a knee-jerk playbook. We have to change things now, so let's pull all the levers—cut staff, get a consultant, reengineer core processes, and shift focus to a new line of business.

I'm not saying any of those individual maneuvers are the wrong ones. But unless you have a well-designed plan that considers input from people up and down the food chain *and* is communicated with everybody in that chain, you will have problems. Again, *don't run to your death*.

What makes great quarterbacks so good? They communicate clearly and calmly in stressful situations. As we say in the Teams, *calm is contagious*. They know the plays that need to be called, and they give the information the rest of the team needs in a way they can receive it. Imagine a drive in the last two minutes of a game. The quarterback comes into the huddle and says, "I don't know what play is going to work, but we have to try something. Just go out there and wing it and we'll try to figure it out."

Those teams don't tend to win, and those quarterbacks don't tend to inspire their fellow players to want to follow and work hard for them.

The best organizations create a vision for change and have concrete steps to execute that vision—and then they *relentlessly communicate* that vision up and down the chain of command. Leaders and managers understand the differences in their roles. It's not fuzzy. It's not open to interpretation. It's not hidden in a forest of clichés and catchphrases.

THE EXECUTION TRAP

An equally common issue crops up with organizations that might have conquered the first problem—delineating the change cause. The leadership team knows what it wants to accomplish, but it falls way short in successfully communicating it.

You know what I'm talking about.

We've all been to the big off-site planning meeting where a leadership team member gets up and announces a big new strategic plan for the organization. We're going to produce a new product, offer a new service, or otherwise completely reorganize the way we do things. The meetings have themes like "reigniting our fire" or "one team"—or something to that effect.

The speech is often accompanied by a slick presentation, newly designed creative, or high-production video. Again, those individual activities aren't an incorrect approach by any means—they are a great way to get the team fired up. But if it stops at the big reveal—and the organization then feels like it's done enough to put the change plans in motion—you will again have major issues.

THE UNINTENDED CONSEQUENCES TRAP

There are many great companies out there that have no shortage of extremely smart and talented people. They know what needs to happen and are able to take immediate stock of the kind of change plans being promoted.

A leadership team can lock itself behind closed doors and come up with a comprehensive change plan, then spend hundreds of hours, and thousands of dollars pushing and promoting the plan but totally *fail* at properly communicating the vision.

Why?

For many of the reasons already noted. Under-communicating. Overcommunicating the wrong things. Lack of alignment. Behavioral and structural barriers. Failures at the data analysis and mission planning level.

Many organizations run into this problem because they believe that having an established reporting structure means they're truly informed about what's happening on the front lines of the business. But if you aren't in the sales meetings or on the shop floor, you don't understand the realities of what those troops deal with every day—especially if communication doesn't flow easily throughout the company. And if you promote a change plan that doesn't embrace those realities, it will be very hard for you to get buy-in. You'll actually get influential people in your organization influencing *against* you.

Let's say for example a large global software company has been going through a series of mergers and acquisitions as part of a major expansion strategy to develop new products, enter new markets, and gain significant market share in a rapidly changing industry. The president of one of the acquired companies is promoted to chairman and CEO.

He assembles a task force to tackle some of the new initiatives around culture integration and creating a unified vision. The new initiative is called "Mission Possible" and has a goal of forging one team, with one culture, one fight, and that is unified behind one mission—to become the most customer-centric global SaaS company in the world.

The organization makes many great strides to get started: off-site leadership meetings, company-wide events where the focal point of the transformation is communicated, emails, newsletters, an intranet. As an added effort, a small consulting team is brought in to assist with this major campaign. But during the initial weeks of their involvement, their interviews with senior and mid-level managers reveal some interesting things.

There seems to be alignment at the top, but if you go down a few levels some employees have a vague idea about the vision, saying, "It's something to do with focusing on customers, right? Not sure, the new mission statement is long and overly complex. Many people aren't really sure what it means exactly or how we will accomplish it. Oh, and senior management just hired someone from outside the organization who will play a major role, but the person seems totally misaligned with what we are trying to accomplish."

A few rungs lower some people say, "New vision? Not sure." And horizontally across departments, many know about the new slogan but have very different ideas about what it means.

Is this uncommon? Not at all. So how can organizations avoid all this and get it right from the beginning? In short, do the opposite of what the software company did.

I call it the *Five T's of Change Communication.*

- **TECHNIQUE**: The communication of a powerful vision is only as good as how it's delivered and how likely the organization is to align behind it. Do vertical and horizontal silos exist that will blur the message? Is the message simple and authentic? Will everyone be able to emotionally connect to the cause? A well-defined internal (and sometimes external) communications strategy should be laid out ahead of time and embraced by senior leaders and the transformation task force before any messaging is delivered.

- **TIMING**: The vision should be powerfully communicated early, often, and always. Some parts of the plan should be rolled out and communicated throughout the process so as not to overwhelm the workforce with information they don't need yet. Saying things like, "More details to come on this, but we don't need to worry about this part just yet." Repetition is important, and not just at every company meeting or in every newsletter. Executives, managers, and change agents from the transformation task force should find multiple opportunities every day to weave the vision into casual conversation. This exponentially multiplies the frequency of communication in many different forums.

- **TOOLS**: As mentioned before, the tools and channels used should vary—especially in today's multigenerational workforce. Leverage social media networks, video platforms, and easily sharable content so employees can digest information at their own pace but also interact with one another when they have questions or want to provide feedback. But again, consistency with aligned messaging is imperative. It doesn't matter what tools or channels you use if you don't get that part right.

- **TEMPERAMENT**: Change can be scary and stressful. The temperament used when communicating will determine how it's perceived. Senior leaders, managers, and members of the transformation task force should maintain a positive mental attitude especially when communicating the bad with the good. When confronted with questions and team members having doubts, those are all great opportunities to reinvigorate employees and get them excited about the mission once again. Again, calm is contagious and having explanations backed by real data is critical.

- **TRANSPARENCY**: Transparency builds trust, one of the most important aspects of an organization that will navigate change successfully. Don't make the communication and progress updates always about how well things are going. If you're hitting roadblocks, and you will, everyone will know it anyway. Get issues on the table, address them in real time and allow the team to influence the processes for improvement. Transparency in feedback goes both ways. Encourage everyone on the team to voice their opinion as needed up the chain.

If people don't accept a vision for change, getting through any of the later stages will be near impossible. The team won't take advantage of new empowerment nor follow through with new tasks that support the mission. Whether it's poorly communicating a great vision or overcommunicating a lousy one, you won't get far and resources will be wasted.

Aligned communication must flow seamlessly up, down, and across the organization for a change strategy to succeed and its initiatives to become ingrained in the culture.

APPLICATIONS FROM THE BATTLEFIELD TO THE BOARDROOM

The reality of "early, often, and always" communication can sound like an exhausting responsibility for a single person or a small group, and it is.

If you're relying on printed materials or a marketing plan to make it work—or a single evangelist to go out and get everybody in line—you'll be disappointed. As previously mentioned, I've created transformation task forces to handle some of these duties.

Let me stress that a task force of this nature is *not* just a run-of-the-mill committee. Plenty of companies grudgingly decide that they have to make some changes, and they outsource the problem to human resources, or to the mid-level managers within the area that is most perceived to need the change. They then ask the relatively powerless committee to send out emails every few weeks reminding people about tactical things they already know.

A real transformation task force has the full attention and support from the leadership group—and includes at least one or more of those leaders on the team. The entire organization needs to see the transformation movement as a serious progression toward a bright future and that the business of the task force will be serious. If the task force doesn't have any power, and its recommendations don't get taken seriously, why would anybody feel compelled to participate—to be engaged? It would prove to everyone in the organization that senior leadership isn't going to follow through.

By constructing the task force with a mixture of leaders, mid-level people, and frontline troops—and giving everybody the freedom to take action—all of those involved can start to feel as if they will be heard. Each group will be able to bring valuable intel about what communication strategies work best for their areas.

▲

For example, let's say you're the leader of a large chemical manufacturing company. Times have been tough. Revenue is in free fall, the stock is crumbling and layoffs are imminent.

You bring on an ace human resources professional to help lead a transformation with the vision of responsible downsizing and a renewed focus on the core areas of the business. When you bring on that pro, the impulse is going to be for you to go to your board of directors and let them know you're taking major steps to turn things around. The new star is going to sort out the organizational problems, and you can spend your time meeting with new suppliers and strategic partners to springboard into profitability.

But by outsourcing the change leadership to somebody else—and a *new* somebody else—you're losing crucial credibility with the rank and file. Instead of leading change, you're simply delegating someone to manage it.

Can a talented human resources person give great advice about what mechanisms to put in place to make a transformation work more smoothly? Of course. But unless the transformation—and communication that goes with it—is both led and managed, it won't work.

What makes up a good task force? I'm former military, so you'll have to forgive me for using an acronym. I call it *PEARL*—players, expertise, adaptability, respect, and leadership.

Players are people who believe in the mission. The players are the fully engaged change evangelists and key frontline managers who are enthusiastic and believe in the cause. Next comes *expertise*—the team members with diverse technical and relevant experience and insight into what changes need to be made and why. Then of course, this team needs all members to have a mindset of *adaptability*—whatever their level. Next comes *respect*. All members of a task force should be highly respected as positive change agents by their peers both below and above them. Lastly comes *leadership*. And I don't just mean senior leaders identified by title or position—although they absolutely have to be fully involved. These team members must act and be seen as impactful leaders within the organization, regardless of rank.

What does this actually look like?

Say you're part of the management team for a growing information technology company. The organization's transformation goal is to reduce costs while also improving both customer and employee retention by a significant margin in the next two years. That's not easy to do, especially in tandem, but most change visions are an appropriate mix of both lofty and feasible goals.

The task force you assemble is made up of yourself (a C-level executive), the CFO, one of the leading data engineers, a new and promising customer rep, a respected mid-level manager who has worked in three different departments, human resources leadership, and the senior VP of marketing.

You adopt the *Six Principles for Communicating the Change Vision* that I briefly referenced earlier in this chapter: simplicity, authenticity, multichannel, repetition, consistency, and gathering feedback. Let's take a quick look at what these mean for your task force's approach.

Simplicity

The first hallmark of the communication strategy is simplicity. The organization's change vision needs to be shareable in a variety of formats. If you can't tell a powerful story about the vision in less than a few minutes, it's too complicated. Once you have the simple, direct story to tell, it can be expanded as necessary for investor meetings, sales calls, interviews with potential high-level hires—and even the media. If you can't articulate a powerful vision in five minutes or less, in which the listener understands and can envision the outcome, you need to go back to the drawing board.

I have seen this go sideways when a leadership team invests many hours in developing a great vision that will align with a solid plan of attack, but then they assume they can communicate this vision once or twice at company meetings. If it takes a long time to develop the change vision, it will also take a long time to communicate it until it sinks in. Keep it simple, and plan to overcommunicate.

Authenticity

Authenticity starts with a leadership team having a good track record and a culture based on trust and accountability. Without these foundational elements, there will be a longer road ahead. No leadership team or company is perfect, so if the track record is a bit muddled, that's fine. But leaders must have situational awareness and understand that consistency will be imperative.

A powerful vision followed by immediate action, behaviors consistent with the new vision, and follow-through are a great way to rebuild trust. Authenticity is also established when the vision aligns with the company culture and values, even if part of that vision is to improve the culture.

Multichannel

Once you've created a variety of formats for this message, you need to choose a variety of channels to share it. The usual suspects—company newsletters, company-wide emails, an intranet, staff meetings, and posters—are a fine starting point, but what you really need is a scheduled, concerted effort from senior leaders, managers, and members of the transformational task force. What do I mean by scheduled? Just like it sounds. Put reminders in your calendar to chat with a variety of people throughout the organization two or three times each day to share both formal and informal stories about the transformation. The more you do so, it will become habitual. As you recall, Telling Purposeful Stories is a core part of the CDT model.

Do the math. If you pass vision statements, information, and progress updates in a quarterly company newsletter, quarterly all-hands meeting, and a monthly company-wide email, that's twenty communication points in a year. But if you have ten key leaders and task force members committing to connecting twice a day with various people in the organization about the cause, that comes out to roughly 5,200 communication opportunities in a year.

Repetition

Repeat. Repeat. Repeat. Use the channels and every opportunity to distill and communicate important information on progress throughout the process, especially if strategies are being tweaked along the way.

I've found that being overly repetitious (although it can feel like you're being annoying) is the only way to make a transformation vision sink in. When repeated regularly and supported by purposeful storytelling and public recognition for early adopters, a well-intentioned vision has a much greater propensity for being implemented successfully and at a faster pace. And you're likely to have the support and assistance of more people. Maybe even everyone.

Success stories are a big part of this. The task force's job is to identify easy-to-understand, easy-to-quantify wins along the way to the transformational goal. For the IT company I mentioned earlier, maybe the specific goal is to reduce costs on a given project by 20 percent. When somebody responsible for making purchases is able to secure an initial deal at a 22 percent cost savings—even if it's a small one—that's a victory to share. It shows people that every goal is a series of manageable steps, not some monolithic, abstract idea taking place in an unknowable future.

It's no different in SEAL training, which is constant. Nothing becomes a habit or muscle memory unless you perform that task repeatedly. When you are in a platoon, you train for over a year before each deployment. And when you're on deployment, if you're not eating, sleeping, or on a mission, you are training. You're in the gym, at the shooting range, rehearsing missions, or reviewing intel reports.

Communicating a change vision requires the same level of repetition. It must happen every day. By continuing to talk about the progress being made, sharing and rewarding success, and reinforcing the message, you're making the change effort second nature. It becomes the new normal.

Consistency

Of course, none of this means anything if the messages you share and actions you take aren't consistent. I don't mean in the sense that they have to be identical, but they need to have a common thread.

I can't stress this enough and it absolutely has to start at the top. Let's go back to the example of the IT services company. Its vision is to reduce costs and improve customer and employee retention, a tricky task because improving customer and employee retention can often require hard cost investments.

Reducing costs can't just involve layoffs and cutting resources. That can quickly lead to an increase in customer turnover, not a reduction. Of course, sometimes head-count reductions are an unfortunate reality. But cost cutting must be considered at all levels. If the senior executives are still lounging in opulence and taking the board of directors on lavish golf getaways, nobody will believe in the vision. And that's just one example. Behaviors, especially of those at the top, must embody the new vision on and off the battlefield.

Gathering Feedback

Another crucial way to reinforce the respect and buy-in for the vision is to be relentless about collecting and reviewing feedback as we have discussed. Command-and-control organizations are good at telling frontline workers what to do and what the changes will be, but they often struggle at listening to their team members.

It's as simple as reflexively asking, "How are we doing with implementation? What kinds of things can we adjust?" The bulk of what comes up might not be worth much, but the act of listening by itself is invaluable. It shows you care—and it gives you the opportunity to get perspectives that you can't track down from inside a conference room or executive suite.

The Power of Influential Communication

Let's put our marketing hats on for a second. Over the past ten years, more and more organizations have been turning to the use of social media and other integrated digital content marketing strategies as a major part of their overall brand marketing efforts. Through technological advancements and multichannel analytics platforms, all of these things are almost infinitely measurable now. Essentially, you can sum it up to getting the right content in front of the right people throughout various stages of the buying cycle. This builds brand trust. That's the same as communicating a change vision—except the "buying cycle" is a *buy-in process*.

One highly impactful part of this strategy is to enlist the help of powerful influencers who are respected thought leaders in a given space. Influential bloggers, citizen journalists, celebrities, and social media stars can be powerful tools for getting the word out about a new brand, product, or service. The statistics change every year, so I'll refrain from throwing numbers at you, but overall, more and more companies are shifting budgets to content marketing strategies that involve key influencers. Research points to the fact that consumers are much more likely to purchase from brands that they trust—brands that provided them with valuable content that is promoted by influencers in the marketplace. My wife follows fashion bloggers who have hundreds of thousands of Instagram followers. She'll purchase items from links in their blogs and Instagram posts because they are well-respected influencers promoting their own brands or brands she trusts. It's that simple.

A CASE STUDY ON THE POWER OF INFLUENTIAL COMMUNICATION

One of our clients at the marketing agency was a large optical company. The company was founded by two scientists in 2003 to answer one question: Doesn't everyone deserve to look good while wearing an affordable pair of glasses? So the brand was born in the San Francisco Bay Area—a natural fit for forward-thinking, tech-savvy companies. The mission was clear: Give people glasses they can actually afford but still make them look fantastic. It started as a small company with big ideas, but quickly grew into a phenomenon. Fashionistas, moms-on-the-go, discerning customers; everyone found that they could get the selection they deserved at prices they could afford.

The company hired us to launch a new search engine optimization strategy that had a huge content marketing component. Like all good marketing strategies, measurable results—online sales revenue—were the main priority. We developed a custom SEO strategy to increase organic traffic and rankings, as well as a long-term link-building and brand-awareness strategy through content marketing efforts. We built a custom content marketing campaign to encourage interaction with current and potential customers. We built an app that housed a nine-question multiple-choice quiz that helped customers answer the question: "What Frames Are Perfect for Me?"

We had software tools that provided massive databases of influential bloggers, writers, and social media icons. Using the search features, we could narrow down a list of very specific influencers who might want to share the content we were creating, or who might even write their own articles about the company and its products. Since I have been a columnist for *Forbes* and *Inc.* for years, my name must have made it into these databases as well. I receive about fifty emails a day with "story ideas" or requests to write about certain brands.

We got the quiz app into the hands of key influencers and it went viral. You don't just create "viral content." You create good, useful content and get it in front of the right people. Then and only then can content go viral.

> The results were unbelievable. In a period of only six months, traffic to the quiz landing page reached more than 570,000 unique visitors—resulting in over $1.2 million in sales. The company saw a 9,655 percent return on its investment in the content marketing campaign.

Imagine how impactful this could be for a transformation strategy! Well-respected change evangelists and influencers deployed across the organization with an important message about the new vision . . . An aligned message reaching across barriers and silos, penetrating the entire organization. Then it goes viral. What could the return on investment be on that?

The sky is the limit.

TALES FROM THE FRONT LINES

If you don't devise a method for open, relentless communication and feedback to understand transformation potential and progress, you're losing the most sensitive tools in the toolbox that help you adapt. And you'll have to adapt.

Resilient teams and organizations plan for change and expect to have to use contingency plans. They're ready. But the only way to know if you need contingencies is to be constantly monitoring feedback and analyzing data against your KPIs.

SEAL Team mission briefings tend to look very dramatic in the movies, but when you're actually in the seat getting information from the team leader or intelligence officer, you're looking for very specific information.

When we hit that house, are there going to be two guys in there, or ten?

If it all goes wrong, how far away is our quick-reaction force?

How far away is the *enemy's* quick-reaction force?

Are we able to assess what the real risk involved is?

Of course, virtually every second of SEAL training is designed to get you ready for *whatever* comes your way. Contingencies are a part of life. They're just as much a part of life in business, and it's your job—whether you're on the front line or in a leadership role—to be open and ready. And readiness requires preparation and seamless communication.

Making It Stick

I was having a conversation about the concept of communicating a lasting change vision with a good friend and client who works for a cloud-based planning and performance management platform for finance, sales, supply chain, marketing, IT, and HR. He also happens to be a former Navy fighter pilot who has done multiple tours of duty. Naturally, we got into the subject of how military philosophies can apply in this civilian context.

"What are the top three or four things you feel the military does very well that business leaders and their organizations can learn from?" I asked him.

He didn't hesitate.

"I could sum it up to three key areas. The first is our relentless focus on training, readiness, and preparedness for change. The next is our ability to compartmentalize and stay focused on the short- and long-term mission. And third, our communication strategies leading up to any kind of transformation. We trust our people with valuable information and empower them to use that information to make decisions and lead change throughout the ranks."

Next, I asked him about how he uses those principles to improve communication across his organization—and what challenges he has faced.

His answer is a great example of how high-performance organizations get it right. He told me that over the past five years the company had experienced a threefold increase in revenue. Employee head count during that time more than doubled. The primary challenges came with talent acquisition bottlenecks. To keep pace with their organic growth, the hiring process became strained. They couldn't completely adopt a "hire slow" approach, but it had to be careful. They had to do some quick firing when the wrong people were let on the bus and made adjustments to the process as they went.

To protect the culture in an organization going through such rapid growth, he outlined five basic communication strategies he used.

1. Constant check-ins and communication using a variety of formal and informal methods. Communicating the good with the bad.

2. Leadership meetings focused on getting and staying aligned and disseminating information from those meetings to the right people quickly.

3. Extreme transparency on the direction of the company and the "why" behind that vision.

4. Continually building upon and communicating the vision of where the company is currently and where it needs to go—and the importance of everyone's involvement.

5. Identifying and celebrating quick wins.

My last question was what I thought was the most important one.

How do you make the changes stick?

"One of the most important pieces of making sure progress toward our vision continued at the pace we needed it to was to use data for tracking progress and measuring for effectiveness," he said. "We used several systems for that—including surveys and analysis of our predetermined KPIs. We used new technologies for internal communication and regularly took a look in the rearview mirror to remind ourselves how we initially defined what success would look like. Had things changed? We measured projected versus actual progress. We updated all reward mechanisms and employee performance standards to match the new behaviors. And most importantly, we made sure to continually remove top-down hierarchies and horizontal silos that started organically emerging as we grew. We wanted to stay nimble."

When a leadership team is able to create that kind of trust through open communication—and by being willing to empower team members to both receive important information and act on it—it creates a truly collaborative, communicative environment.

Yes, those words are easy for anybody to say.

But if you establish those expectations and mindsets and build real structures to support them, you're essentially future-proofing your organization for the long-term transformation adventure. And then your chances of success in the later stages go up dramatically.

You're ready.

PART 3

WINNING
THE CHANGE FIGHT

rganizations can gain significant momentum during the early stages of a transformation life cycle. They successfully align the culture with the strategy, gain initial buy-in from as many people as possible, plan the mission with the best possible data analysis and intelligence, and consistently communicate mission intent.

But then somewhere along the way things start to fall apart. Participation starts to dwindle because the process takes longer and costs more (hard and soft costs) than anticipated, fatigue and fear start plaguing the minds of early adopters, naysayers become emboldened by the potential of mission failure (the "I told you so" mentality), and competing priorities start to distract even the most senior leaders from fulfilling the vision.

In Part 3, you will learn more valuable tools for leading through change—and making that change stick. You will learn systems for ensuring participation lasts throughout the entire process, and how to combat change battle fatigue, keep the team energized, maintain discipline, and ultimately build a resilient organization.

7

INCLUSION: THE POWER OF PARTICIPATION AND ENGAGEMENT

My loyalty to Team is beyond reproach.
—NAVY SEAL ETHOS

We desperately want to believe in saviors. We want a leader to whom we can be loyal and follow into battle. And those leaders want to believe they have a loyal and fully engaged team standing beside them on that battlefield.

Struggling companies often hire new CEOs who will be the turnaround expert that saves the business. Sports teams bring in new general managers and coaches to change the culture and fix a losing record. And countries elect new visionary leaders who will redefine the future.

From the outside looking in, it seems that they alone boldly lead the team to victory. But the complex problems and issues any organization faces today can't typically be solved by a single leader. Great leaders are masters at the art of team engagement.

Today, it takes more than leadership—and more than management. Management and business books are filled with stories about legendary leaders, like GE's Jack Welch or Apple's Steve Jobs. The tails of heroism often make it seem like they came in and single-handedly made the company an industry leader—turning an organization from a failed state to flourishing nation.

Of course, they didn't do it alone, and even if they did, the strategies required to do it that way just don't work today. Lording above the troops from a corner office and issuing orders is a losing plan in a time when every organization faces complex, fast-changing terms of engagement.

Obstacles come quickly, and the solutions require a variety of skills and perspectives. A single person doesn't have the combined experience, knowledge, or expertise to do it alone. There are too many moving parts.

You need a team. You need to engage as many people in the organization as possible. That's another great advantage we have in the SEAL Teams—100 percent employee engagement.

We've talked at length about the importance of participation from senior leaders and influential team members as part of the transformation task force—participation in developing the vision, defining the mission, and communicating the intent. But it doesn't stop there. Without the participation of most people in an organization, transformation efforts will fall short or fail entirely.

▲

As I have previously touched on, globally, managers are missing out on the full potential of the majority of their teams. Employee engagement must be a top priority for all leaders and managers—but never more so than during transformations. According to Gallup research, on average about fifty percent of employees aren't totally sure about what they are supposed to do at work every day. Only one third believe they communicate to their managers what they need to succeed in their roles. And when an employee's manager actively helps them set clear performance goals, active disengagement nearly disappears and engagement increases to upward of seventy percent. But if its that simple, why is engagement such an issue?

A senior VP at one of my client firms—a hedge fund based in London—reached out to me to talk about the culture transformation strategy the organization had been working on for the past few years. Their vision was a renewed focus on developing leaders throughout the company and working to break down some of the silos that had started to grow. The vision also included a plan for aggressive growth over the next five years—which required a more nimble and collaborative team environment. The culture needed to align with that strategy. Leadership needed to be delegated and distributed throughout the ranks.

The company had been experiencing massive growth thanks to creative research, formidable intelligence gathering, and relentless business development, but that growth had also started to slow them down. The speedboat was turning into a cruise ship. The fund had billions under management but still the same head count as when they were generating half the business. After doing a series of diagnostics, it seemed they had made it about 60 percent of the way toward hitting their transformation goals but then hit a wall.

I asked my client about what she thought seemed to be going well and what barriers were blocking progress. She told me that while most of the employees were excited about the new vision and wanted to be fully engaged in its successful implementation, the feedback was that there were just too many roadblocks standing in their way. We dove deeper and I took notes as she talked.

When she finished her thoughtful analysis, we went over to the whiteboard and started mapping it all out.

The end result was a list of typical barriers that stand in the way of employee engagement and participation during organizational transformations. I wasn't surprised by any of them because they align with my theories on where companies tend to get ahead of themselves by not addressing these upfront.

I call them the *Five Roadblocks to Employee Participation and Engagement*.

The most effective managers actively focus on creating an engaging workplace, constantly ensure the team has what they need to succeed and remove structural and behavioral barriers standing in their way. Each of these barriers has a varying impact on a change effort. Some companies do a decent job of proactively addressing some of them, but usually not all of them. At least not at the onset of rolling out a transformation strategy. These are the roadblocks.

Culture

The first roadblock is cultural—and it's why we spent so much time talking about it in Part 1 of this book. When organizations don't perform a culture diagnostic analysis in the beginning to identify strengths to be leveraged and weaknesses to be removed, change efforts will eventually run into resistance. And again, managing culture is never more important than during a major change effort. If the culture is misaligned with the new vision, the team will struggle.

Structures

The second roadblock comes in the form of the existing structures that don't line up with the new vision. Behavioral and structural barriers have to be addressed at the beginning so as to understand how they may impact forward motion for change. If, for example, collaboration and innovation are a key component of leading successful change, managers must ensure that vertical and horizontal silos don't impede this part of the initiative.

Systems

Then come the legacy systems that may have worked for the old model but don't work with the new vision. Most powerful of all are usually HR mechanisms and reward systems. Systems that no longer work could include performance evaluation processes that don't address new behaviors that need to be rewarded, compensation and bonus decisions based on risk-averse attitudes, subjective or misaligned promotion decisions, and talent acquisition strategies that don't fit the new mission profile.

Naysayers

The fourth roadblock is a people problem—the naysayers. You'll often see managers or other influential team members stand in the way of employee engagement because they don't agree with some or all of the transformation strategy. Because they hold a certain rank or have significant influence, their lack of participation spreads quickly. It makes people think, "Maybe I should just stay in my bunker and see what happens before doing anything." Or worse, these people—the actively disengaged—will actually instruct those around them not to adopt the new ways of doing things.

Training

The final roadblock is know-how. Almost all transformations require employees to have to learn new things and adopt new mindsets, skills, and behaviors. Many organizations are simply afraid (or too financially short-sighted) to invest the time and money for the proper professional development needed to set employees up for success. Or, they don't provide enough training—or offer plenty of training that doesn't necessarily address the new skills that will be needed. It's hard to get the team to participate successfully when they don't have the tools or skills to get it right.

Just like in the Navy SEAL mission planning process, organizations and their transformation task forces must identify what stands in the way of achieving mission success. Using that information, they can then develop risk mitigation strategies to eliminate as many roadblocks as possible. Addressing these five areas is critical.

When roadblocks are removed and employees are truly engaged, they will go "all in" on the transformation effort. They will be more productive, profitable and will maintain a customer-focused attitude. And most important, they will embrace the suck and stick around much longer.

THE TAKINGPOINT PRINCIPLE

In the SEAL Teams, engagement is not some human resources initiative, it is part of our culture. We are all in, all the time. It's how we do business. SEAL Teams are the result of the most selective, comprehensive training program in the world. We have no shortage of expertise.

But what SEALs also have is total and committed buy-in from the newest training graduate to the top leadership group at the U.S. Special Operations Command. SEAL leaders take a collection of very capable operators and put them in the best position to both use their skills to accomplish the mission and bring back intelligence and feedback that improves tactics for later missions.

Every person on the team is part of a continuously improving process—one that thrives on change.

Obviously, replicating that kind of buy-in and emotional connection to the cause in the business world is very difficult. SEALs (and world-class athletes) come to their organization hardwired with motivation and commitment to a simple, clear-cut team and individual goal.

Winning.

An NFL player wants to win the Super Bowl. A SEAL wants to purge the world of evil. It's that simple.

In the civilian world, the missions aren't so clear-cut. The work isn't always as glamorous. Not everybody on your team is there for the same reason, and sometimes they don't have both hands on the rope—nor pulling in the same direction.

In virtually every organization, you're going to find amazing, intelligent, motivated people who are committed to doing terrific work. You're also going to find average contributors who scrape by—people just putting in time for a paycheck.

And let's not sugarcoat things. Work is work. Everything isn't going to be engaging, exciting, and worthwhile. Plenty of it is plain boring and unpleasant. That's just as true for a SEAL as it is for an accountant, customer service representative, or banker.

The best organizations understand their strengths and limitations and build a structure that both reinforces those strengths and acknowledges human limitations. They build systems that reward collaboration, collect data from every corner of the organization, and use leverage in the truest sense of the word. They *include everyone in the fight*.

And not surprisingly, according to more Gallup research, work groups with high levels of engagement experience 17 percent greater productivity and therefore about 20 percent higher profitability.

One of my clients—a global aerospace, defense, security, and advanced technologies company—brought me in to present to a large team of emerging human resources leaders. They had a new vision for helping their leaders at all levels gain a deeper connection to how their work supports the warfighter on the battlefield. The emerging leaders would play a key role in evangelizing this new engagement strategy, so they had to first have an intimate understanding of this themselves. Essentially, we were engaging and empowering them to engage and empower others. We would be equipping them with the tools and training to become change agents—and then deploy them across the organization.

It's no secret that the most current research points to epic levels of disengagement among the workforce. The fact that only 15 percent of the workforce globally is actively engaged is because the majority of frontline workers don't feel empowered, and don't have a deep understanding of how their work matters in the overall pursuit of the organization's goals.

In a large company like an aerospace and defense firm, engineers and strategists in the R&D division might have an intimate understanding of how their products and technology improve the warfighter's ability to engage the enemy, but someone in finance or accounting might not. This goes back to the importance of an aligned narrative behind the vision of the organization. Everyone should be able to articulate it easily.

But when people and virtual or physical roadblocks aren't addressed, successful change implementation isn't possible. Influencing employee engagement and participation can work both ways. Either barriers are reduced, the transformation task force has the right people, and key change agents are deployed to war-torn areas of the organization, or the opposite occurs. Culture issues, structural constraints, reward systems, naysayers, and training aren't addressed early on and the transformation train derails.

Influential people or groups that haven't been engaged in the planning process or don't agree with the majority of the change effort can be the company's worst enemy. Conversely, when the task force and change agents are successful in communicating the vision and recruiting everyone around them to prepare for the change battle, the chance of success goes through the roof.

This is where the CDT model comes back into play—when you need to audit and measure the team's level of engagement. Managers should look at engagement in a hierarchical structure, starting with basic needs and moving up to professional growth—all of which impact an employee's ability to help drive change.

MEASURING EMPLOYEE ENGAGEMENT

When an employee can make the following statements with confidence, they are much more likely to be engaged.

- **PROFESSIONAL GROWTH** This past year, I have been given many opportunities to learn and grow, both professionally and personally.

  My manager regularly discusses my performance and progress with me and asks if there is anything else he can do to make my job easier.

- **TEAM ORIENTATION** I believe my fellow team members are engaged and want to do great work.

  I am clear on the mission and purpose of this organization and know how my work impacts mission success.

- **INDIVIDUAL NEEDS** I know what is expected of me in this role.

  I have the training and resources to excel at my job.

  I receive both recognition and constructive guidance.

  My manager cares about me as a person.

When employees know they have what they need to be successful, feel that they are cared about, trusted and empowered, they will almost always be engaged. And engagement isn't just critical for leading change, it's a core function of companies that dominate their battlefield.

APPLICATIONS FROM THE BATTLEFIELD
TO THE BOARDROOM

For any SEAL mission to succeed, it requires 100 percent participation from everyone. From the assault team and support elements to allied forces and the decision-makers in the TOC (tactical operations center), all must be engaged. That isn't a problem, because all believe in the mission and narrative that supports the vision. Does everyone always agree on the details? Of course not. But one thing that is never lacking is full participation.

On one particular mission, our task unit had been assigned a dual DA (direct action) capture or kill mission. The two platoons in the task unit would split up and simultaneously breach two different apartments in a massive three-tower complex that was built in a U-shape configuration. The fourteen-story towers were surrounded by a ten-foot wall, and the only entrance was via a guard gate at the southeast corner. Successful execution would require the participation and coordination of many different assets—from ground troops and air support to blocking forces and other military divisions in the area of operation. If any one particular unit or person isn't fully engaged, these missions can go sideways in a hurry.

We left our compound at 1:30 a.m. for the thirty-minute drive to the apartment community. On final approach, we noticed the gate was down, so the convoy stopped and the guys in the lead vehicle dismounted to address the gate issue and assess breaching options. The assaulters from the other three vehicles dismounted and set security.

The gate opened easily and we moved in on foot. My platoon would be taking the apartment on the tenth floor in building one—which meant we'd be getting our exercise this night. Naturally, there were no elevators—not to mention, while a bunch of heavily armed Team guys riding up in an elevator with a little background music might be hilarious, it would be a tactical disaster. The other platoon was taking a first-floor apartment in building two. Lucky bastards.

Once we were stacked outside our target on the tenth floor, we radioed the other team—"Green, green, green"—which meant we were in place and ready to set charges. Once the charges were set, we radioed again: *Three, two, one. Execute. Execute. Execute.*

BOOM!

The concussion of the simultaneous blasts blew out nearly all of the windows in all three towers! Imagine standing just a few feet away. No wonder TBI (traumatic brain injury) is such an issue! Both teams flooded the target apartments. Our target was a dry hole—some family members but no high-value target (HVT).

The other platoon captured their guy. (Lucky bastards!) We quickly exfilled off target to RTB (return to base). We had only been there for eleven minutes. Not bad.

Speed, surprise, and violence of action.

As we were driving back, we got word we were being spun up for another hit that night. After thirty minutes at base—to check gear, listen to a briefing from our agency contact, and make our plan—we headed back to our vehicles. The only intel we had was that the HVT was a high-ranking official and was in a two-story house in an upscale neighborhood. That's it. He'd been on our list for a while, so we didn't hesitate.

We pulled onto the street about a hundred meters from the target house and got out to move in on foot. The street was narrow and dark. Only a couple of dim streetlights illuminated the area. It was a black night with no moon, so we pulled our night-vision goggles down and took in the scene with a fuzzy green hue. The front gate was open, so the assault team stacked up along the wall while the breaching team moved to the front door.

The breacher set the charge on the door, backed off, and blew it completely off the hinges. We hit the doorway and went into the house.

It was a mess.

Glass and smoke everywhere. Some of the family members had been sleeping in the front room. One woman was sitting on the couch with a large, triangular piece of glass sticking out of her right eye—yet she didn't make a sound. We moved through the house, which was one of the largest and most complex floor plans we had seen.

We found our HVT hiding in one of the rooms. He came out with his hands high, but started moving toward us quickly, yelling in Arabic. A muzzle strike to the chest folded him like a rag doll, and we cuffed him and took him out into the yard.

Our corpsman and I moved back to the front room to tend to the family members that were wounded. He quickly started treating the woman with the eye injury, while I slung my rifle and picked up two little girls in their pajamas. The floor was covered in glass, and they didn't have any shoes. I moved them to one of the other rooms where a few other family members were being held. These are the unfortunate realities of war. It was heart-wrenching.

We began our SSE (sensitive sight exploitation) to look for any valuable intelligence, computer hard drives or documents, and any other relevant information we could find. We finished quickly and returned to base for our after-action review on both missions.

These two back-to-back missions were successful in large part to the full participation of all assets involved—despite the high levels of uncertainty. We didn't have any structural or behavioral roadblocks. We had powerful influencers—officers and senior enlisted leaders who communicated the mission intent clearly—which gave us direction but let us adapt to the changing realities of each mission. Everyone was fully engaged and operating on all cylinders.

It's easy to talk about creating that sense of teamwork and inclusiveness, but how do you actually build it? It comes from concrete decisions about how an organization is structured and run, and from coaching people on the team about how to change mindset.

Let's start with some of the more concrete elements of the process. Say you're a part of that IT firm I referred to in the last chapter. That transformation vision is all about being known for legendary customer service—being an elite leader in the space.

But unless you make some significant structural changes in how you measure and reward your people, how you train them, and how you push information up and down the chain of command, you won't get there. You might get an initial bubble of engagement about the change because it's new, but if all employees don't see that they're rewarded based on the new goals, they won't stay engaged. And if you aren't measuring actual consumer-based metrics to see if you're making progress? How will you be able to broadcast your wins, or make adjustments if you're falling short? This goes back to the importance of real-time data analysis and aligning that intel with predetermined KPIs.

No single word can make people go to sleep faster than *training*, but it's a ubiquitous part of the corporate world because it's so necessary— just like in the SEAL Teams. If an organization changes systems or processes, or is looking for a different approach, how can that happen without specific training about *which outcomes* the organization is trying to promote?

But it shouldn't be training that focuses only on new systems and processes. The best organizations also incorporate behavioral training into the mix. Training that transforms the way people think and view the world around them. Training that provides them experiences that transform mindsets and attitudes. It's not just some management consultant giving the leadership team a laundry list of things to make the employees do. It's concerted training designed to get everybody to understand a new mindset. It's training people to think in a new way and look at the world around them through a new lens.

One of my clients, a national financial management consulting firm, brought me in for a full-day event that included a keynote presentation and workshop. The event was designed to be the catalyst for incorporating the new transformation vision. The company has been around for about twenty years and is one of the most respected privately held firms of its kind. When the new chairman joined the company, he launched his version of a culture diagnostic and began analyzing areas of opportunity the firm could capitalize on.

He quickly determined that the organization struggled with its approach to talent acquisition, training, and performance measurement. Most employees joined the company as analysts and worked their way up. They were provided standard training and measured on their technical and analytical capabilities. But when they moved up the ranks and eventually earned the title of director, they were measured solely on sales and business development.

The problem?

Those employees got virtually no training in those areas. The lack of training combined with the pressure to move up was creating one of those barriers we have been talking about. The new role and expectations (for which no training was provided) didn't match reward mechanisms.

The firm's director of human resources described the new vision for becoming a "sales culture." Senior leaders wanted to reinvent the organization. The healthcare side of the business was going to be spun off so they could focus on their core business lines and become more nimble.

But until now, they were struggling to plan and communicate the details behind this vision.

They wanted to become a *sales culture*. OK, so what does that mean? How were they going to accomplish that? What resources were required to achieve this? What metrics would be used to measure progress?

Were the answers to all these questions locked away in one of their many silos or in the visionary minds of senior leaders?

Maybe.

We organized the event to include all of the employees from each branch across the country. We wanted to get everyone in one place and engage them in the process for better defining what this mission looked like. We wanted to give them a voice in developing actionable steps toward achieving this new vision.

Before we could even plan this event, I made it clear we needed to ensure that all senior leaders were aligned on this vision and how they felt it could be accomplished. Once that was clear, we could create a meaningful event that engaged as many people as possible in the planning process. Did they have a transformation task force? Who was part of it? What resources did they have and how much authority over budgeting and decision-making?

The event served its purpose well. It provided a venue for early-stage engagement that produced buy-in and the foundation for later-stage participation in the successful culture transformation.

All of these structural and process changes should be working together to empower people up and down the chain of command to take ownership of their own areas of expertise. And it can't just be words.

"Empowerment" gets thrown around an awful lot by organizations that don't really give their people the autonomy to take action. If you tell a team that they're in charge of their microenvironment but then micromanage them to death, they'll stop participating in any meaningful way beyond following orders. Or if you empower them with projects that have little value and let them run with the ball, they will see through it and quickly disconnect.

The flow of information will become one-way—from the top down—and the organization loses its most important asset in valuable, fully engaged team members giving it their all.

I see this all the time with even the most well-intentioned organizations. They go through the process of articulating the change message within the leadership group and come up with a plan for sharing that message with the rest of the organization, but it never fully makes it out of the boardroom.

Why?

Because the leadership group couldn't even establish true alignment or come up with coherent steps for communicating the vision.

It happens all the time. A leadership group gets together and comes up with a consensus, but there's no action plan. There's no specific discussion about how and when to get the message out to the rest of the organization. There's no framework for specific actions to be taken—and who will be accountable or responsible for those actions.

All of the good ideation, collaboration, and decisions in that meeting often die right there in the room. Not because of ill intent, but because of lack of follow-up.

Most often, it's because people are busy, and they have to move on to fight the next fire. Because their responsibilities to take action are unclear, they don't communicate with their people until days or weeks later—when the message isn't as clear in their minds. Or they don't say anything at all, which leaves the frontline people to hear a trickle-down message that may or may not square with what they've heard through the grapevine.

There's no alignment in the message, so the tendency is to ignore it and keep on with the status quo, especially if this is a consistent occurrence in the company.

That's the opposite of the way the best organizations run. Those teams operate by always looking at what happens next. They have the freedom to define the "micro-vision"—their part of the story—without having to get sign off. They're empowered. They have the resources.

They take action. That action is evaluated and adjusted if necessary, and information flows in both directions.

Rinse and repeat.

There is never going to be total buy-in all the time. There are cultural and historical factors at play. You're going to have naysayers who say something isn't the right thing to do, or it's being rolled out improperly. If those people are influential in the organization—say a mid-level manager from a division that's important to the transformation—that's somebody who is going to passively or actively work against the transformation. If that person is really influential, they could be holding twenty or fifty people back with them, just by being the manager who ultimately reviews those under him or her!

So how do we do all this? We take decisive action to ensure the participation of as many people in the organization as possible.

Five Ways to Empower and Engage Employees to Lead Change

The modern business environment requires giving a broader range of people more power to drive change. That's the textbook definition of empowerment. Inspiring the team is one thing, but physically and psychologically giving them more autonomy to participate in the transformation process is critical for success.

On the battlefield, mission success hinges on the participation of everyone from frontline troops to the top leaders thousands of miles away. The same applies in business—especially during times of change. So let's avoid this pitfall and now talk about how to better empower employees to take ownership and effect positive and lasting organizational change.

1. Communicating a Powerful Change Vision

Again, this is where it all starts. In the last chapter, we talked about the six principles for communicating a powerful change vision. Keeping it simple and authentic is crucial, as is using multiple channels for communication and finding ways to repeatedly weave the vision into everything the company says and does. The transformation task force guiding the change initiatives must also change their behaviors to be consistent and aligned with this new vision.

One of the most powerful elements of Navy SEAL culture is simple: a shared sense of purpose and total alignment on the mission. Everyone has a voice, and we encourage transparent communication from the top down and bottom up. When the team is aligned and bought into the mission, that's when beliefs change. New beliefs lead to new actions being taken, and those actions lead to the desired results.

2. Aligning Systems and Structures to the Vision

This is often where it can get tricky. Many of the organizations I evaluate do a good job of getting to this part of the process but fall short when it comes time to build systems, processes, and structures that align with the new vision.

Let's say an innovative HVAC company is growing exponentially, and leadership wants to take the organization nationwide over the next five years. One of the most important parts of their change vision is to be considered the leader in customer service and innovative maintenance solutions. So they develop a customer-first vision plan. They begin to execute this plan but it begins to stall about halfway through and nobody seems to know why.

The leadership team brings in some consultants, who quickly uncover the issue. The company is still using many of the structures they put in place when they were a start-up. Human resources systems and compensation models have almost nothing to do with rewarding customer-first behavior. They don't have a seamless system for regular customer feedback.

You see where I am going with this.

During organizational transformation, it's often a requirement that legacy systems have to be upgraded to align with the new vision.

3. Providing Training for the New Systems and Structures

Building those new structures is just one step. Without training people on how to best utilize new systems, it's a wasted investment. Even when organizations have the foresight to commit to extensive training, that training is often either not extensive enough or isn't focused in the *right* areas. They focus on the few technical skills required to "operate the tool" but don't teach team members to think differently and understand how to use the tools adaptively.

4. Handle the Anti-Change Agents

Respected, influential team members can be powerful forces within a change environment. If they buy in, they can evangelize the message and bring waves of team members with them. But when influential, highly competent team members resist the change message, they can do catastrophic damage. It can come in the form of vocal opposition or quiet, passive-aggressive resistance.

Either way, it can be a cancer.

To address it, transparent, straightforward communication is crucial. Experienced, influential team members gained that status for a reason. Mining your most experienced team members for their feedback accomplishes several important goals. It reinforces that their voices are being heard, and it provides frontline intel about the change process—potholes to avoid, issues that need to be resolved.

It also offers the chance to fully explain the "why" behind the transformation. At this point, they either get on board and see the light, pretend to get on board and quietly oppose the actions being taken, or continue to outwardly oppose the new plans. If it's anything but the first option, they must be removed. That's not an easy thing to do. There will be political and personal implications. But such is the burden of command.

5. *Actually Give the Team Ownership Over Specific Projects*

As I have emphasized already, empowerment has to be authentic or shouldn't be attempted at all. This is where leaders need to adopt a more adaptive mindset and inspire the team to be accountable and take ownership.

As long as the battlefield commander's intent (in this case, the change vision) is clearly and regularly articulated, more autonomy can be given to responsible frontline leaders. With the proper "lane markers," they can and should be allowed to innovate within the given structure. Mistakes will be made. But true autonomy can't really exist within a command-and-control leadership mechanism.

With truly empowered employees, winning the change fight is much more likely. And the organization will be well equipped to combat fear and change fatigue, which we will talk more about in the next chapter.

TALES FROM THE FRONT LINES

It isn't hard to see why the Naval Special Warfare community is such a tight-knit group. We've all been through the same brutal training process, and on every mission, you're relying on the buddy next to you to win the fight and get back alive. And he is relying on you.

That's a fantastic way to create a group of empowered, accountable, and enthusiastic operators. It's also expensive, time-consuming, and hugely selective. It costs millions of dollars to train a single class. Tax dollars at work.

In the real world, organizations need ways to realistically build these qualities into their teams—to come out with cohesive, tightly bonded groups that are open to being more collaborative and better equipped to handle more responsibility for the change mission.

One of the ways to do that is by getting more creative with the training—thinking out of the box. We've talked about the concrete training organizations can undertake *within* the corporate structure to get people to better understand exactly what their functions and roles are. But just as important is getting culture-focused "outside" training that helps people think differently.

When I'm called in to work with an organization, only part of my work comes in the form of keynote speaking or conventional workshops. If requested, I also conduct different kinds of "boot camps" and experiential events designed to get people out of their comfort zone and working together more collaboratively. I've done this all over the world with organizations ranging from multinational banks to professional sports teams. It is mindset training designed to unlock new habits and eliminate old ones that stand in the way of mission success.

One of my first experiences running this kind of training came in Hong Kong, for a group of senior leaders from the global bank I referenced in Chapter 1. I was contracted to come in for a series of keynote presentations, workshops, and breakout sessions. The president who hired me also happens to be a fitness fanatic, so he wanted to incorporate an early morning beach boot camp.

The client wants some pain? No problem!

It started with a 6 a.m. muster at a beach in an upscale area of the city. The goal was not to beat these senior leaders and mid-level banking managers into submission, but get them out of the office and working together in teams. The message? Breaking down cultural and physical barriers to improve communication and collaboration.

I designed the boot camp to be a BUD/S-style beat-down session— but catered to average fitness levels. (One guy even showed up in khakis and a button-down shirt! I guess he missed the memo about active- wear. But he rolled up his pants and dove in.) After a safety briefing, I broke the group into equal boat crews of six or seven and told each crew to assign their own leader. Each leader's role was to motivate the team and pass detailed instructions to his or her crew about each exercise or evolution.

"Boat crews, get wet and sandy! Now!"

I sent the crews through a series of very physical drills and races that required total cooperation within the teams to succeed. I gave the requirements for each drill to each boat crew leader, who then had the responsibility to transmit that information to his or her team.

In an exercise like this, you see very quickly which crews have leaders who can communicate the right information—plus provide organization and motivation—and which ones fall into disarray. And it almost never has anything to do with physical ability. I'm just as likely to see a bunch of fit, active people struggle as I am a group of less-than-fit people who nail every requirement. It's about coordinating the team and aligning them under one mission.

Every participant quickly realizes that the boat crew is only as strong as its weakest link, and that working together is the only way to survive each test. The boats that come in last in a given drill are required to get wet and sandy. The winning crews can choose to sit out the next evolu- tion and get a short break—which motivates everybody to keep trying. It's very much designed to reward winning—and to produce a collabo- rative mindset to get to the win. And we always do an AAR afterward to discuss key learnings.

Since then, I have done many of these types of events. For one particular client, a national law firm based in Los Angeles, I was contracted to be the keynote speaker and to run the attendees through a boot camp workout. I followed my usual process. It's always fascinating to see how teams respond. Who steps up—and who gives up. During this event, it happened to be raining, so after my keynote address the hotel staff cleared out the entire ballroom. Attorneys don't like getting wet, apparently.

During a particular relay race, one of the boat crew leaders fell out, barely able to catch his breath. He knew he could no longer effectively lead and would be a weak link, so he benched himself while still shouting instructions and motivating his team. One of his team members immediately stepped up and took charge, and she ultimately led her team to victory.

Sand and sweat isn't always required to achieve collaboration. I had another client coming into San Diego for an off-site leadership event, and aside from being their keynote speaker, they asked me to create an outdoor challenge for people who wouldn't be able to shower and change clothes after.

This was a group of fifteen senior leaders from a publically traded Fortune 500 medical device manufacturing company. This team oversaw the company's largest division—responsible for more than $10 billion in revenue. Some were new to the team, and the organization wanted to focus on improving leadership, trust, accountability, and communication.

The group CEO was a former college football player and Secret Service agent, so I worked with the director of training and human resources to put together something both fun and challenging.

What I came up with was essentially a photo scavenger hunt, but no self-respecting SEAL can call it something like that. No. This was an *intelligence gathering surveillance and recon mission* behind enemy lines.

I created a mission briefing packet for each team, and essentially they would be tasked with performing "surveillance" of particular targets. The Seaport Village area in San Diego was the designated area of operation and was under ISIS control. Some of the mission requirements were very specific, while others required interpretation and problem-solving. Each team picked a leader for their group, and I gave each of them an individual briefing on the parameters of the mission—what intel they needed to collect, and what problems they needed to solve. The mission had a definite time limit, but the teams were free to organize themselves however they saw fit—and solve the problems with whatever strategies and tactics they felt were the most appropriate. The groups were required to meet at the "extraction point" at the assigned time, or the boat (their 6 p.m. dinner cruise) would leave without them—and the team who accumulated the most intelligence was the winner.

These activities usually reveal interesting team dynamics, and you can quickly see who among the teams is taking charge. It isn't always the "official" leaders. You'll see people take ownership of the mission plan. I provide guidelines, but teams are free to determine how they solved the problems.

This medical device group—all highly educated and capable leaders—was learning how to communicate dynamically, and to assemble and disseminate useful information in a fast-paced environment. The event was designed to be the catalyst for dissolving silos and opening the lines of communication—and ultimately to create alignment.

The message being communicated in these exercises is that leaders and managers are there to provide lane markers, but teams need to have the ability—and the empowerment—to confidently solve problems in the best way they see fit.

Leaders and managers need to learn to sometimes get out of the way!

How much can something like a beach boot camp or intel mission change an organization? By itself? Not much.

But when an organization embraces the *idea* behind this type of training and acts on those ideas, they can completely and totally transform. They're the ones that fully embrace the commitment to time, resources, and accountability.

On the other hand, organizations that go through the motions of managing change and hire a consultant to check the box—doing the training to say they did the training—are destined to fail.

They might have changed some rules and made some of the correct moves, but they didn't change the culture, and they didn't create engaged believers inside or outside the company.

8

FATIGUE: MANAGING FEAR AND STAYING ENERGIZED

I will draw on every remaining ounce of strength to protect my
teammates and to accomplish our mission.
—NAVY SEAL ETHOS

Most organizational change efforts take longer and cost more money than leaders and managers anticipate. In fact, more recent research from McKinsey & Company shows that it's actually closer to 70 percent of change efforts that fail or fall short. Why?

For many of the reasons we have covered: a weak culture that isn't aligned with the mission, lack of participation and buy-in, under-communicating a powerful vision, overcommunicating a poor vision, not enough training or resources, and so on. But one very critical roadblock standing in the way of bringing a change vision to fruition is what I call *change battle fatigue.*

Change battle fatigue is the result of many elements such as past failures plaguing the minds of employees, the sacrifices made during the arduous change process, and rollout strategies taking longer than antic-ipated. When a transformation is poorly led, fatigue can set in quickly.

According to older but still relevant 2008 research from IBM, the need to lead change is growing, but our ability to fulfill a change vision is shrinking. Hence why people often get discouraged and eventually give up. Even when companies make great strides while building a change culture and preparing for the change battle, fatigue can derail even the most valiant efforts for change—essentially leading to losing the change battle.

When change efforts have failed in the past, people often grow cynical. They start to mutter under their breath, "Here we go again . . ." or "Here comes another flavor of the month . . ." or, as one senior manager told me, "We're lying low until this new fad blows over and leadership gets distracted by something else."

It's difficult for managers and staff to get motivated when they believe that the latest "new initiative" being preached from above is going to die just like the last one—no matter what they do. Fear makes change intensely personal. People become concerned about their jobs, families, and long-term career path. When people are afraid, most can't hear or think as well. It's much harder for them to absorb important information when panic starts to set in. This can be a big distraction that undermines the team's ability to focus and stay productive. And times of change are when you need them more focused than ever.

This is a fundamental reason why SEAL training is so hard. Everything you do is live fire, live explosives. When you're moving dynamically through the "kill house" (a training facility for practicing close-quarters combat) taking out targets, those aren't blanks we are shooting. One misstep and people can get shot. When you're in the desert or fields of Arkansas doing land warfare training, you're running and gunning for sixteen hours a day. It's hot, exhausting, and loud as hell. And when you get tired, mistakes can happen—like say forgetting to change out your barrel. But the level of intensity serves a specific purpose. To prepare you for war. As the Navy SEAL Ethos says, "We train for war and fight to win."

You don't realize how well trained and prepared you are until your first gunfight. The training is designed to mitigate fear and fatigue so that you stay focused and have the mental and physical endurance to defeat the enemy. So you maintain the ability to move, shoot, and communicate effectively as a team—channeling the natural tendency toward fear into focused aggression.

Though many Americans may not have realized it, December 28, 2014, marked what the U.S. government called the official end of the war in Afghanistan. That war has been the longest sustained conflict in U.S. history—but despite the announcements that the formal conflict was over, America's war there is far from finished. That perplexing distinction—that formal combat operations are over but that the U.S. still remains in an armed conflict—in many ways exemplifies the manner in which we have approached these conflicts for the last sixteen years.

As we speak, there is a debate about how many more new troops to send back to Afghanistan. Or, as Kabul-based journalist Matt Aikins once put it, referring to Afghanistan: "a 'formal' end to the war means the beginning of an 'informal' war, without aim or end, founded on the premise that we are no longer at war."

Iraqi prime minister Haider al-Abadi declared victory over ISIS in Mosul. But what's around the corner? More fighting? Humanitarian crisis? One can only imagine the level of battle fatigue many of our brave men and women in the armed forces experience. But unlike many business organizations, the military has droves of new recruits coming in every day—energized and ready to take the fight to the enemy. Seasoned soldiers rotate back to civilian life and the new blood takes over.

Unfortunately, that kind of turnover can have a detrimental effect during a transformation effort, and to a company's culture in general. Business isn't war, but the uncertainties and challenges that come with it today can create their own kind of persistent fatigue within an organization. When teams are subjected to a relentless barrage of competing priorities, messages about "reinventing" and "pivoting," and stacks of new requirements to go on top of their everyday duties, they break.

This "change battle fatigue" is one of the biggest challenges organizations face—even when they've made some good decisions about ongoing strategy and built a solid case for transformation.

When this fatigue begins to set in and momentum starts eroding, it's easy for the entire change effort to fall apart. And when all of that effort is wasted and the members of the team feel like they're back at step one, it makes the next change effort that much harder to launch and gain momentum.

The next time, it will take longer. Cost more. The people who don't believe in the changes will be ready with their I-told-you-so's, and even those committed to getting the organization moving in the right direction can get discouraged. It generates a cycle of failure.

So how do the best leaders and managers mitigate change battle fatigue and keep the team engaged and energized?

By doing three things: *identifying and celebrating early successes, creating cultural experiences that support the vision,* and *leveraging emotional intelligence and increasing situational awareness.* All of these strategies keep the change train on track.

THE TAKINGPOINT PRINCIPLE

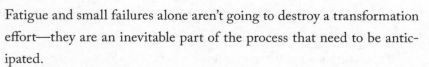

Fatigue and small failures alone aren't going to destroy a transformation effort—they are an inevitable part of the process that need to be anticipated.

Every elite athlete experiences failure on the path to winning a world championship, an Olympic gold medal, or a Super Bowl. But the best don't turn failures into permanent downturns. They don't let the weight of fatigue keep them down. They have the emotional intelligence to see the signs—both within themselves and those around them—and take corrective action.

SEAL training is hard for those same reasons—and to produce those same outcomes. The instructors make the training almost incomprehensively miserable in the early stages so that the people who make it through understand that they can push through almost any amount of pain, fear, and fatigue. We learn how to channel those things into the fuel we need to fight—focused aggression.

That's what we're going to be covering in this chapter. You probably don't need focused aggression so much, but celebrating early successes, creating transformative cultural experiences, and leveraging the powers of emotional intelligence will help you block change battle fatigue, channeling it into something productive for you and your team. And ultimately escaping the cycle.

Mary, a visionary emerging leader at a global packaging company, has just been promoted to be the VP of operations. She has also been appointed to be part of the transformation task force that is leading the strategy behind the company's new rebranding mission. The vision is to transform their internal and external brand perception from being "a boring old packaging company" into an innovative industry leader with the goal of attracting new customers and hot new talent. The strategy includes everything from a series of acquisitions and an overhaul in operations to completely reworking the look and feel of their branding. Basically, they were becoming a new company.

During one of the first task force meetings Mary attends, she decides to observe, listen, and learn. The transformation has only been under way for four months so there will be plenty of time to assert her influence over the process.

Eventually, she chimed in and asked about the overall plan, priorities, and any initial milestones that have been identified as "low-hanging fruit." The CFO, also a well-respected leader in the company, throws around some fairly ambiguous answers about the plan to hire a great creative agency and a few of the operational improvements that will streamline their packaging design center. None of them specific and none time bound.

"So who is accountable for each of these initiatives and how will they know when they have achieved some of these goals?" she asked.

It quickly became apparent that none of this had been clearly defined. The transformation the company was taking on was no small task by any means, and it seemed that although they had the foresight to create a task force and influential senior leaders were fully involved, they didn't yet quite have a handle on how to tackle all of this. Bringing in consultants was being discussed, but it would be extremely costly and the CEO didn't think the investment would be worth it.

"I know I've only been here a couple years, but does anyone mind if I explain the experiences I had at my last company?" Mary asked.

"By all means. We are all ears!" said the CFO.

"Well, we were facing a very similar transformation that we knew was going to take at least four years. Realistically, we knew it was going to probably take longer. The leadership team assembled a task force similar to this one that included senior leaders and a solid cross section of key people throughout the company. About a year into the effort, we had made some progress, but not as much as we had hoped. The change evangelists that were not part of the task force but actively promoting the effort throughout the ranks began to lose hope. The cynics gradually became more emboldened by the perceived failures," she said.

She went on to explain that they eventually decided to pump the brakes and do a quick analysis of what wasn't working. It seemed that course correction was needed. After doing so, the task force realized that they were making more headway than even they realized. If this was the case, that meant not many people in the company could possibly know what the quick wins were either.

Why?

Because during the planning process they had failed to identify and even manufacture specific early milestones that could be achieved and celebrated at the six- and twelve-month marks. Nobody had specific ownership over early stage wins that could be leveraged to tell their story of progress. Additionally, even though the company was going through a complete operational and cultural overhaul, no cultural experiences had changed to match the new vision.

"Wait, what do you mean by cultural experiences?" one team member asked Allison.

"It can be almost anything from company meetings and internal communications strategies to off-site events and the seating plan. Any experience that either supports the desired culture and vision or detracts from it," she answered.

The task force unanimously decided then and there that they had a lot more work to do before moving ahead. This was going to be a long change battle and they needed to be prepared. Early victories needed to be identified and communicated broadly across the organization and new cultural experiences needed to match their vision for being an innovative industry leader.

Stories like this are not uncommon and illustrate why so many trans-formations fail in the long run. Without celebrating quick wins, creating or changing cultural experiences that support the vision, and having an emotionally intelligent team that has situational awareness, people have a very hard time continuing to believe in the mission.

The Purpose Behind Identifying and Celebrating Early Successes

One of the questions I always get from my mentees about SEAL train-ing is how anyone manages to survive BUD/S. What was the hardest part and how did I get through it? Did I go in the first day expecting to make it through the toughest elite military training program on the planet? Yes, I did, but that attitude was only part of why I was able to do it. The fundamental reason was because I took one day at a time and viewed each passing day as a small victory. Every time another guy quit, my morale went up. Getting through each day meant I was one day closer to the finish line. I blocked out distractions and maintained focus on the long-term vision (becoming a SEAL).

That might sound simple, in a way, but it's something most organi-zations struggle with. I've come in to work with dozens of clients who have undertaken huge rebranding campaigns or an attempt to restructure their entire operation—and they've spent hundreds of thousands of dol-lars in research, come up with an elaborate plan, and marketed the new vision both internally and externally. But when it came time to execute the change vision, they never talked about the intermediate goalposts and cheered their people for making progress. In those situations—where people are already frazzled about being asked to do new things—a lack of communication and encouragement quickly leads to fatigue.

It doesn't take a big, elaborate plan or an Academy Awards–caliber prize ceremony to accomplish this. A good management team pulls the mission plan apart and figures out where the intermediate milestones are. One client—a large software engineering company—needed to create a new client support program that pulled data together from a half dozen different independent platforms. They made a change plan, and the first goalpost was to have a new seamless data management solution selected within ninety days—meaning the budgeting, research, and final decision needed to be made in that time. When it happened in eighty-two days, the organization told the story of how it was accomplished and rewarded the team responsible with a Friday off at a company-sponsored day spa retreat. People saw tangible signs of progress and the surpassing of early goals.

Identifying early milestones and quick wins starts during the mission planning process. If these projects are not clearly defined, time bound, and owned by specific people, the chances of being able to celebrate early successes diminishes. It starts with asking simple questions such as:

What are our top priorities for the first twelve to twenty-four months of this transformation?

What projects—that will show measurable progress—can we plan to complete at the six- and twelve-month marks? Or even earlier?

Who is going to own these projects? Who is accountable, responsible, and informed?

What will our internal communications strategy be when we do accomplish these goals?

Saying communication is important is almost a cliché at this point. But again, many organizations struggle with this critical piece of the strategy. When you're going through dramatic organizational changes, it's crucial to continue to tell the story behind the changes to both internal and external participants.

The companies that navigate change the most successfully have leaders who are constantly telling the story of the change message—both formally in meetings and casually at the water cooler. They're telling the story of progress and team accomplishments. Sending out an email written by the human resources or public relations staff and calling that communication just doesn't get it done.

For example, if one of the early milestones for a vision to create greater efficiencies is to roll out a new collaboration software, break that project down into micro-projects that have specific due dates. Designate a budget. Research. Cost analysis. Tool selection. Implementation and training. Then celebrate these wins with aligned communication from the top as well as telling stories about the accomplishments. Acknowledge the people who made it happen. Then put specific metrics in place for measuring the tool's effectiveness. Look at the data and report progress.

These are tangible and measurable steps toward showing transformation progress. This goes back to the difference in roles between leaders and managers. Leaders are keeping an eye on the vision and ensuring alignment on how to get there while managers are making sure these types of projects get done on time and on budget.

So what are the purposes behind identifying and celebrating early successes?

First, doing so validates the vision for transformation and gives the task force and evangelists ammo for supporting their argument, keeping the powers that be on board and shutting down the naysayers.

Second, it provides the needed momentum to lessen change battle fatigue and keeps the team energized. When people see and hear about progress and understand exactly how that progress supports forward motion toward success, they will remain emotionally connected to the cause.

Third, like any project management process, the early milestones can provide valuable data about what's working and how the plan might need to be adjusted.

The Purpose Behind Creating Cultural Experiences that Support the Vision

When performing the Culture Diagnostic Analysis, identify what aspects of the culture support the vision, detract from the vision, or add no real value either way. Then you need to decide what needs to stop, start, and continue.

For example, I was brought in to work with a large manufacturing company that had a renewed vision for improving accountability and collaboration to support plans for rapid expansion. Their R&D division would play a pivotal role in the successful completion of the transformation. But when I visited their offices, all I saw was an ocean of cubicles with high walls and a series of small conference rooms around the exterior of the space. Everyone was sitting at their desks with headphones on doing their work. While this office setup is quite common and works fine for many companies, it didn't seem to fit well with a vision for accountability and collaboration.

I immediately asked if there was interest and budget in transforming the space into something that screamed collaboration—a quick win. Reluctantly, they decided to create a budget and hire a local office space design firm. I gave them some suggestions based on what we had done at one of my companies. The result was amazing.

They removed all of the old cubicles, replacing them with a network of workstations that created an ecosystem for formal and informal collaboration. People could actually see and talk to each other without using Google Chat to communicate with a person two seats over! All of the exterior conference rooms had large glass windows—collaboration became more visible. There was even a large war room surrounded by glass walls right in the center of the space. In one corner was a comfortable "living room" area with couches, bean bag chairs, a picnic table, and flat screen TV. The TV was used for live streaming between other offices. The walls were repainted and covered with snippets from the new culture and vision statements. You could see and feel change happening.

By doing this, the company was creating new cultural experiences that specifically supported the vision for improved collaboration. It didn't take much interpretation for everyone in the office to understand why this was done.

The Purpose Behind Leveraging Emotional Intelligence and Increasing Situational Awareness

Emotional intelligence is widely known to be a key component of effective leadership, especially when navigating change and uncertainty. The ability to be perceptively in tune with yourself and your emotions, as well as having sound situational awareness, can be a powerful tool for leading a team in VUCA environments. The act of knowing, understanding, and responding to emotions, overcoming stress in the moment, and being aware of how your words and actions affect others is described as emotional intelligence. Emotional intelligence consists of these four attributes: self-awareness, self-management, social awareness, and relationship management.

For example, a study of over forty Fortune 500 companies showed that salespeople with high emotional intelligence outperformed those with low to medium emotional intelligence by 50 percent. The same study showed that technical programmers who fell in the top 10 percent of emotional intelligence competencies were producing new software at a rate three times faster than those who fell in the lower ratings.

One of my clients has been using personality assessments in an attempt to reduce turnover in its sales force but with marginal success. But they never did anything with the data. Their transformation goals included rapid growth, but sales turnover was obviously killing that piece of the vision. When I encouraged them to actually start assessing emotional intelligence and investing in training for improvement in areas like stress management, self-awareness, and social skills, the company was able to increase retention by 67 percent. I haven't seen the numbers myself, but the claim is that they have saved over $20 million in a three-year period.

Emotional intelligence also improves employee satisfaction, something vitally important during any change effort. A West Coast bank I spoke to was forced to cut almost one-third of its staff due to the economic downturn (understatement) in 2008. Determined to survive the change battle, the leadership team invested in assessing the remaining staff for their levels of emotional intelligence. The results supported their transformation goals to ensure they not only had the right people on the bus but that those people were in the right seats—doing jobs best suited to their capabilities. The company survived and is now more productive and more profitable with fewer employees.

A major car dealership I have worked with had a renewed vision for exemplary customer service to support rapid expansion goals. The dealership utilized emotional intelligence tests and new interviewing techniques to uncover high levels of empathy in candidates. A year later, the dealership was rated in the top 10 percent of the auto company's two hundred–plus dealers for both sales and customer satisfaction.

As a Navy SEAL veteran, entrepreneur, and leader of some of the fastest growing companies in the country, I have experienced many emotions and become very aware of how those emotions can have a positive or negative effect on my ability to inspire and lead a team. Many individuals try to shut off their feelings, but as much as we distort, deny, and bury our emotions and memories, we can't ever eliminate them. Nor can we emotionally connect with others.

You can learn to be emotionally independent and gain the attributes that allow you to have emotional intelligence by connecting to core emotions, accepting them, and being aware of how they affect your decisions and actions. Being able to relate behaviors and challenges of emotional intelligence to workplace performance during change is an immense advantage in building an exceptional team. One of the most common factors that leads to retention issues is communication deficiencies that create disengagement and doubt. And as we have shown already, engagement and participation are crucial for successful transformation.

Leaders lacking in emotional intelligence are not able to effectively gauge the needs, wants, and expectations of those they lead. Leaders who react purely based on emotion with little to no filter can create mistrust among their staff and can seriously jeopardize their working relationships. Reacting with erratic emotions can be detrimental to overall culture, attitudes, and positive feelings toward the company—and the change vision. Good leaders must be self-aware and understand how their verbal and nonverbal communication can affect the team. As the Navy SEAL Ethos says, "The ability to control my emotions and my actions sets me apart from other men."

To help understand your emotional intelligence competencies required for effective leadership, I would recommend determining where you stand on the following elements.

1. Self-Assessment

This can be defined as having the ability to recognize one's own emotions, strengths, weaknesses, values, and drivers and understanding their impact on others. Without reflection we cannot truly understand who we are, why we make certain decisions, what we are good at, and where we fall short. In order to reach your maximum potential, you must be confident in who you are, understanding the good with the bad. Those who have a strong understanding of who they are and what they want to work on can improve themselves on a regular basis. And are more prepared to lead through change.

2. Self-Regulation

Also known as discipline. This involves controlling or redirecting our disruptive emotions and adapting to changing circumstances in order to keep the team moving in a positive direction. Leaders can't afford to lose their cool. Being calm is contagious, as is panic. When you take on a leadership role, you can no longer afford to panic when things get stressful—one of the many burdens of command. When you stay calm and positive, you can think and communicate more clearly with your team.

3. Empathy and Compassion

Empathy is the ability to put yourself in someone else's shoes and understand how they may feel or react to a certain situation. When one has empathy, the capacity to feel compassion is open. The emotion that we feel in response to suffering ignites a desire to help. The more we can relate to others, the better we will become at understanding what motivates or upsets them.

4. Relationship Management

You can't make deep connections with others if you're distracted. Many of us have families, other obligations, and a crazy to-do list, but building and maintaining healthy and productive relationships is essential to one's ability to gain higher emotional intelligence. You must have the ability to communicate effectively and properly manage relationships in order to move a team of people in a desired direction.

5. Effective Communication

As we have discussed, in the SEAL Teams you have to do three things flawlessly to be an effective operator and team member: move, shoot, and communicate. Communication being of the utmost importance. Studies show that effective communication is 7 percent the words we say and 93 percent tone and body language. When you're in the cold, dark waters underneath a large ship at night, you can tell who everyone on the team is just by how they move. So remember, body language is just as important as the words we say.

Misunderstandings and lack of communication are usually the basis of problems between most people. Failing to communicate effectively in a workplace leads to frustration, bitterness, and confusion among employees. Effective communication can eliminate obstacles and encourage stronger workplace relationships. When employees know their role within a company and understand how they benefit the overall direction and vision, there is a sense of value and accomplishment. Good communication results in alignment and a shared sense of purpose—and it dramtically improves trust and engagement.

Emotional intelligence is a powerful tool critical for exceeding goals, improving critical work relationships, and creating a healthy, productive workplace and organizational culture. And from a leadership standpoint, it is imperative for leading through change.

Identifying and celebrating early successes, creating cultural experiences that support the vision, and leveraging the powers of emotional intelligence will help mitigate fatigue and fear and keep the team energized.

APPLICATION FROM THE BATTLEFIELD
TO THE BOARDROOM

SEALs run a wide variety of missions. Multiday sniper over-watch. Dangerous rescue missions. Long-range reconnaissance where you're behind enemy lines for days. Nighttime direct action assaults that can flow into the following day. Developing sources and gathering intelligence. Maritime interdiction and ship attacks. Training allied forces. Protecting foreign officials. The list goes on. And again, the training is designed to eliminate fear and keep you energized and focused.

A Goat Rope

"Goat rope" is a term we used in the Teams for a mission or situation that was a total mess. Or, according to the Urban Dictionary: *A confusing, disorganized situation often attributed to or marked by human error. A convoluted issue that is contested by many parties. A rodeo event in which competitors attempt to lasso a goat, usually for younger participants.*

Well, the mission I am about to describe had all of that. Literally. Things don't always go as planned—and that's when short-term fatigue can set in.

We were tasked with capturing a HVT who was funding and arming anti-coalition groups and who had close ties to al-Qaeda in Iraq. We departed for the hit at 1 a.m. The target location was a farmhouse (and known weapons cache) in a rural area outside of Al-Fallujah, and we were using vehicles as our insert platform.

Here is how this goat rope mission went down. You can't make this stuff up.

> **STEP 1:** One of the Humvee tires blows out on the way to the target. Stop. Throw in some chewing tobacco. Set security. Change tire.

> **STEP 2:** About a mile out from the target, the AC-130 Spectre gunship providing air support radios that people are moving on target.

> **STEP 3:** Arrive at target. Assault team inserts about one click (1,000 meters) from the target house and moves in on foot.

> **STEP 4:** There were not one but three structures on target. We reconfigure into a skirmish line and move through the target area, clearing one structure at a time.

> **STEP 5:** While moving toward a small structure with my squad (four-man fire team), I maintain focus on the main door. As I move closer, I fall waist deep into a cesspool.

I'm covered in human waste. Only a few minutes into the mission and it had become a *crappy* situation.

STEP 6: The AC-130 gunship radios that we have six squirters (people running off target) heading north. They drop several 40 mm grenade rounds to stop the squirters' movement. One squad hops into a Humvee and races off to go round them up. The AC-130 talks them in to the enemy location. It was just two women and four children—unharmed.

STEP 7: We finish clearing the main target house, finding only one male. Not our guy.

STEP 8: During our SSE (sensitive site exploitation) we encounter heavy resistance—from cows, goats, and llamas. They were not happy about our presence.

STEP 9: We find dozens of SA-7s, AK-47s, RPGs, and grenades under large tarps in the small farmhouse. No bad guys but at least we found the weapons cache.

STEP 10: I'm still covered in human waste.

STEP 11: We load some of the weapons into the Humvees and pile the rest in the main house. EOD (explosive ordinance disposal technician) sets explosive charges to destroy the weapons.

STEP 12: Before blowing charges, we decide the humane thing to do is herd all of the enemy cows, goats, and

llamas into a pen on the far side of the property so they
don't get incinerated.

STEP 13: Heavily armed Navy SEALs attempt to herd
livestock. It does not go well. I specifically recall one of
our guys—rifle slung—trying to drag a pissed-off goat
across the yard using a rope that had been placed around
its neck. Hence the term *goat rope*.

STEP 14: Our lead breacher—and big-time cowboy—
comes out of the house and takes over, successfully
herding the animals into the pen like a pro. It was
impressive.

STEP 15: Pile into the vehicles and begin exfil off target.
Charges blow, sending a giant fireball into the night sky.

STEP 16: One of the vehicles—a $300,000 fully
armored Mercedes G-Class carrying our agency guys
and their source—goes off the road. The intel guy at the
wheel had limited experience driving wearing night-
vision goggles.

STEP 17: The Mercedes is damaged and has to be towed.
While towing it behind one of the Humvees, the rural
farm road narrows, and it rolls off into a ditch—with the
agency guys and their source in the vehicle. It's now lying
on its side in a six-foot-deep ditch. Its occupants have to
crawl out of the side windows.

STEP 18: I'm still covered in human waste—but at least
it's starting to dry.

STEP 19: We get out cargo straps, attach them to the Mercedes, and are able to pull it right-side up and out of the ditch using one of the Humvees.

STEP 20: The convoy resumes exfil and starts heading back to base. The sun is now coming up. We enter an urban area and traffic is starting to pick up. Rush hour!

STEP 21: The convoy increases speed (standard procedure in an urban area) and the Mercedes hits a curb and goes halfway off the side of a bridge. Unbelievable!

STEP 22: Convoy stops, we dismount, throw in some chewing tobacco, set security, and start directing traffic. Humvees attach cargo straps but can't budge the heavy SUV.

STEP 23: I flag down a guy with a large cargo truck to help. He was reluctant to say the least. Maybe it was my smelly pants that turned him off—not sure.

STEP 24: For two more hours, we direct morning rush hour traffic and attempt to get the Mercedes off the side of the bridge. It's now 10 a.m. the following day. Already above 100 degrees.

STEP 25: We eventually say screw it, remove radios and sensitive material, and leave the SUV behind. We would have to come back later and get it.

STEP 26: We arrive back at base. I take my disgusting pants off and throw them in the pit where we burned our trash. I walk back to the tent in boxers and body armor. Fatigue setting in.

STEP 27: A few of us and some Army brothers with a flatbed head back out to retrieve the Mercedes on loan from our agency partners.

STEP 28: We arrive at the bridge only to find that some innovative individuals had been kind enough to dislodge the Mercedes from the side of the bridge. The only problem was that it was completely stripped! No doors. No wheels. Engine gone.

STEP 29: Return to base.

STEP 30: Write big check to agency partners.

What a goat rope!

And while missions like these don't compare to what we consider significant ongoing battle fatigue, it's a humorous way to illustrate my point. All plans come into conflict, which leads to fatigue and uncertainty—and most change efforts take longer than expected. And that's where resiliency comes in, which we will talk about in the last chapter.

Managing Fear

Outside of identifying and celebrating early successes, creating cultural experiences that support the vision, and leveraging emotional intelligence, there are a few things leaders and managers can do to keep employee fear at bay.

First, acknowledge that fear exists. Empathy is a key factor in emotional intelligence, which is imperative for effective leadership during times of change. Taking the team's feelings into account, especially when making decisions and communicating progress, plays a big role in managing fear. Actively acknowledging that fear exists and letting the team know what measures are being taken will make them feel safe. If they feel safe, they will stay focused on their objectives.

Second, be strong for the team. You don't have to act like a robot, but I've found that remaining calm under pressure beats panic every time. Panic is wildly contagious and shows immaturity in leadership. Have the big debates with other senior leaders behind closed doors, get aligned, and then communicate what needs to be said in a positive manner. This also goes back to understanding your own emotional intelligence and ability to control or redirect your disruptive emotions. Embodying confidence is key.

Third, overcommunicate. Again, leading a company through times of adaptive change can be long and arduous. And like any other plan, things change. You won't get everything right the first time. Create an environment where communication flows both ways.

Fourth, focus on the positives. At some point during a transformation, a time comes when focusing on the past is a waste of time. Once you begin moving down this path, the focus must shift to the positive outcomes that will result from this somewhat stressful time. Business must go on. Keep doing great work and rewarding the team for their accomplishments.

TALES FROM THE FRONT LINES

The mission described earlier might sound like nothing more than a hard day at the office (of course, with automatic weapons in a war zone), but navigating a mission under less-than-ideal circumstances, when everybody on the team has every reason to be tired and frustrated, is the very definition of what happens regularly in most business organizations today.

It's about surviving and thriving when things *aren't* perfect.

One of my clients, a retinal image scanning technology company, is about as far away from a grubby farm in central Iraq as you can possibly get, but my friend Quinn Lyzun, Optos' deputy CEO, shares stories with very similar threads.

"Two principles I always talk about are that change creates opportunity, and change equals pain plus a plan," he says. "Instead of looking at it as something scary, we have a culture where people say, 'Great, let's see what happens next.'"

Optos had all the typical start-up struggles leading up to the economic downturn in 2008, but its innovative product—a scanner that can quickly capture eye images for doctors to diagnose medical issues—kept it afloat despite some leadership challenges. "Years ago, when we were publically traded, every May we'd go through some kind of restructuring because we missed our numbers, and the CEO would want to show he was doing something to address it," says Lyzun. "It was always some kind of change in head count, and it was completely demoralizing. Our people were exhausted. But after a change in leadership, the new CEO recognized how toxic that was to the culture. He changed the focus to the customer, and looked inside the organization to find people who understood the business. He empowered us to take accountability and run with it."

The company flourished and was ultimately purchased by Nikon in 2015. Thanks to its strong culture of accountability and emphasis on communication, the company didn't experience many of the cultural tremors that come when a Western company is acquired by a larger Eastern parent.

"My philosophy is to be open with people and tell them the truth face-to-face, like it or hate it, and get to where we need to be faster. We only use email for following up. I call it 'managing by walking around,'"

Lyzun says. "After meeting with the Nikon people six times for a total of twelve weeks, and understanding that they appreciate what we do and didn't want to change us, I took that back to our people and told them what I thought. Of course some people were skeptical and were waiting for the other shoe to drop, and it took a year for things to settle in. But since the acquisition, we haven't lost a single person. Everybody stayed. That's almost unheard of in this kind of transaction."

The principles of identifying and celebrating early successes, creating cultural experiences that align with the vision narrative, and leveraging emotional intelligence are all key drivers in mitigating fear and keeping the team energized—and moving together toward the finish line.

9

DISCIPLINE: FOCUS AND FOLLOW-THROUGH

We demand discipline. We expect innovation.
—NAVY SEAL ETHOS

As I have stated before, although the principles in this book are displayed as a chronological process, they are not meant to simply be followed as such. Disciplined leaders and disciplined teams are required from beginning to end in any successful transformation evolution. I highlight the principle of discipline here as it relates to maintaining focus on the vision, mitigating distractions, and staying the course.

For any organizational transformation effort to succeed, discipline and accountability must become the bedrock of the culture.

How do determined young men become Navy SEALs? How do elite athletes achieve peak performance? One word. Discipline. They cut out everything in their lives that doesn't add value to fulfilling their goals—the people, behaviors, and distractions that draw them further from greatness. People and organizations that lack discipline have made a conscious choice for that to be their reality—for a lack of discipline to drive substandard performance.

When I made the choice to transition from corporate America to the Navy to become a SEAL, I had to make a significant mindset shift. Anything that stood in my way had to go—with no exceptions. My social life, diet, and training regimen were all redesigned to fit one vision. Becoming a SEAL.

As I write this book, brave and disciplined young men are joining the ranks of the SEAL Teams every couple months. As a member of the executive board for the SEAL Family Foundation, I have the honor and privilege of attending these graduations. You can't accurately describe in words the feeling and emotion that permeates the training center on graduation day.

For most, the journey has been years in the making. For all, earning the SEAL trident is a reward for discipline, focus, and an unrelenting pursuit to achieve a singular goal. They understand that the trident is our symbol of honor and heritage—that it is a privilege they must earn every day.

We have an informal tradition that usually takes place after the formal ceremony. The trident has three quarter-inch pins on the back used to secure it to the uniform. Those pins have backings that snap on to ensure the trident doesn't come off. Behind closed doors, new graduates will remove those backings so that the sharp pins are exposed to the flesh. Other seasoned frogmen attending the graduation will line up and pound the trident into the graduates' skin as hard as they can with their fists—or at least this was my experience. This symbolizes that the trident is now a part of you. The discipline that led you to this day doesn't stop there. It is only expected to increase.

In a presentation I gave to The North Face's elite athletes in Moab, Utah, I used the example of my friend and teammate David Goggins (the SEAL and ultramarathon runner), referred to in a previous chapter. The North Face team is made up of ultramarathon runners, skiers, snowboarders, climbers, and cyclists, so it was no surprise they knew David and some had raced against him. His journey to becoming a SEAL and elite athlete was no different than any of theirs.

For any person or organization with a desire to grow or change, discipline requires consistent behaviors that align with achieving goals. Then those behaviors become habits. And when productive goal-oriented behaviors become habits, it's hard to stop them. That's why they are called habits. Like the healthcare company mentioned in an earlier chapter that started referring to their core values as habits. That was done by design because values are only as good as the words and actions that support them.

In Part 1, we covered the process for measuring and improving trust and accountability as it relates to preparing your organization for change. With these pillars as the foundation of a company's culture, focus and discipline are more likely to be achievable. But like anything else, creating a disciplined team culture starts at the top.

In his book *Good to Great*, Jim Collins said that "a culture of discipline is not a principle of business, it is a principle of greatness." Those words might resonate with many leaders who are feeling frustrated about aspects of accountability, follow-through, attention to detail, collaboration, or some other area in their organization. The reality is that discipline must start with the habits and routines of leadership.

Let's say, for example, a sales director announces the closing of the firm's largest new client in a company-wide meeting. What's wrong with that? The reason that this is undisciplined behavior is because the senior leaders had already collectively agreed that new business had to stop during the early stages of their transformation so the company could focus on the important initiatives and gain momentum. They were all aligned in this decision—or so they thought.

Unfortunately, one of those senior leaders couldn't resist bringing in this business. When the sales director brought forth the opportunity, he actually dropped everything for a month to focus on helping close the deal! Instead of being a productive member of the transformation task force, he shifted gears completely to do the one core thing that the company had decided to temporarily stop doing.

Competing priorities will plague a change effort from beginning to end. Without disciplined behavior that aligns with the vision, the mission fails every time. Discipline and consistency are the path to greatness.

THE TAKINGPOINT PRINCIPLE

A big part of my consulting business is meeting with senior executives at organizations that are struggling in certain areas and to help them both come up with a plan and develop the skills it takes to *lead* into the plan.

They have to be able to make change operational.

One of the first questions I ask is what they think are the root causes of their problems. The five "whys" exercise. And any time I talk to senior executives who complain that their teams are falling short of meeting specific goals, I ask them what they feel the root causes are. Lack of accountability, trust, and collaboration are typical answers. But when you dive deeper you typically see that these behaviors aren't being exhibited at the top. How can any organization expect to have a culture of discipline when it doesn't exist among senior leaders?

It can't.

Disciplined leaders provide consistent messages and support the front line by making the tough decisions that keep a change initiative on track. Disciplined team members hold themselves accountable and don't need to be steered around like sheep. With more horizontal leadership and control, you create ecosystems of empowered leaders and managers up and down the food chain. If they understand the framework for success—what the goal looks like, and what defines a win—the leadership team can get out of the way and let greatness happen.

Of course, the other side of that coin isn't quite as shiny. Undisciplined leaders wander off message and make decisions that hurt the team.

They promote undisciplined behavior down the chain of command—or tolerate it when it should be addressed and corrected. Behavior that is tolerated is what will define a culture, for better or worse. Like a director from one of my client firms once said to me in a conversation about the lack of discipline plaguing their organization, "Honestly, that's just the way it is around here and I don't really see it changing."

In *Good to Great*, Jim Collins focuses on the three fundamental areas of discipline in an organization. You can only form a disciplined foundation if you have the right people on the bus, who are themselves self-disciplined. Applying this over time, you will be able to cement this into the company culture.

Those three areas are:

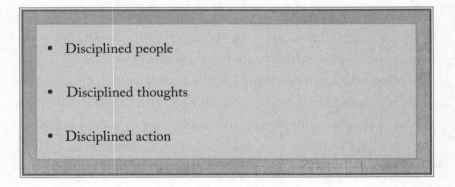

- Disciplined people

- Disciplined thoughts

- Disciplined action

Self-disciplined team members who are accountable don't have to be managed as much. As we have discussed, when you decentralize controls and create ecosystems of empowered leaders and managers throughout an organization, all you need to do is provide the framework within which the team can operate—then watch the magic happen. But when undisciplined leaders and employees exist within that framework, things fall apart. People lacking discipline have to go. When discipline is an issue at the top, however, the chances of success are dismal.

When gathering intelligence and planning the change mission, the stop-start-continue exercise I mentioned earlier plays a critical role in defining actionable steps for achieving the change vision. I take clients through this exercise regularly, and the actionable solutions that emerge can be monumental. But it is then on them to be disciplined and follow through with those defined solutions.

How to Execute a Stop-Start-Continue Exercise

The best way to outline this exercise is to first list the top three to five core objectives of the transformation strategy. This can be done for any goal-oriented activities but in this context we are focusing on a change effort. This activity can be done by the transformation task force, small teams in different divisions, with all leaders and managers across an organization—or in smaller firms, company-wide.

Once the top priorities have been listed you can begin. For each priority, have a category labeled *STOP, START,* and *CONTINUE.* Then discuss each priority by listing the systems, processes, mechanisms, mindsets, and behaviors that must stop, start, or continue in order to reach the specific goals. This is a time for true collaboration and most importantly transparency—a time to put everything on the table. But what happens after the exercise is completed is what matters. Execution. Discipline.

The activities listed in the stop category are among the most important because they detract from the mission. Those activities will usually fall into one or all of the following categories:

- They don't align with the vision.

- They have a negative impact on the desired culture.

- They add no value to the mission.

- They distract people from focusing on the "win."

The struggle is that those activities are usually the by-product of years of behaviors and mindsets based on an outdated vision. This is one of the main reasons organizational change efforts fail, even when a company has made significant progress in early stages.

For example, very few of the contestants on the hit TV show *The Biggest Loser* actually keep the weight off. They typically have lacked discipline throughout their lives and fail to transform their mindset to focus on a new reality. They don't rid themselves of old habits and adopt new ones. The same applies for failed change efforts.

But with disciplined people acting in a disciplined manner, chances of mission success skyrocket. Less oversight is required, freeing leaders and managers to focus on activities that push the change train forward. Given the proper resources and training, people can innovate within a given framework. This is why elite special operations units are so effective and why great organizations crush their competition.

They have discipline.

You're reading this and saying to yourself, "That's fine, but how do we improve discipline in my organization? How can I personally become more disciplined?"

It's not magic. It's a series of small decisions that build on themselves. I was listening to a radio interview with my friend actor Terry Crews—with whom I did Mark Burnett's NBC reality show, *Stars Earn Stripes*. The host asked him how he stays so fit with his crazy schedule. His answer was simple: discipline. He makes the time. But he reminded listeners that his been doing this for thirty years. Start with something small every day—even ten minutes.

From an organizational perspective, discipline perpetuates. The most agile companies set goals, build systems to support those goals, and fill their teams with people determined to achieve those goals. When the goals are achieved, they're able to show how it happened—based on good data, decision-making and discipline. Discipline is rewarded as a trait, which can inspire those with potential—but who lack discipline—to become more disciplined.

What does that look like in practice? Take the removal of a member of a team for performance reasons. That's a sensitive subject that can create resentment and chaos in any team—even if the player clearly needed to go. If the reasons behind a team member leaving are never made clear, the standards by which everybody is judged can seem to be opaque. There's no clear connection between expectations and the behaviors that either are or aren't tolerated.

The best organizations use these seemingly negative outcomes to create positive behaviors—not by fear, but by transparency. If a team member isn't disciplined and needs to be removed, it's an opportunity for the leadership team to confirm the mindsets and behaviors required for achieving the organization's goals. The behaviors that align with the culture, values and mission. And this is most effective in high-trust organizations.

On a personal level, improving one's discipline requires the same kind of incremental decision-making day to day. It's developing self-awareness and honesty with yourself, and being relentless despite setbacks. After I gave a keynote address for a group of leaders at one multinational corporation, one of the people in the audience pulled me aside afterward. He told me how grateful he was to hear my talk, because what I had said about undisciplined managers applied to him. He saw himself, and how he was falling short. He realized his approach was detracting from true empowerment and team discipline. He wanted to learn, and he wanted to improve. Every month for the next year, he emailed me with a detailed account of what he was doing to address his weaknesses, and how those changes were impacting his team with measurable results.

That's discipline. It's a choice.

APPLICATIONS FROM THE BATTLEFIELD
TO THE BOARDROOM

It goes without saying that it takes discipline to prepare for and successfully complete SEAL training, and to thrive as an operator on a team. And there's no doubt that all the men I served with had one thing—*grit*.

When you show up to BUD/S, you've already been intensely preparing for what you know will be the most challenging stretch of your life, physically and mentally. There's no gliding into it. Grit comes from having—and developing—a disciplined mind.

The instructors tell you that winning will be a conscious decision. Outside of getting seriously injured, it's in your mind. You make up your mind that you're going to pass, or you make up your mind you're going to fail. There's no coming into BUD/S thinking, "Well, I hope I make it," or "I'm just going to do the best I can."

Does that mean you don't have doubts, or voices in your head telling you to give up? Of course not. Everybody has them. The voices tell you that it's too tough. That it would feel so good to get warm and just sit out for a day or two. To go an hour without somebody yelling at you. And usually those voices aren't just in your head—the instructors are trying to convince you that "this isn't for you."

But discipline is not listening to those voices.

One of the great honors of my career is being able to be a mentor to young men preparing for or going through BUD/S. My goal is to give them some advice and perspective about what they're going through, and to be a sounding board for the questions they have.

It's equally inspiring for me to select the most disciplined candidates and watch them pursue their goal with relentless, unwavering focus and aggression. Nothing stands in their way. Before they arrive at BUD/S I help them understand the culture of the community, its history, and what challenges they will face. Of course, there is only so much you can explain in words. They have to experience it themselves. I help them focus on that singular goal and work backward to break down the mental and emotional barriers standing in their way. To quiet the voices telling them to "stand down" and take a path of lesser resistance. That the magic only really happens outside of our comfort zones and only discipline will push them through to the other side—where bravery in the face of adversity becomes second nature.

As we discussed earlier in this chapter, the steel of that kind of discipline comes from a series of small steps. In BUD/S, it is reinforced over and over again that every decision you make leads to the correct path. You don't blow anything off, and you don't take anything for granted. Attention to detail matters.

Let me give you an example.

In training, we learn how to "combat dive"—to navigate pitch black water to take out a target and get back to the extraction point. The instructors pound it into your head that you have to *plan your dive and dive your plan*. Deviating from the plan—without a good reason to fall back on contingencies—can lead to mission failure, and often heading off a mile in the wrong direction.

That's because it is terrifyingly easy to get into the dark water with your swim buddy, with nothing but your attack board (device housing your compass and stopwatch), and start second-guessing. Am I going the right way? Is my kick count off? Over the years this all becomes second nature but during the second phase of BUD/S (when you've only been in training for a couple months), this is all brand-new territory.

You quickly learn to communicate well with your swim buddy underwater. This is obviously primarily nonverbal communication through hand signals. But there are times when you start second-guessing your route that things can come undone. When discipline and focus start to falter.

Breathing pure oxygen through the Dräger diving apparatus actually has some adverse effects—one of them irritability. My swim buddy and I were typically top performers when it came to combat diving. We always hit our targets and arrived at the extract point before other pairs. But not without the occasional friction. On more than one occasion, we would literally get into underwater arguments yelling at each other through our regulators. I think I actually reached for my knife once. Not really, but it crossed my mind. We were being undisciplined.

You have to have the discipline to keep yourself calm and say, over and over, I planned this dive for a reason. I'm not going to deviate. I'm going to follow the plan. Because when you deviate for no reason (decisions not based in reality or on actual data), you'll usually end up in the wrong spot, encountering a problem you didn't plan for. That's a recipe for disaster.

That's not to say discipline is mindless. Adjustments are important, but they need to come from informed decision-making. You have to let the data and feedback dictate it, not the competing priorities and gut "feelings" we've been discussing.

The same applies when leading an organization through change. So let's take a look at some of the types of "organizational discipline," their importance, and how to improve discipline to better navigate change.

THREE TYPES OF ORGANIZATIONAL DISCIPLINE

- Self-discipline: This is the ideal situation where the employees themselves are motivated enough to regulate their actions like time management, priority setting, and follow-through so management doesn't have to oversee every little thing.

- Task discipline: In this situation, the employee has to be responsible enough to do their job in the best way possible. In an ideal scenario, this would be described as flawless execution.

- Group discipline: Group discipline is teamwork. Most projects in an organization require a team approach, so group discipline is of the utmost importance.

IMPORTANCE OF ORGANIZATIONAL DISCIPLINE

- Security: Having a disciplined workforce ensures that the work environment is peaceful and provides a sense of security. This couldn't be more true than during the uncertainty of change.

- Improves performance: Discipline eradicates issues such as absenteeism, missing deadlines, and poor work quality.

- Increase in productivity: Improved performance results in higher efficiency and productivity, and therefore profitability.

- Promotes appropriate behavior: Following a set of conduct naturally makes sure that all employees exhibit behavior fitting the organization's culture and brand image.

STEPS FOR IMPROVING DISCIPLINE

- Eat the elephant one bite at a time: Breaking larger, more daunting tasks into bite-size chunks allows the team to

move more seamlessly toward the ultimate objective,
gaining new productive habits along the way. Those goal-
oriented habits improve discipline.

- Reward disciplined behavior that achieves goals: You can even
  challenge top performers with innovative new projects that
  the organization has never attempted before but that align
  with the vision. Give them the resources to execute and
  tell their story of success once the goal is achieved. Talk
  about the areas of self-discipline, task discipline, and group
  discipline that were required to win.

- Reward activities and behaviors: Reward activities, behaviors,
  and attitudes that align with the achievement of the vision
  as much as the achievement of the goals themselves.

- Remove undisciplined people: Those who lack discipline
  and who seem like they will never have it must go. It's a
  detriment to mission success and disrespectful to those
  who are executing their duties and exhibiting behavior that
  aligns with mission success.

Organizations lacking in discipline have a very hard time cementing
long-term change into the culture. As I have mentioned, culture transformation starts at the beginning of the transformation effort but doesn't
really stick until the end. Until disciplined mindsets and behaviors have
led to specific achievements. And as Jim Collins says, you have to have
the right people on the bus.

TALES FROM THE FRONT LINES

In a recent conversation I had with my friend and colleague who is president and CEO of notably the oldest fast-food chains in America, I was asking him about the concept of discipline when it comes to a major corporate turnaround strategy. How important is discipline for leading change?

For fifty years, the brand was one of the premier fast-food restaurants in the country. During the 1970s, it had more locations than McDonald's, and it was a staple of many midsize Midwestern towns. But by the 1980s, the brand started to struggle. It shrank, and eventually was absorbed by a large holding company in the fast-food space.

The strategy was to roll out co-branded restaurants that included two restaurants under the same roof. This brand was the smallest brand in the portfolio, and was already getting less attention. Then, they moved away from the co-branding strategy, which further alienated his brand. By the end of the holding company's ownership, the company only had two full-time employees dedicated to managing it on the corporate side.

So, in 2008, when a large franchise group decided to try to buy the brand and reinvigorate it, they needed a plan. My colleague had been an executive with the company before it was acquired by the large holding company, but he had moved on when it looked like things weren't headed in a direction he supported. Now, the potential new ownership group looked to him to come on board and help them with the acquisition, then stay on to run the new company when it was successfully liberated.

He was excited to come back to work with a brand for which he had a passion, and honestly, he was looking forward to the challenge of salvaging what the brand was for generations of customers. He wanted to take on the transformation challenge. And most importantly, he had strong relationships within this franchise group. There was already an existing foundation of trust. He knew if he gave them his commitment, they would in turn give him the autonomy and resources necessary to win.

To say it was a tall order is no exaggeration.

Under the previous ownership, the morale of the frontline managers and franchisees had withered. They hadn't gotten any attention, so they were either doing the bare minimum to get by, or they had come up with their own way to operate.

To take back control of the brand and offer customers a consistent experience, he had to gain the rank and file's trust—and impose some discipline on the operation.

"So what was the strategy? Clearly the franchisees and frontline managers had lost some trust and knew they had become a bit of an afterthought. At this point, trust had to be at an all-time low with complacency at an all-time high, right?" I asked.

"Oh absolutely," he answered. "Here's what I did."

He explained his process start to finish. It was time to analyze the culture, assess current levels of trust and accountability, gather data, assemble the team, and plan the mission. He pored over years of data that had been gathered by analysts and outside consulting firms. The problem of course is that no one had ever done anything with the data. He performed a SWOT (strengths, weaknesses, opportunities, threats) analysis and then hit the road to validate it.

With low morale, declining sales, and plenty of analysts predicting the brand's demise, it would have been easy to get demoralized and give up. He could have gotten distracted by some elaborate and outlandish plans to grow the company outside of its core.

For the next two years, similar to Jeff Campbell's strategy, he traveled to every store location, meeting with the frontline troops and getting their feedback.

This was a "boots on the ground" strategy. He had to better understand the current state of their mindset and know what he would be dealing with. Their voice had to be heard and the information, he knew, would be invaluable.

During this time, he had assembled his executive team—his transformation task force so to speak. He brought on a field marketing person, a paralegal, and three field managers who had been with the brand since before it had been acquired. They had probably the greatest level of situational awareness than anyone else at this point. Together, using the data and feedback gathered from key frontline troops, they developed the mission plan and defined the vision for their transformation.

Their vision for rebuilding the singular brand would require discipline and consistent action. Without discipline and aligned communication, rebuilding trust and engaging the franchisees and location managers would be impossible. They had been ignored and provided few resources for years, so this would be no simple battle.

He and his team planned and launched a franchisee convention to use as a platform for the launch of this new turnaround vision. The four pillars of the new vision were:

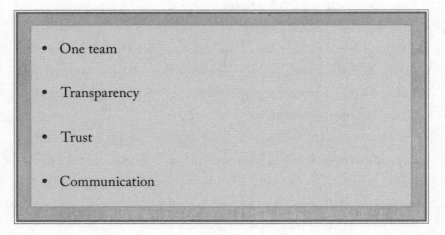

- One team

- Transparency

- Trust

- Communication

Sound familiar?

With this one team vision supported by complete transparency, rebuilding trust and improved (and consistent) communication, they were able to dissolve the vertical and horizontal silos that had developed over the years. The promises that were made to the organization and the new systems that would support the four-pillar vision would require discipline, focus, and extreme follow-through.

The company made a commitment to hire "behind the curve," promising that nobody would ever lose their job because management increased head count too aggressively. The leadership communication strategy was simple and effective and an example of where many companies get it wrong. They held biweekly leadership meetings to find alignment on five or six key initiatives or provide updates that needed to be disseminated. Immediately following these meetings, those leaders and managers would meet with their teams—in person—and pass the word, highlighting what they, too, should pass down the chain or to franchisee partners.

They held quarterly meetings to discuss and provide updates on key initiatives relevant to the transformation. They used these opportunities to communicate early success and reward quick wins. They developed a new systematic rewards process that ensured consistent public recognition for those exhibiting behaviors and mindsets that supported the new vision.

Leaders from the core "support center" would deploy to the front lines and work a full shift each quarter. Doing so allowed them to have face-to-face interaction with key frontline managers, get their hands a little dirty and better understand all the mechanisms that drove day-to-day operations.

All of the new systems, policies, processes, and ways of doing things have taken the company from dire straits to impressive profitability over the last five years. Using their four-pillar vision and taking a disciplined approach to improving accountability from the top, sales have increased 30 percent and total unit volume is up 35 percent.

Disciplined leaders leading disciplined teams ensure that distractions are mitigated, duties are executed, follow-through happens, and transformations are achieved. As the SEAL Ethos says, "the execution of my duties will be swift and violent . . ." Undisciplined behaviors must be eradicated as swiftly as possible before and during any transformation effort—and quite frankly in any organization with a desire to achieve winning results.

Discipline is the path to success, happiness, and achieving seemingly impossible goals.

10

RESILIENCE: THE PATH TO LASTING CHANGE

I will never quit. I persevere and thrive on adversity. If knocked down, I will get back up, every time. I am never out of the fight.
— NAVY SEAL ETHOS

Regardless of the type or magnitude of the transformation an organization is facing, one of the ultimate goals is to prepare the company for long-term strength and agility. The goal is not to simply navigate today's needed changes but also to create a resilient organization poised for more change. A team that is ready for the next battle—whenever that may be.

If it's true for the SEALs, it's certainly going to be true in the civilian world, where the stakes are different and it isn't life and death. Even with the best intentions—and even the best leadership—change initiatives can stall. They can fail.

It happens when you don't have resiliency. An openness to adapt and change and get up again when you experience a short-term failure.

I see it in many of my client companies. They do a tremendous job figuring out what to change, getting buy-in from all the important contributors and administering the rollout. They get the organization ready and willing to change. But then, the momentum slows. Either the front-line troops sink back to the positions they were in before the change, or they find some comfortable middle space to occupy. Things are better than they were, but not where they should be.

I have had the honor of working alongside the greatest warriors and toughest men I have ever known. Men who have been severely injured only to fast-track their rehab to get back to their units. My wife, Nicole, is highly resilient. Our eldest son, Tyler—resilient. Our nineteen-month-old son, Ryder, is a total bruiser—also resilient. But my three-year-old daughter is one of the most resilient people I know.

During the Q&A session after one of my keynote presentations in Singapore, someone asked me what the toughest thing I have ever been through is. Unexpectedly, I immediately started feeling emotions rise and had to collect myself before answering. The answer was not what he expected.

Sure, there have been experiences from my time in the Teams that bring to surface the realities of war—the loss of good friends, taking life, attending funerals, and working closely with SEAL families (through the SEAL Family Foundation) who have lost a husband, father, or brother. But none of that was what consumed me with overwhelming emotion in that moment.

As a parent, nothing compares to when your children are in danger. When my wife was fifteen weeks pregnant, I received a call from her one afternoon while I was at the office. She told me that the doctor's office had called and that I needed to come home immediately—we had been told to come to the hospital. When I got home, she told me that the nurse who called told her that her blood work had come back and protein levels had spiked. We knew this wasn't a good sign but were not yet aware of what this could mean for our unborn baby girl.

Thirty minutes later, we arrived at the fetal and genetics department at UC San Diego hospital and sat in the waiting room with several other parents looking grief-stricken. The anticipation was nauseating. Finally, we were called back. My wife and I sat in one of the offices consoling one another. A few minutes later, a grief counselor entered. A grief counselor! We hadn't even met with the doctor yet.

She handed us some brochures and proceeded to tell us that when protein spikes in the initial blood work, it means that the fetus is experiencing some kind of birth defect. She went on to detail the various types of birth defects our baby might have: spina bifida, brain damage, and paralysis. This list went on.

Eventually she left and said the doctor would be in soon. We were devastated. How could this be happening to our baby? To our family? Was this God's plan?

Soon after the doctor came in.

"OK, before we go any further, I want to let you know that you guys are going to be fine," she said.

Naturally, that did little to alleviate our fears about what she was going to say next. She told us that the baby had gastroschisis. "Gastro-what?!" I asked.

"Gastroschisis is a birth defect of the abdominal [belly] wall. The baby's intestines are found outside of the baby's body, exiting through a hole beside the belly button. The hole can be small or large and sometimes other organs, such as the stomach and liver, can also be found outside of the baby's body," she explained.

My wife was sobbing uncontrollably, and understandably so. The doctor explained all of the inherent complications that could impact the pregnancy and our baby's entire life. It would be a stressful pregnancy, to say the least.

My wife was at the fetal and genetics department two to three times a week during the entire pregnancy so they could run tests and monitor our daughter's progress. Typically, gastroschisis babies are born premature, so we had to prepare ourselves for that reality.

One Friday afternoon, I was sitting at lunch with a client discussing an upcoming event when I got the call. My wife had gone in for her last checkup of the week. Her fluid levels were low and they told her she wouldn't be leaving the hospital without a baby that weekend. It was happening.

As one could imagine, this was not as joyous an occasion as it could have been. The pediatric surgeon who would potentially be working on our daughter had told us that we wouldn't really know what complications we were facing until she was born. Some of the intestine could be dead or damaged due to months of exposure to the amniotic fluid. But we wouldn't know until he could examine her upon delivery.

That evening my wife began going into labor. The following afternoon, she delivered our baby girl, Parker Rose. As soon as she was delivered, I kissed my wife and escorted Parker to the surgery room. The surgeon examined her and said she was in good shape for a "primary closure." Which meant she was going to have immediate emergency surgery to insert her intestines and stomach back into her body cavity.

Watching your newborn be prepped for major surgery is gut-wrenching. No pun intended. But watching this unbelievable team of nurses and doctors stay so calm under pressure was fascinating and gave me strength. As soon as she was ready, I had to leave the room.

I returned to our hospital room where my wife, her parents and brother, and our oldest son, Tyler, were waiting. The minutes seemed like hours. Just forty-five minutes later, the door opened and the pediatric surgeon walked in with a big smile on his face. I looked at my watch and asked half jokingly, "What, you're done already? Do you have dinner reservations, or something?!"

He told us that everything went perfectly and she was in recovery. The feeling of relief was overwhelming. But we still knew we had a long road ahead.

Parker spent twenty-five days in the NICU (neonatal intensive care unit)—half of the average time gastroschisis babies are usually there. She was our warrior baby. As resilient as they come. A year later, she had more complications and had to have yet another emergency surgery. But she recovered well and is now a happy, strong-willed little princess who loves dance and gymnastics. She's had none of the inherent digestive issues that the majority of gastroschisis children often experience.

What can I say? Warrior blood runs in her veins.

Resilience is an interesting thing. Some have it. Some don't. But all who tackle life's challenges head-on and rebound from adversity with strength and determination will develop it. And learn to never lose it. This applies to our personal lives, professional lives, and to any organization with a strong desire to achieve greatness. That is why this final chapter is so important. Again, it's not just about navigating the obstacles you face today, but preparing for the ones coming tomorrow.

THE TAKINGPOINT PRINCIPLE

As the Navy SEAL Ethos says, "I stand ready to bring the full spectrum of combat power to bear in order to achieve my mission and the goals established by my country. The execution of my duties will be swift and violent when required yet guided by the very principles that I serve to defend . . . I am never out of the fight."

Navy SEAL training is designed to create warfighters that anticipate, prepare for, adapt to, and bounce back from adversity better than anyone else on the battlefield. Why? Because resilient organizations require resilient team members.

While *resiliency* may seem like an obvious trait for any company to pursue, it seems to be easier said than done. It's more important than long-term planning because as we all know, the best-laid business plans come into conflict—especially when navigating the inevitable obstacles that require organizational improvements or major transformations. That's not to discount the importance of planning, especially when those plans involve looking to the horizon for threats and opportunities.

As I alluded to in an earlier chapter, I had the privilege to speak at a leadership meeting for one of those battle-scarred-but-successful companies last year. Through hard work, openness, risk-taking, perseverance, and some pain, they have built an amazing infrastructure that supports and rewards resiliency.

This software manufacturing company spent more than two decades as one of the undisputed leaders in their corner of the marketplace. But massive shifts in technology made their most profitable products obsolete in a matter of months. Dozens of new worldwide competitors were pecking away at their market share, and it was conceivable that one of the most respected brands in the business could disappear from the market.

The company's leadership team made a dramatic, risky decision to eliminate an entire line of business and shift its resources to emerging business in a different space. The short-term results were painful—they intentionally walked away from 35 percent of their top-line revenue and had to say goodbye to dozens of huge customers.

But their approach to this new market wasn't a decision. It was a long-term strategy. It was an investment—and one with significant upside.

Each part of the strategy required resiliency and perseverance. The organization needed to cut ties with valuable customers, lose employees from the discontinued product line that had been loyal to the organization for decades, and invest millions in research, marketing, and infrastructure improvement for the new business lines.

By being willing to make changes—and seeing those changes through—the organization opened itself to a market three times the size it previously occupied. After three years, they had not only replaced the lost revenue but actually increased revenue to a level 40 percent higher than their previous best year.

As we've been discussing, disruptive change is a fundamental part of business today. It has arrived. For organizations to last, they need to not just accept this reality but embrace it, prepare for it—and profit from it.

When you can navigate change with well-prepared, disciplined, courageous teams, you can do it without many of the disruptions that set other organizations back. You can build teams of dedicated, loyal team members who will lead you into those challenging waters, not just wait for direction about what to do.

Of course, you don't build this culture of resiliency with a snap of the fingers. It takes a dedicated effort to ingrain the strands into the corporate fiber. I've done it with my own organizations, and it's a fundamental part of what I do in my consulting work.

To get there, an organization's leadership team needs to have a comprehensive understanding of the current cultural makeup of the team. Why? Because the default for any person under extreme pressure or stress is to fall back to the easiest or most comfortable position. During times of adversity, people don't typically "rise to the occasion"—they fall back to their existing levels of training, preparedness, and mental fortitude. Understanding your culture means you understand the baseline— and where things will go if you don't have the right structures in place.

I've seen companies spend years communicating the vision for change, implementing new company practices, adding and removing people from the team, and executing the plan to a T. They've seen tangible victories and great results in every metric, from product quality to efficiency to profitability.

They get to that point and people on the leadership team start high-fiving each other about successfully achieving the transformation vision, and they immediately get comfortable in the "new normal." This can be a significant pitfall during transformations—thinking you've reached the finish line when you still have a ways to go.

The "new normal" also isn't supposed to be a forever plateau. It is the foundation for making the next necessary transition. And if you haven't built the new cultural structure to be comfortable with ongoing change, you've missed a huge opportunity.

You also run the risk of falling completely out of the new normal and back into the "old normal"—what the organization was before the transformation even happened. It's a lot like what happens when a person who isn't really interested in fitness decides to get a personal trainer—for "motivation." It's a great idea to get some help and guidance, but without forging the discipline and mental fortitude necessary for making long-term gains, it becomes a wasted effort.

If you have a dedicated and talented transformation task force in your organization, they can create tremendous momentum and rally impressive performance. But that can overshadow the fact that real change roots aren't growing throughout—especially when talented managers are helping drive the plan forward. The momentum can actually mask the fact that the long-term foundation isn't being set.

How can you tell if the roots are real and growing? I follow a five-step *"growth tree."*

Recognize

Most permanent cultural change happens nearer the end of the change process, not nearer the beginning. When you recognize that fact, you are less likely to get lulled into a false sense of security after some big early changes.

Results Matter

If you don't define what the victories are and when they need to be accomplished, you're missing a chance to imbed resiliency into the team. Without specific metrics and consistently measuring performance against those metrics, how can you know what real progress has been made or how close you really are to the finish line? That personal trainer you hired? What good would it do for the trainer to tell you that in six months, you'll be in shape—without giving you intermediate goals and steps to achieve them and rewarding you with praise when you met them? Intermediate goals also help build in motivation to get back up again if you fall. If one aspect of the transformation goal is to increase customer satisfaction by 5 percent by the end of the first year, and you only improve .5 percent in the first quarter, you know where you stand and that adjustments need to be made. Without predetermined milestones, quick wins can't be celebrated, nor do you have evidence that course correction may be needed.

Draw the Picture

What does the new culture look like? What does a win look like? When you model it, it becomes real—even before you reach the goal. When people know what the change vision is and can literally feel it, they can keep the goal in their sights when they face an obstacle or start running out of steam.

Stock the Team

Organizational change is complicated and takes more time and resources than most anticipate. Culture change to support those initiatives is no different. It takes a long time to build a culture and therefore a significant effort to change a culture. During times of change—especially radical change—it is often necessary to bring in new people that embody the new vision and shared values. Careful recruiting and selection is very important. Similarly, sometimes the company has outgrown those who don't share the new vision and are unlikely to change. Or worse, will attempt to derail the new vision.

Build It

If you don't have a system in place to reward people for the things you want them to do, you won't get the desired results. If new expectations are put in place but compensation and HR mechanisms aren't aligned to support those performance expectations, old behaviors will come back. And why wouldn't they? Build a specific model to ensure the culture and the people supporting it align with the new vision and strategy.

▲

Resilient organizations have sound leadership at all levels and strong cultures founded on trust, accountability, and agility. They have a foundation of meaningful core values that ALL members of the team believe deeply in and a sense of team unity beyond what you find in many organizations. They also have a tendency to show consistent and better-than-average returns year after year.

Business organizations with a desire to grow, remain competitive, adapt to emerging technologies, and find new ways to manage and engage multigenerational workforces must all discover new ways of building resiliency into the culture.

My experience as a business leader and research of other organizations has helped me identify the *Fifteen Fundamental Pillars of Resilient Teams*.

1. They have a focused sense of urgency and anticipate change well. They believe a little bit of paranoia is a

good thing. They are always looking to the horizon for opportunity and threats. Complacency does not exist.

2. They see beyond what other organizations would see as limitations and have an anything-is-possible mindset.

3. They actively weave accountability into the fabric of the culture. And it starts at the top.

4. They delegate leadership responsibility and authority down the chain of command. They give decision-making capability to frontline troops and provide the resources for rapid execution.

5. They don't waste time on activities that can't be measured. They invest in the strongest areas of the business and improve or eliminate the weak areas.

6. They exist in a constant state of transformation and reset goals every few years. Every time they do, they set a clear time-bound vision and communicate it regularly. Information is disseminated quickly and they involve as many people as possible in mission planning.

7. Once they have the vision and mission well defined, they stay the course as long as market conditions and data support it. If not, they adjust.

8. They embody a people-first approach. Employees, then customers, then shareholders . . . in that order.

9. Resilient teams attract, empower, and retain courageous people willing to do bold things.

10. They bounce back from adversity stronger than before. They tackle challenges head-on and always take the fight to the enemy.

11. They think and act horizontally. They actively break down vertical and horizontal silos and approach work and communication cross-functionally.

12. They self-correct quickly and adapt before problems become unmanageable.

13. Resilient organizations are made up of lifelong learners. They encourage transparent feedback and use that data to constantly improve the business. They give everyone a voice.

14. They neither allow nor reward mediocrity. Performance expectations are clearly defined, and they always recognize and reward above-and-beyond behavior.

15. Resilient teams define excellence as the constant pursuit of perfection. They are never satisfied with the status quo.

Resilient organizations last longer and navigate change better than anyone else. They are well prepared and disciplined, and they have courageous teams that embrace change and a culture founded on trust and accountability. They have aligned leaders who show courage in the face of unimaginable obstacles and gain participation and buy-in from all levels of the organization. They thrive in adversity and are never out of the fight.

To further reinforce the *TakingPoint* principle of resiliency, let's more clearly define what the resilient organization of tomorrow looks like. What are the top priorities?

Priorities for the Resilient Organization of Tomorrow

As we have discussed, disruption and VUCA environments are now the norm. Organizations facing the need for change (pretty much all of them) have the opportunity to lead change effectively to remain relevant and competitive while simultaneously building a more resilient team.

Hyper-connectivity and technology are driving transparency. Employees have almost global opportunities, and talent acquisition and retention is becoming increasingly difficult. Having a compelling purpose and structures that allow for constant growth are imperative. Traditional hierarchical structures are fading away to give way to purposeful networks and communities of people working together to achieve a shared purpose—the one-team-one-fight mentality. The cumulative impact of these forces demands a new mindset and competencies for leaders to be able to stay relevant and make a positive difference to people and hence, their businesses.

Leaders and managers who will drive peak performance and the best financial returns will have to transform their organizations into resilient high-performance teams that embrace change. So what are the priorities that must garner the most attention?

The first and most fundamental foundation of the resilient organization of tomorrow is having a compelling vision. Not just the vision for change but the higher purpose behind why they exist, the value and purpose behind their work and how that work connects everyone to the cause. Leaders will begin to remove slower-moving hierarchical structures and develop ecosystems of empowered teams with leaders at all levels. Those networks will be given the resources and autonomy to make decisions and execute in decentralized environments.

Leaders and HR teams will develop new and more strategic talent acquisition programs that align with the vision of the organization. They will improve the ability to screen for "culture fit" while ensuring a healthy amount of diversity in the team. Even more important, they will improve retention of their best people by investing heavily in personal and professional development. They will design learning cultures that provide developmental resources 24/7 through the use of technology and digital platforms. Development will not only focus on subject matter expertise and specific technical skills but also emotional intelligence, behavioral skills that fit the needs of the company, and leadership. Leadership development will be accessible to all, regardless of title or position.

Leaders and managers will create cultural experiences and engagement mechanisms that allow for better collaboration. Cross-functional teams will have real purpose and be empowered to solve real problems and innovate within given structures. And new rewards systems will be put in place that focus on supporting these behaviors, attitudes, and activities just as much as they will on output and execution.

High-performance resilient teams will not only learn to function well in VUCA environments but actually thrive in adversity. These teams will be trained how to think and act in the ever-changing business environment and will constantly look to the horizon for what lays ahead. Leaders will adopt a future-thinking mindset and eliminate a constraints-focused mindset. Opportunity and the "white space" will be their focus while maintaining situational awareness on the reality of their existing situation. This will give them the ability to create change, not react to it when external forces require it.

The resilient organization of tomorrow will develop a better customer-centric approach while still prioritizing the team. They will regularly gather feedback from inside and outside the organization and constantly develop actionable insights from that data. And then they will execute—swiftly. Violent execution will become the norm—but founded on sound principles and proper data analysis.

And most importantly, while doing all of these things they will be moving, shooting, communicating, clarifying, and reclarifying the entire way. When knocked down, they will get back up—every time. They will draw on every remaining ounce of strength to accomplish the mission and will never be out of the fight.

APPLICATIONS FROM THE BATTLEFIELD TO THE BOARDROOM

The most vivid way to talk about resiliency and toughness is to point to the most prominent examples of it—Navy SEALs, professional athletes, noncombatants living in war-torn countries, and visionary Fortune 500 leaders and their organizations.

Of course, the problem with doing that is it might imply that only people (and organizations) with some extraordinary level of fortitude, intelligence, or skill can pull it off.

Are our servicemen and servicewomen, national championship sports teams, and top-performing companies fortunate to have special and talented individuals affiliated with them?

Absolutely.

But talent is only the start, and it isn't even the most necessary piece when it comes to building a tough, resilient team.

In BUD/S we had plenty of physical marvels and world-class athletes. We had guys with genius-level IQs and advanced martial arts training. We had guys who looked so scary that they could clear out a bar without saying a word or lifting a finger.

And we also had relatively slight guys who looked like accountants (accountants who liked to work out, but still . . .). And guys who were more reserved than vocal, and guys who didn't come across as being one of the smarter people in the room. One guy in my class had the nickname "Iron Marshmallow." It was of course a term of endearment. Especially when he would crush us all in fifteen-mile ruck runs in the desert!

The people who make it in any walk of life are the ones who combine emotional intelligence, situational awareness, discipline, resilience, and a baseline level of talent for the tasks they're going to be required to do. And then they work their asses off.

You can have talent, and you can have skill. But if you don't have a willingness to prepare, work hard, and get up when you fall, talent and skill won't save you. My friend and former teammate, David Goggins, whom I've referenced before, doesn't like to run. In fact, he hates it. And if you recall, he is an extreme athlete and ultramarathon runner! So why does he do it? It's about giving to causes bigger than himself, sacrificing to raise awareness for causes he believes in, and pushing boundaries to inspire others to overcome adversity. It's about reminding people that life can suck sometimes—get over it and go do something great. Be resilient.

And rather than regale you with stories about resilience on the battlefield and the horrors many of our warfighters have faced over the last sixteen years, I prefer to reflect on the humor often faced during one's military service.

On one particular deployment, I spent time in Kenya, Africa. It was not your typical platoon or team deployment. A few SEAL brothers, a SWCC team, and I were assigned to a small Navy base near Malindi, Kenya. Let's use the term "base" loosely in this context. Our primary mission was to train the Kenyan Navy in maritime interdiction. Basically, how to police their waters against piracy. There were other reasons we were there that can't be discussed, nor are they relevant to this story.

We resided in a camp on the far end of base that consisted of several small buildings. One was used as our TOC (tactical operations center) and to store our weapons, and the others were used for our "accommodations." More or less huts built from plywood. But we had air conditioning and electricity, which was nice. We had three ATVs and several Jet Skis—which of course we painted camouflage and mounted M60 machine guns on. Why? Why not?!

The boat team had two rigid-hull RIBs (rubber inflatable boats) and the mother of all boats, the Mark V (a high-speed boat used primarily for inserting and extracting SEALs in low- to medium-threat areas of operation).

One day, early on in the deployment, I was out for my morning run on trails and dirt roads that wove throughout the base's many acres of undeveloped land. I rounded a bend and came upon a group of fifteen or so large chimpanzees who were gathered in the middle of the dirt road. It seemed they were having a town hall meeting of some kind. They all turned and gave me inquisitive looks. I immediately slowed my pace, trying to decide if I should proceed with caution or go back the way I had come.

I decided to proceed and slowly circumvented the group of curious primates—careful not to look them in the eye. I passed them and then picked up my pace, changing course for the more well-trafficked paved road that ran through the base.

A few minutes later, I came across a female patas monkey and her two babies lying on the side of the road. It seemed she had been hit by a vehicle. Upon closer inspection, it was clear that she wasn't breathing. Her two babies, however, were still alive, clinging to her chest with their tiny paws. Each could fit in the palm of my hand. I scooped them up, wrapping them in my shirt, and headed back to our camp.

We aptly named these tiny creatures "NAZRAT" (Tarzan spelled backward) and "Iron Mike," after the world-famous boxer Mike Tyson. Although they were deemed our new camp mascots, I fell quickly into the primary caregiver role. Using eyedroppers to feed them milk, we slowly nursed them back to health. Eventually, I transitioned them to solid food, giving them fruit from those tin mixed-fruit cups where you peel the top off. Needless to say, I had no monkey-rearing experience from SEAL training, so this was a "figure it out as you go" situation.

NAZRAT eventually fell ill and passed away. It was a sad day. Iron Mike on the other hand was living up to his name and getting stronger and bigger every day. He was exhibiting his *monkey resilience*. We made him a karate uniform (seemed like the thing to do) from the white cloth of a T-shirt and gave him large orange slices for lunch. He would eat until he literally would pass out. I was jealous of his lifestyle.

He slept in my bunk with me every night, usually nestling in my armpit or curling up on my chest. I had to be careful not to roll on top of him while sleeping. Like all babies and toddlers, when they want something they let you know immediately. He had a high-pitched screech that he used to let me know it was feeding time. In the early mornings, he would crawl up onto my face and grab my eyelashes, pulling them up hard to wake me up! You get used to it eventually.

During the days we didn't leave camp or were on breaks between training, I would place him on top of my head so he could hold on to my longer-than-usual hair and go for a ride, leaving my hands free to do whatever it was needed doing. I figured that's how they do it with their parents so why change routine.

As he got healthier and grew bigger, he became more independent and self-absorbed. Adolescence! When the time came to redeploy back home, I knew I couldn't take him with me. I asked about the parameters but it was a complicated process. We said our goodbyes, and I left him in the care of a few Army guys who had provided extra security for our camp. But he could take care of himself now.

▲

You often forget more than you remember when it comes to experiences like these, but this story—and the experiences my daughter has been through—came to mind while researching the meaning of resilience in great organizations.

And there are many case studies from which we can derive great value and better plans for the future—while learning from the failures and success of others. And while the need for resilience isn't anything new, we just often don't strategically plan for resilience using the *Taking-Point* principles covered in this chapter. It's often not an actual part of the business plan. But it should be.

A CASE STUDY

Cisco Systems Inc. (an American multinational technology conglomerate headquartered in San Jose, California, that develops, manufactures, and sells networking hardware, telecommunications equipment, and other high-technology services and products) is a perfect example of a well-executed business resilience strategy. There is plenty of detailed information on this case study on their website, but the highlights are important for supporting the case for resiliency to become an overall part of the business strategy.

In the case study, they refer to "disaster recovery" as only one part of an overall business resilience strategy. Resilience in large part is about how an organization is prepared for and reacts to unforeseen events. Adversity and VUCA environments will always have an effect on employee satisfaction and performance, customer retention, and shareholder perception. But when an organization can become more resilient through strategic planning and action, events that can have a negative impact on productivity, efficiency, and profitability can become less "unforeseen." They can be predicted—especially with good data. A business resilience strategy covers more than just infrastructure and resources—it gives workers secure and reliable tools for communication, collaboration, and access to enterprise applications and data anytime, anywhere.

The case study also further clarifies this by stating, "Like other companies, Cisco Systems relies on its network and IT infrastructure to keep its business running—but Cisco also uses its network to increase worker, application, and collaboration resilience. Cisco addresses its challenges for business resilience through a combination of proactive planning, well-designed procedures, and extensive use of its own products and technologies."

And as Cisco's chief network architect Craig Huegen put it, "Designing the network and IT infrastructure for the stability of Cisco's business is our number-one goal." This is both Cisco's resilience challenge and opportunity. Cisco's enterprise network serves approximately 36,000 employees in more than seventy countries worldwide, carrying enormous volumes of data, voice, and video traffic. To assure business resilience, Cisco IT has developed extensive disaster recovery plans that prepare for a wide range of potential disruptions across the company, from the failure of a single network device in a local office to a major earthquake at the company headquarters in San Jose, California.

Just like we do in the SEAL Teams, much of Cisco's business resilience strategy is built around redundancy. As we say in the Teams, *two is one and one is none*. At Cisco, network resilience is based on a high-availability network design, with a redundant architecture that automatically recovers or reroutes communications around failures.

Without going into the technical details behind their strategy, Cisco continues to see measurable results from its ongoing business resilience strategy. Resilience is both a mindset as well as an investment in ensuring the company's capabilities and reputation remain intact should unforeseen events occur. Some of those results include:

- Enhanced application survivability through mirrored data centers and distributed content

- Survivable voice communications through local call processing and PSTN (public switched telephone network) gateways

- Protection of network and business assets with comprehensive security mechanisms and practices that address a wide range of threats

- Employees who can work anytime, anywhere for both daily mobility and fast relocation to alternative sites under variable and unpredictable circumstances

"At the highest levels, Cisco supports business resilience by promoting network availability, mitigating the impact of security threats and information loss, and protecting the company's corporate reputation," says John Stewart, information security director for Cisco Systems.

At Cisco, technology deployments, plans, and processes for resilience are continually evolving to serve a growing company, advancing technology, new types of security threats, and new business needs.

Essentially, Cisco knows the importance of proactively planning and being well prepared to execute in VUCA environments. And while many organizations may not be as disciplined and detailed in their approach to resiliency, the best companies out there understand that it can be learned and constantly improved upon. Like "Iron Mike" and Parker Rose have done, they bounce back from disaster (regardless of how big or small the volatility may be) and become stronger. They become more resilient and learn how to prepare for the inevitable obstacles they will face.

TALES FROM THE FRONT LINES

One of my client companies, Paramount Residential Mortgage Group (PRMG), is the definition of a resilient organization. Since 2001, PRMG continues to be a leading lender in the mortgage industry. As a privately held mortgage banker and residential home lender, PRMG has successfully helped many borrowers purchase and refinance their homes throughout the United States. Like many start-ups, when they first opened their doors, they had a staff of three. Today, PRMG employs nearly 1,300 people and has close to ninety branches throughout the United States.

So how did they prepare for and fight through the worst recession since the Great Depression? How did they navigate change and not only survive the battle, but thrive in adversity? Resilience.

I was instantly intrigued to begin working with this organization when my friend and colleague Chris, a senior executive who runs their national retail division, told me that his son was just about to graduate SEAL training and join the Teams. As soon as our call was over, I called my team member (Cindy Axelson—fallen SEAL Matt Axelson's widow) at the SEAL Family Foundation to make sure my wife and I were on the invite list for the graduation dinner.

During several calls leading up to the event with PRMG, I asked Chris many questions about the history of the company, its culture, and most importantly how they survived and thrived through the implosion of the housing market.

"I remember when I was in graduate school, our professors [mostly academics] were generally in line with other real estate industry professionals that doom was pending. That a recession was coming and the housing bubble was leading the way. My dad, who has been in the real estate investment advisory business his entire career [and notably an expert in the field], was no different," I said as I led into my first question.

"But so many home builders were still launching new projects and investing in new opportunities, even as the signs of collapse started emerging. So many builders, investors, and banks were still drinking their own Kool-Aid and acting with a broad sense of invincibility. So how was PRMG different? How did you anticipate or prepare?" I asked.

He paused for a moment and then answered thoughtfully by saying, "Anyone saying they could accurately predict the recession in its totality and severity is lying. But one thing that was different about this company was the senior leadership's foresight to anticipate change. Literally, from initially launching the company they prepared for a rainy day, even when there were absolutely no signs of disaster on the horizon. The market was only growing."

Chris went on, "This conversation reminds me of one of Aesop's fables, *The Ant and the Grasshopper*, where a hungry grasshopper begs for food from an ant when winter comes and is refused. The situation sums up moral lessons about the virtues of hard work and planning for the future. And that's exactly what our founders did from day one."

"What did you think of the movie *The Big Short*?" I asked as a quick aside.

He laughed. "One of the best scenes in the movie is when they hit the road to test their theories and head to places like Florida that had been experiencing some of the most significant growth. When Steve Carell's character is interviewing the stripper and she tells him that she has not one, but multiple homes, that's when it clicked! When *everyone* is getting in, that's when it's time to start thinking about cashing out."

I went on to ask Chris if there had been a specific strategy for survival, and his answer seemed so simple that it made me wonder why so many didn't follow the same path. The issue of course for many was that once many companies realized that the worst was actually happening, it was too late.

"Essentially, our preparedness and financial solvency is what continued to give banks confidence that we could deliver, that we were going to not only survive but maintain consistent focus on our core functions," Chris said.

The model for PRMG's resiliency became abundantly clear as he explained their story of survival. Consistent actions coupled with a sound financial position (that had been years in the making) equaled trust. Banks trusted them. Their customers trusted them.

"Consistency matters and building a great reputation creates new opportunities, even during the worst of times," Chris said wisely.

"So what role did leadership and culture play in this journey?" I asked.

"We didn't really have to transform our culture to match a new strategy. Our main shift was to ensure we got back to the basics, focus on our core values and what we do best. We quickly realized that survival meant a renewed focus on our customers, the loan officers that needed our support and resources. We wouldn't survive if we tried to solve these problems by being a jack-of-all-trades—trying to be all things to all people. It was about extreme focus," Chris said.

"How did senior leadership attack this battle? What role did they play in building and maintaining resiliency?" I asked.

"They played the most important role of all. Resiliency starts at the top. They maintained a positive mental attitude and enthusiastic vision for the future. And they communicated that vision and how we would fulfill it constantly. This was about continuing to push forward with a sense of purpose, rolling our sleeves up and hard work. If winning meant getting up earlier and staying later than the competition, that's what we did. Some team members thrived in this environment and some couldn't handle it. Those that didn't add value were removed, even people in senior roles," Chris said.

By thinking and acting with discipline and resiliency, PRMG has more than doubled in size since the 2008 downturn. They have gained significant market share and are now one of the largest privately held mortgage companies in the country. They have a deeper and wider foundation and a stronger culture for it.

The company has absolutely no "legacy" issues as a result of the recession like many competitors. Their growth has also been 100 percent organic, not the result of a single merger or acquisition. They have no debt and a confident team of brand evangelists helping to communicate their vision and recruit amazing new talent.

A great story about resiliency and overcoming the odds.

◢

When you have confidence in your ability to adapt and you have a structure that supports that ability, you can start to see beyond the horizon. You can identify potential problems and deal with them before they become unmanageable. That kind of action also trains your change "muscle" and makes you more able to deal with unanticipated obstacles.

When you can metabolize failure and adversity—analyze it, put it in the proper context, and use it to improve your process—you're creating an entire stockpile of *change fuel*. Informed change fuel.

You're constantly asking yourself questions, in a state of analysis:

- What is the data telling us?

- What course correction is needed to accomplish the mission?

- What potential threats are lurking around the corner?

- Are we properly managing and measuring all important KPIs?

- If we aren't, what do we need to do?

- Once these goals are attained, what's next?

I don't want you to get to the end of this book and think the process ends with these words. Because if you do these things correctly, you're creating a new, powerful cycle of analysis, action, and improvement. Once you've met the goal, you move the goalposts and do it again.

You've become "future-proof."

CONCLUSION

The *TakingPoint* principles outlined in this book and supported by stories from literal and figurative battlefields are just that—principles. My goal is for this book to provide you with a guide for leading successful and lasting transformation. *TakingPoint* is not just a model for leading change today but for redesigning organizations into modern organisms that will thrive in the information age.

Regardless of the approach any leader and their organization takes to adapt to adversity and navigate the uncertain waters of change, it all comes down to culture, mindset, and the willingness of bold, disciplined people coming together behind an aligned narrative and singular mission. Cultures and attitudes must shift to align with new strategies, and great organizations will build new structures that support their vision.

When a military unit, small business, or global organization can learn to infuse the ideals of trust and accountability into their culture, they will be well prepared for the change battle. When they assemble high-performing groups of empowered people and engage them in the planning and execution of that battle, victory is likely to be the outcome.

When leadership and decentralized decision-making is diffused throughout the organization and tactical moves are made by frontline troops, leaders can better focus on the strategic vision—and look to the horizon for what lays ahead. By keeping the team energized and aligned behind the ultimate vision, fatigue dissipates, energy remains, and the fight can be won.

So go forth onto your battlefield and take the fight to the enemy. Through discipline and resilience you will win this change battle and many more to come.

Good luck!

ACKNOWLEDGMENTS

It didn't take long for me to realize that writing a book is a complex journey involving many people—it's a *team* effort in every sense of the word. But my inspiration began with the humbling experience of being blessed to have served alongside some of the greatest warriors this world has ever known. Our servicemen and servicewomen—and their families—who give so much in service to a cause much greater than themselves, will always touch me with great emotion. They stand ready to answer our nation's call and defend us against enemies who wish to destroy us. And some, of course, give their lives. We sleep peacefully at night because of those brave men and women who willingly run to the sound of gunfire and set aside their own selfish desires to protect our way of life and the freedoms we enjoy.

I could never have accomplished this rewarding effort without the loving support of my wife, Nicole, and our three amazing children, Tyler, Parker Rose, and Ryder. Writing is a creative process that often requires quiet and solitude, not something that comes easily in a household of five. Without the uncompromising support and leadership of my wife, this vision could never have become a reality. I'd also like to thank my parents, who made me the man I've become; and my in-laws, who are always willing to take the children far away from my home office!

I owe special thanks to my amazing team. My literary agent, Farley